# EXCAVATIONS

# EXCAVATIONS

*a book of advocacies*

BY

CARL VAN VECHTEN

*Essay Index Reprint Series*

BOOKS FOR LIBRARIES PRESS
FREEPORT, NEW YORK

INTERNATIONAL STANDARD BOOK NUMBER:
0-8369-2336-7


LIBRARY OF CONGRESS CATALOG CARD NUMBER:
71-156726


PRINTED IN THE UNITED STATES OF AMERICA

FOR MY BROTHER
RALPH VAN VECHTEN

*"A workman with his spade in half a day*
*Can push two thousand lagging years away;*
*See, how the tragic villas, one by one,*
*Like sleepy lizards, creep into the sun."*
LEONORA SPEYER.

*"God, what a rain of ashes falls on him*
*Who sees the new but cannot leave the old."*
EDWIN ARLINGTON ROBINSON.

*"But, besides those great men, there is a certain num-*
*ber of artists who have a distinct faculty of their own*
*by which they convey to us a peculiar quality of pleasure*
*which we cannot get elsewhere; and these, too, have*
*their place in general culture, and must be interpreted*
*to it by those who have felt their charm strongly, and*
*are often the objects of a special diligence and a con-*
*sideration wholly affectionate, just because there is not*
*about them the stress of a great name and authority."*
WALTER PATER.

## PROEM

The papers in this book, it seems scarcely necessary to state, are not essays in criticism. Rather, they were written to provoke the reader to share my own enthusiasm for certain, at the time of writing, more or less obscure figures in the literary and musical world. In some instances, notably in the cases of Edgar Saltus and Ronald Firbank, this purpose was successful. A few of these papers, however, may be called Excavations only in the sense that they have been dug out of old books and magazines. I have not reread the authors discussed herein. Reflection, however, has urged me to make pertinent alterations and reservations, and I have added occasional footnotes of protest or timeliness.

Erik Satie is lifted from Interpreters and Interpretations; Edgar Saltus, from The Merry-Go-Round; A Note on Philip Thicknesse, Oscar Hammerstein: an Epitaph, Sir Arthur Sullivan, and Isaac Albéniz, from In the Garret: these books are out of print and will not be reprinted. The paper on Ouida served originally as a preface to In a Winter City, in the Modern Library (1923). Thanks are due to Mr. Horace Liveright for permission to republish it. The paper on Matthew Phipps Shiel served originally as a preface to Alfred A. Knopf's edition of The Lord of the Sea (1924). The Ronald Firbank paper is a composite of a paper (the first to be written in America about Firbank) published in the Double Dealer for April, 1922, a review of The Flower Beneath the Foot, in the New York Tribune, June 24, 1923, and the preface to the first edition of Prancing Nigger, Brentano's; 1924. Sophie Arnould served originally as a preface to Philip Moeller's

[ix]

## *Proem*

charming comedy, Sophie (Alfred A. Knopf; 1919). On Visiting Fashionable Places out of Season, The Later Work of Herman Melville, Henry B. Fuller, Arthur Machen: Dreamer and Mystic, Léo Delibes, and A Note on Dedications have not previously appeared in a book. The first was printed in the Reviewer, the second and third in the Double Dealer, the fourth, in the International Book Review, the fifth in the Musical Quarterly, and the sixth in the Bookman.

CARL VAN VECHTEN.

*March 10, 1925.*

[x]

# Contents

## On Visiting Fashionable Places out of Season

It is the incredible custom of a certain unimaginative group of civilized mankind to devote itself wholeheartedly to any single environment for but a few brief weeks each year, a period which has come to be designated as "the season." So brief are these fashionable invasions that the season in one part of the world rarely conflicts with the season in another, thus providing opportunity for particularly ambitious and vigorous persons, with nothing else to do, to visit the proper places on the proper days throughout the entire twelvemonth. On the other hand, there are individuals who derive a peculiar pleasure, melancholy or otherwise, through finding themselves in these localities, arbitrarily set aside for the entertainment of the idle class, during the months that these restless folk attempt to amuse themselves elsewhere. These casual guests wander, not without awe, through the mazes of splendours and palaces, the windows of which are boarded up, whether against the attack of banditi or dust has never been made quite clear. The look, the feeling, of the absent owners hover about these edifices like the ghosts of royalty that haunt the castles of the middle ages.

The villagers, who depend for their livelihood upon the outsiders, but who never unbend during the rush of the season when so much is demanded of them for which they are overpaid, are doubly polite to the straggler who happens in during the odd months which occupy so much the

### Fashionable Places

greater part of the very long year, for a year lasts an eternity in such a spot.  Now the price of victuals and drinks automatically tumbles.  Carriage and boat fares are subject to amazing depreciations.  One is fêted, so to speak. The stragglers, indeed, help to fill the coffers with unexpected gain; moreover they are somewhat of an antidote for boredom, a tiny trickle of excitement at a time when excitement is not anticipated.  They are the surprises.  The regular trade of the season is received with more reserve.  Tradition, belike, exacts the toll of reticence in this regard.  Paying trade, of course, is paying trade, even in bulk, but when there is a crowded cottage and hotel list to satisfy with food and amusement it may be taken for granted that innkeeper and shopkeeper will greet each newcomer with less apparent enthusiasm.

Through no conscious effort on my part, rather through chance, which assuredly, however, has coincided with my desire, I have never visited one of these exotic places save out of season.  My sole visit to Scheveningen, for example, was paid when that Dutch sea-coast town exhibited unpeopled stretches of brown sand pounded by angry waves.  The celebrated bath-chairs of exclusive design, the high backs of which serve to effectually conceal the figures of their occupants, rhythmically dotted the dunes by the old Voetpad, giving, when approached from behind, the illusion of a crowd of bathers.  The strand, however, exploited no lovely ladies in exposing bathing garments.  The weather was bleak, and the sober silence of a Dutch fisherman or two and the screaming of the wheeling gulls complemented my not too unenjoyed spleen.  Lunch in the Kurhaus was a solitary ceremony.  The vast dining-room with its scores of tables held but me and the waiters, three of whom bore

[2]

## *out of Season*

in my Côtelette à la Joncourt so soon after I had scanned the bill of fare that the service seemed magical. In this lonely grandeur I began to sense my resemblance to Max Beerbohm's justly admired portrait of Queen Victoria, in which the late Empress of the Indies listens to Lord Tennyson reading In Memoriam in a hall of a size which would very well accommodate a Handel festival. I felt, indeed, even smaller than they looked, for, after all, the authors of In Memoriam and Edward VII were personages of such portentous importance that the Sahara Desert would not appear to be entirely empty were they set down in the centre of it. However, unless one happens to be Victoria or her favourite poet, one becomes pensive and forlorn in the face of a vacuum, and Scheveningen, out of season, is certainly a vacuum. Did it, I wondered on this occasion, exist at all? Surely Tosti's Good-bye must have been written in this void Kurhaus dining-room, untenanted save for the rows of tables and chairs and the black-coated waiters.

Nice, in the winter, is frequently too cold for comfort. In the summer, on the other hand, it is usually delightfully cool; I am informed that the temperature during the hot months rarely rises higher than it does at Paris. Yet no one with any pretense to smartness could afford to be seen in Nice in the summer. To be sure, consuls, bankers, and others of foreign nationalities must perforce remain the year there, buoyed up by patience, hope, and alcohol, but to all intents and purposes Nice in midsummer is a bourgeois French village, without the charm and patina of such French villages as are never awarded the favour of fashion.

White walls, green shutters, and boarded windows occlude the eye on every street. The life that glows so

[3]

radiantly in January is quite extinct in July. The ambient palms strive to retain their royal splendour, but, out of season, they look manifestly self-conscious in the gardens of the hotels with the extraordinary names, Hotel of John the Baptist and the English, Hotel of Rome and St. Peter, Hotel of the Prince of Wales and Mary Magdalen. The Promenade des Anglais, mentioned somewhere in any novel the scene of which is laid on the Riviera, is as quiet as Riverside Drive on a Tuesday morning. Nay, quieter. Meanwhile, like the polar bear in the Arctic winter or the caterpillar in the cocoon, Nice waits, tranquilly and stupidly, for the awakening.

Cannes, which during the season depends so much on white-flannelled English boys for its glory, is apparently even drearier. A person lacking imagination will derive no normal pleasure from a contemplation of Cannes in the summer, unless it may be an enjoyment of the view of the mountains which o'ertop the town. Some of us, however, experience a certain abnormal satisfaction in surveying such a place in its most grim-visaged aspects. It is with a similar pride that certain women remember that they have caught glimpses of royalty in its undergarments.

Monte Carlo, I fancy, is never entirely out of season. The passion for gambling, ebulliently and personally, against a throne, as it were, is too strong at all times to be circumscribed within the limits of a month or two. The Casino, therefore, is invariably crowded, even when the Opéra is closed and the owners of the play-cottages and fairy-villas are far away. I have been told by a singer who has appeared frequently at Monte Carlo that the Opéra is used merely as a decoy. The prospective

[4]

booker of places is informed that all seats for immediate performances have been disposed of and is urged, often with success, to purchase stalls for the following week. Thus his visit is prolonged and his amateur expeditions to the gambling-house continued, while inveterate gamblers and acquaintances of the tenors and sopranos may have blocks of seats for the asking. In July, however, when I visited Monte Carlo with friends, there was no opera.

I shall never forget my first view of the principality of Monaco from the motor, high on the Route de la Corniche, the city lying like a tiny, glittering jewel on the promontory butting into the deep purple of the Mediterranean. It was twilight when we descended, and I recalled that Arthur Symons once advised his readers to approach a strange city only at night, good advice which I have followed not only in regard to Monte Carlo, but in regard to Paris, Venice, and Naples as well.

The salles de jeu in the Casino exhibit a shifting series of fascinating moving pictures. New figures are constantly added to the groups, but certain types recur with rigid regularity. These have been described in Middlemarch and elsewhere: hard faces and soft faces, young faces and old faces, duchesses and commoners, but on the majority of these faces only four emotions are to be observed, curiosity and greed, hope and disappointment. The professional gambler, on the other hand (and in July these predominate), wears a mask. He is superior to any humiliating display of feeling. His expression never alters. It undergoes no metamorphosis, whatever his fortune. These stand, a little aloof from the tables, or sit, huddled over them, watching the inscrutable countenance of the croupier as he announces the fall of

[5]

the ball with his "Rien ne va plus," or rakes in the heaps of gold louis and paper notes, old women with hooked noses and dowdy gowns, old men with visages riddled with wrinkles, handsome younger women in elaborate robes, doubtless with the insigne of Lanvin, Callot Sœurs or Redfern stitched within the belt, shimmering in gold and silver brocade, with scarfs of kincob, young men in dinner jackets, or young men in shepherd's plaid or white serge.

I determined to discover what I might do with one gold louis and luck was with me, for I played three hours with this capital, amassing, from time to time, a considerable pile in front of me, but at eleven o'clock even my louis was gone. Then, although still fascinated by the spectacle, sordid and somewhat disgusting like all brilliant spectacles, whether in the nature of a coronation, a durbar, or a bull-fight, I strolled out into the gardens. The Café de Paris, where I might have nibbled a lobster for fifteen or twenty francs or tasted a peach for eight, loomed opposite. The orchestra was performing; that year it was the Méditation from Thaïs and Un peu d'amour, but you know what one is likely to hear from all Café de Paris and Ritz orchestras. The names change, but the sentiment persists through the decades. . . . I hovered about the bosky terrace of the Casino until nearly one, trying in vain to convince myself that I was not longing to witness a suicide. No unlucky fellow was obliging enough to shoot himself that night, however, and so finally, confessing to myself that I was keenly disappointed, I returned to my hotel.

In the morning, hot, white Monte Carlo in the sunglare gave me a sense of the uncertain pleasures of off-seasons. The honey which, with croissants and coffee, made up my breakfast, was tepid. The garden, where I sat, was torrid. A walk along the shore of the sea, with the rays of heaven bearing down directly on my head, was almost unbearably unpleasant. An encounter with the comic-opera soldiers of the principality, in their incredibly gay uniforms, decorated with torsions of gold cords, served somewhat to alleviate my discomfort.

The Italian Riviera is actually popular in the summer, for interior-bred natives seek their sea-coasts during the warm weather. I visited Spezia in August and I should not have known that it was not the season. The piazza on a Sunday evening offered a kaleidoscopic, human spectacle, with its crowds of women, for the most part without hats, sailors in white, and gentry and shopkeepers sauntering under the eucalypti and plane-trees, while the band played in a central pavilion. Nor were the smaller towns without visitors. A peculiarity of hostelries in these Italian villages is that the chambers connect one with the other; no space is wasted on corridors. In one of these, troops of Roman matrons on their way to the ocean, clad in bathgowns, accompanied by children wrapped in towels, traversed my room early in the morning. It was in this same hotel that I slept in a bed with the Virgin and Child painted on the headboard and Cupid and Psyche on the footboard!

A city like New York, or Paris, or London, is never entirely out of season. Paris might be so regarded in August, but all signs fail, for even then the city on the Seine is thronged with visitors, and even a few sly Parisians creep furtively back from Deauville or San Sebastián to enjoy the ostensible immunity of the month.

## Fashionable Places

Nay more, certain cocottes, finding that it pays to avoid the intense rivalry at Trouville or Aix-les-Bains, return to drive in the Bois in August.

So with New York, popularly supposed to be deserted in the summer, by women at any rate. Some one, on that account, has called Manhattan a paradise for men from the end of May to the middle of September, all the pleasures, but none of the responsibilities. The phrase is a pleasant one, but now, when a rickey, fashioned of gin manufactured in New Jersey, costs one dollar, almost unwarranted. To be sure, it was the war and not prohibition which originally destroyed the erstwhile summer atmosphere of New York. During the course of the European conflict one met here all the silly stragglers, the bounders and bumpers, who usually mess up the Savoy Grill or the Carlton in London, or who sit on the terrasse of the Café de la Paix or frequent the Ritz and Armenonville in Paris. In the bar at the Beaux Arts, in the Knickerbocker (alas, no more), they gathered. One encountered them motoring in Central Park or supping at the Midnight Frolic. One was sure to run into them in the smart shops of Fifth Avenue or its cross streets, ordering stationery at the Japan Paper Company, old earrings, fashioned of hair or coral, at the Louis XIV Shop, wrist-watches at Dreicer's, hats with the coque feathers of the Bersaglieri at Tappé's, jugs of Egyptian enamel at Noorian's, amber crystal bowls for live fish or green salad at Ovington's, or stuffs of foreign dye at Wanamaker's, to be cut into divers garments, robes for walking, robes for tea, robes for dancing at the Cascades of the Biltmore, robes in which to visit Evangeline Adams to demand a reading of the stars.

[8]

## *out of Season*

One autumn during the long war years my wife was engaged to make a moving picture in the Bahama Islands and I seized the opportunity to accompany her. Our destination was Nassau on the island of New Providence, a town which boasts a season in February and March, when it is utilized as a sort of annex to Palm Beach. If the idle rich tire of Florida, an excursion to Nassau is suggested, and the suggestion, occasionally, is acted upon.

September is *not* the season. The weather is uncomfortably warm; in the sun the temperature often registers 115 Fahrenheit. There are three thousand or more islands in the Bahama group, many of which are minute and uninhabited. The total population reaches fifty-eight thousand, of which fifty thousand must be black or mulatto. Nassau, the largest city and the seat of the Governor and Parliament, has a population of ten thousand or more. Here, there are two large hotels and several smaller ones and, during the brief period of invasion from the continent, everybody takes in boarders, but there is little hospitality of this kind offered in the summer or early fall. The two superior hotels are then closed tight; the only sign of life about them is the stir made in the upkeep of their elaborate gardens. Even the minor hotels are reticent about remaining open and the stray visitor to Nassau will be hard put to discover a place to eat and sleep. Out of season, indeed, Nassau is the most uninhabitable, unsociable town I have ever visited and yet, so perverse is my nature, I am sure that I would prefer it to Nassau in season.

After much searching and more discouragement, we finally settled in the half-closed Hotel Nassau, from the balcony of which I might gaze across at two pink stucco houses, mysterious, shuttered villas, suggesting a suitable setting for a tale by Arthur Machen. Between these cottages lay a garden, with a banana-tree and a palm, beyond which a view of the indigo harbour opened, the masts of the schooners, rising in a design of parallel vertical lines, the sails, half-unfurled, bellying in the soft breeze. Further on, wide stretches of water shone vivid emerald-green or sapphire, creating, with the indigo, the iridescent colouring of the darkest black opals; and yet beyond extended the low green line of Hog Island, over which, in rough weather, the surf of the ocean broke.

I had expected to encounter parrots and monkeys, tropical fauna. They were missing. The three monkeys on the island existed in a state of captivity. The hovering presence of humming-birds, king-fishers, and gulls compensated for the absence of the parrots. The fish and the flora assuredly were exotic. At the market, a pavilion erected in the Spanish style, one might purchase anything edible the island offered, from a live pig to an alligator pear. The display of fish was particularly tempting, piles of scaly fellows with scarlet throats and tourmaline fins; conches which offered their flesh to the kitchen and their effulgent shells to the collector's cabinet.

The streets, moving pictures of lazy grace, were an unfailing source of interest and delight to me, picturesque in the sense that most villages under a hot sun become picturesque, for the sun in the tropics seems to soften every outline, performing the office of the twilight in the temperate zone. The buildings were all low, usually no more than two storeys, and they were painted in the bland roses and yellows that give the Italian scene its air of charm. As in the case of the Italian houses, part

[10]

## *out of Season*

of the colour was always worn away, but the clear light, far from making this condition repulsive, softened and melted it into a state very pleasing to the eye. Often a gazebo, protected from insects by wire-screens and from the sun by green shutters, jutted from a house. Everywhere black-fibred palms, bananas, the strange silk-cotton trees, with their fantastic roots heaved high above the soil, mangos, and bread-fruit trees flourished. Along the upper streets, for the roadways climbed from the sea to the top of a low hill, surmounted by the Governor's palace, which elsewhere would be described as a modest bungalow, I discovered handsome residences set deep in lovely gardens, in which flowers and shrubs were thickly planted. The crumbling pink walls surrounding these estates reminded me of Tuscany, but no cypresses dominated the landscape, although pines, often grown in monstrous shapes, somehow were incongruously present. Sauntering over the crest of the hill to the south side of the island, I came upon a forest of these pines, slender saplings, with naked trunks and only feathery tufts of green at the tops, growing in a rocky swamp with clumps of palmettos, in lieu of hazel-bushes, springing up between their roots. If Heine had visited this eccentric forest could he have written his song of contrasts about the palm tree and the pine?

Returning to the town, I sought refreshment, finding it in a room at the back of Harold E. M. Johnson's grocery. Picture the dirtiest back-room of a New York Bowery saloon in the good old days: a few round tables, wiped off infrequently, a few rude chairs, all in the space of ten square feet. The damp and dirty plaster of indeterminate colour was peeling from the walls. The floor was strewn with cigarette butts. The air was pervaded

[ 11 ]

with a foul, musty stink. An open door faced a blind wall, the ground beneath scattered with refuse and broken bottles. The windows, the shutters half-open, let in the burning light and through them also drifted the titillating street cries, while within, men in white garments sipped ginger ale in which cut limes floated, and wished they were back in God's country. Had you been there, you would have fancied yourself, as I did, in the heart of a South African melodrama or a story by Rudyard Kipling.

Outside, the Negro women pedlars, their heads bound with red and yellow bandannas, over which they wore straw hats of huge dimensions, sat at the corners of the streets, vending fried fish, baked breads, small fruits, alligator pears, guavas, green peppers, and peanuts. Other Negro women, casually balancing great burdens on their heads, and men, balancing flat baskets containing three or four live, white cocks, their feet securely tied, passed. Two-seated vehicles, and donkey-carts, driven by Negroes, rolled slowly along the glistening shell roads. Bay Street, the main thoroughfare, was lined with haberdashers, shoe- and grocery-marts. The islanders boasted quaint names. French cognomens had crept in from the outer keys. I encountered a Negro who called himself Irving l'Homme. Other common Negro names were Jean-Baptiste, or even John-Baptist, Cecil, Cyril, Reginald, Percival, Harry, Veronica, Muriel, Evelyn, and Mildred. The keeper of a pub had caused his full name, Timothy Darling Orlando Garrick Elder, to be painted on the sign over his door.

The island of New Providence, I discovered, was protected from the open sea by Hog Island, exactly in the manner that Venice is shielded from the Adriatic by the

## *out of Season*

**Lido.** It was a mile across the harbour to Hog Island,
and then only a narrow strip of land separated me from
sea-bathing, a strip of land wildly entangled with oranges,
almonds, eaten green, and guavas which, when cut and
placed in bowls, form a colour combination suggestive of
a Japanese print, a delicate salmon-pink enclosed in a
rind of yellow-green.

The bathing accommodations on Hog Island were primitive, for, during the season, the Hotel Colonial offered
its own bath-house to visitors from Palm Beach. The
bathing itself, however, was of a variety seldom vouch-
safed to mortals. Here Venus might have risen radiantly, her nether portions magnified in the transparent
water. The beach was clean, shining, shimmering sand;
the water was warm and the depth sloped gradually.
The favoured spot lay in the curve of a bay where, even
when the ocean was rough, the water remained limpidly
smooth. Those who desired surf bathing might satisfy
this craving further up the shore where the breakers rolled
in with great intensity. Out of season, at any rate,
there was no bar against bathing nude, and many of the
Negroes came here for that purpose, although the majority of the blacks took advantage of the more accessible
beaches on the shores of New Providence, those gracious
dominions known as Prospect or Labouchere, a mile or
two west of Nassau.

Wonderful in their lithe nudity, these Negroes, gleam-
ing in their bronze perfection: I never could sufficiently
admire their swimming prowess. Their stay under water
seemingly could be prolonged indeterminately. Water,
it appeared, was as elemental to their natures as the air
they were more accustomed to breathe. Assuredly, they
were amphibious. Their dressing was accomplished with-

[13]

out the aid of towels, their bodies drying quickly in the sun, their thick, metallic skins apparently immune to sunburn. At the beaches where clothing was required, they did not employ bathing garments; such as they were, they wore their street clothes, consisting, usually, only of a shirt and a pair of ragged trousers, and these, too, dried rapidly after emergence. Like Negroes everywhere, they sang a great deal, but I heard no folksongs. Rather they sang Tipperary, or Good-bye, boys, I'm going to be married tomorrow. I was amazed to hear one youth—he could have been no more than twelve—lustily whistling the Marseillaise, with especial emphasis on those stirring phrases which underline the words, Aux armes, citoyens!

One night, on request, the natives arranged a "fire dance." This is a ceremony celebrated in secrecy during the season, when, according to report, the bucks and their doxies dance naked in some secluded nook in the forest, if a sufficient purse has been collected to make it worth their while. In the summer the young girls and boys prance for enjoyment before a bonfire, kindled for illumination rather than heat. They were quite willing to permit the spectacle to be observed, but the gate-receipts apparently were not adequate to encourage disrobing. The music was furnished by a drum, made by fitting a skin over the head of an empty cask, and beaten with extraordinary rhythmic effect, and by the clapping of hands and singing of the group of native spectators. When the skin of the drum became loosened, it was held over the fire to dry taut again. The words of the songs were often indistinguishable; sometimes, indeed, they consisted merely of harsh cries. I can perhaps

best designate their nature by appending a rude
sample:

> He's gwine roun' dah circle!
> Tum ti tum tum, tum tum tum!
> He's gwine roun' dah circle!
> Tum ti tum tum, tum tum tum!

Monotonously, this primitive jingle was reiterated, until
the dancers tired.  The tunes did not vary greatly in
effect, not at all in time, and they bore some esoteric, inexplicable relation to Russian folksong.  As in so many
of the Russian dances, one dancer performed at a time,
indicating his successor by a nudge in his or her direction.
There was not much variety in this exhibition, obviously,
in its inception, symbolic of manifestations of sex.  The
movements included wild leaps, whirls, contortions of the
body, girandoles, occasionally suggesting the barbaric
Polovtsian dances in Prince Igor.  Almost invariably,
the arms were held close to the sides, sometimes with the
forearm horizontal to the body, but seldom higher.  A
man advanced slowly, one leg dragging behind the other,
with a curious suggestion of lameness.  One of the girls,
a savage creature, with a mass of untutored hair, danced
with a peculiar clawing motion of the hands.  In one
of her figures she stooped almost to the earth, continuing
her odd rhythmic clawing as she shuffled around the
circle of hand-clapping, shouting hysterics.  Her thin
arms and legs, her angular, awkward grace, if not her
wild gestures, brought to mind the marionettes which are
employed in Ceylonese shadow shows.  When the crowd,
excited, bent forward, encroaching too much on the central space, one of the boys snatched a fiery brand from
the bonfire and with a swift sweep of his arm singed the

[15]

bare feet of the eager spectators.  They spread back
with alacrity.

I passed an hour or two in the court house, listening to
the English magistrate while he sentenced black boys to
hard labour for minor offences, but, naturally enough,
interest anywhere centres after a time—and I spent three
weeks in Nassau—upon something other than a round
of street and court scenes and Negro dances.  I sought
diversion in reading and a little stationery shop, occupying the ground floor of one of the pink houses across
from my hotel, was one of the two—and perhaps the better of the two—shops where reading matter was on sale.
In addition, the local newspaper, filled for the most part
with advertisements and stale news from the front, appeared twice weekly, supplemented by a bulletin of the
war news which was posted every day on the wall of the
post office.  In the little shop it was possible to buy
books by Marie Corelli, G. A. Henty, Robert W.
Chambers, or Hall Caine; the Ladies' Home Journal, an
institution everywhere, like John Brown or Lillian
Russell, and the London Illustrated News were similarly
offered for sale.  I even discovered a copy of Vogue with
an ancient date.
It was in the library that I found the Forum and the
English Review, the Century, the Atlantic Monthly,
Harper's and Munsey's.  There, too, the best of the
London newspapers were on file, besides the New York
Times and the New York Herald.  I enjoyed many
pleasant hours in this library, an octagonal structure with
shelves, chairs, and windows in each of the eight di-
visions.  It was a decidedly agreeable experience to sit
alone in one of these, removing books at random from

the shelves. It was, I should surmise, an accidental library, odds and ends from Government House, left behind as successive Governors departed, with perhaps a few additions grudgingly presented by townsfolk with a feeble spark of local pride. Still, here and there, I found books to interest me, stowed away between ponderous three-volume novels with villainous titles by authors now forgotten. Almost all the books were very much worn with handling. Henry James's The American Scene was an exception. Was the book, I wondered, a virgin? Was I the first to despoil it? I skimmed slowly through its vague contents until I sat with Mr. James in a theatre (name not mentioned) on the New York Bowery, observing an actor (name not mentioned) in whom he was interested. The style of the book reminded me of the ethics or orders of a newspaper where advertising is solicited at so much a column, so that the cub reporter is warned not to drag in the names of shops unless they be decidedly germane to the course of his narrative. Yet, I recall reading, in the description of a fire printed on the first page of the New York Times, the phrase, "in the very shadow of Abraham and Straus's." . . . The Golden Bowl was also available but I did not examine it. I reached, instead, for William Beckford's History of the Caliph Vathek, and for the next two hours I lived with enchantment. What more appropriate volume could one select to read in a Victorian library in a tropical clime? This supplementary Arabian Nights' tale is very moral, for it instructs us that if we yield to the temptations of the senses we are henceforth damned perdurably, but let no prospective reader, who dreads moral books, be deterred on that account from perusing Vathek. As for myself, I was held so com-

pletely captive by the quaint naïveté of the narrative, the
oriental colour, the afrits,[1] dives, peris, houris, and
goules, the wicked and hideous Giaour, the beautiful
Nouronihar, the ladies of the harem in their cages, hung
with chintz, Vathek's vicious mother, Carathis, who
practises cocoonery in her tower, surrounded by Ne-
gresses, mutes, and serpents, and the wondrous halls of
Eblis where that subterranean monarch ("a young man,
whose noble and regular features seemed to have been
tarnished by malignant vapours; in whose large eyes appeared both pride and despair; whose flowing hair retained some semblance to that of an angel of light; in
whose hand, which thunder had blasted, he swayed the
iron sceptre that causes the monster Ouranabad, the
afrits, and all the powers of the abyss to tremble") sat
upon a throne of fire in a vast tabernacle, curtained with
crimson and gold brocades and carpeted with leopard
skins, that I never dropped the slender volume until I
had arrived at the final page, where Vathek, the complete
Manichean, his heart encircled in everlasting fire,
languishes in the lower depths of a Mohammedan .hell.
Afterwards, I was not at all surprised to learn—so seemingly spontaneous is this performance—that Beckford,
after beginning to write Vathek, had never laid it aside
until it was completed, two nights and three days later.[2]
This was in 1782 when the author, an amateur of letters

---

[1] Sir Richard Burton gives ifrít as the correct phonetic spelling of
this word.

[2] This was the author's boast, but he may have meant that he wrote
the final draft at such a sitting. By means of certain autograph
letters preserved in the Morrison Collection, Dr. Garnett was able to
show, on the best of all authority, that of Beckford himself, that the
writing of Vathek occupied several months, at least; in all probability,
fully a year.

and an eccentric in life, was but twenty-three years old. If André Gide's definition of genius, that it is the feeling of resourcefulness, may be regarded as authentic, William Beckford was assuredly a genius. Byron admired Vathek; so, apparently, did every other coeval, but fashions change, and probably only those fortunate individuals who bury themselves in watering places out of season read it today.

The morning after this adventure I espied a book on magic in this library, and then Howells's Italian Sketches, or Travels in Italy, or whatsoever it may be called, turned up, and reading the pages on Verona I was happy to discover that Mr. Howells, too (somehow I had followed him, without being aware of it, in this opinion), preferred the Arena at Verona to the somewhat more celebrated Colosseum at Rome. It is with a charming pen that Mr. Howells draws his pictures, but I put the volume down eventually to inspect a paper by one F. A. Wright in the Edinburgh Review on Greek music, a most interesting paper in which the writer compares Bellini and Donizetti to the Athenians, because they preferred the human voice to the orchestra, and then suggestively couples a number of composers with a corresponding number of Greek dramatic poets. Bach and Pindar, I remember, and Mozart and Euripides, Mendelssohn and Æschylus, Richard Strauss and Aristophanes. . . . Beethoven and Sophocles is a conjunction that would occur to any one. . . . But, now that it is too late, I regret that I did not examine the three-volume novels, for there were certain titles in this library that I have never met with since; I am reminded in this connection of a passage in Philip Thicknesse's book about his journey through France and Spain: "From many parts of the road we had a view of the Mediterranean Sea, and the Golfe de Royas, a fine bay, over which the heads of the Pyrénées hang; and on the banks of which there seemed to be, not only villages, but large towns; the situations of which appeared so enchanting, that I could scarcely resist the temptation of visiting them;—and now I wonder why I did not, but at that time, I suppose, I did not recollect I had nothing else to do."

Fortunately, for my peace of mind, I can read three-volume novels—if not precisely the same titles—elsewhere, as easily as I might have done in the old Victorian library at Nassau. I can, indeed, by rummaging around in ancient bookshops in New York acquaint myself much more readily with literature that for some reason or other is out of season than I might in some untenanted watering place.

In 1795 there appeared in London a novel called The Monk, written by one Matthew Gregory Lewis, who was then just twenty. This romance became fashionable and famous at once, even more fashionable and famous than Mrs. Radcliffe's The Mysteries of Udolpho, which had been the sensation of 1794. Horace Walpole's The Castle of Otranto (1765), Clara Reeves's The Old English Baron (1777), and William Beckford's Vathek were other forerunners. In 1804, Lewis himself furnished the work with a successor, The Bravo of Venice. These tales, bursting with rich fancy, miraculous adventures, and fantastic exploits, bide their time well. The colours cling to the canvas in their original brilliance, while the hues of more realistic fiction, evirated of all imaginative quality, have faded. How pleasant it is to return to their romantic delights!

## out of Season

The rare first edition of The Monk, lacking the emendations and deletions made by Lewis at the behest of his father, who found too many references to rosy breasts and nuptial couches to suit his Sir Roger de Coverley tastes, may have supplied its contemporary readers with proper joy, but the pleasure one derives from this rococo history today, when many an author fears that his public may be unable to follow him if he undertakes a journey on a magic carpet, are at least doubled. Lewis made no effort to restrain his wanton fancy or to give the episodes in his book any arbitrary air of credibility; rather, he plunges the reader at once into a milieu where the Baron Munchausen himself would feel embarrassed. The reader, sufficiently grateful for this ingenuous appeal to his good nature, is quite ready to believe anything by the time he has finished the fiftieth page, and from then on he dashes along with the author at breakneck speed, refusing to be unseated by collision with any phenomenon, however unnatural.

The tale, like Vathek, is moral, proving that pride goeth before a fall, that those who have never sinned are uncharitable towards peccancy in others, and that it is easy to be virtuous if one is never tempted, but, as in the case of Vathek, no potential reader need hesitate because of this apparent flaw. Indeed, probably only one reader out of nine thousand, even after he has been warned, will perceive this improving purpose of the author. The Monk is a first-rate thriller in three volumes with a monk as the weak hero and the devil himself as the villain. We assist at the wild, midnight elopement of Don Raymond, the Marquis of las Cisternas, with the bleeding nun, a spectral substitute for his beloved Agnes, the horses running away during a tempest in the mountains, or, in contrast to this scene, we listen while the middle-aged Baroness Lindenberg, on her knees, supplicates the favour of Alphonso, a scene which suggests a somewhat similar episode in Bel-Ami. We shudder, the more so because we are powerless to succor her, while the beautiful and pious Antonia, drugged like Juliet to simulate death, is despoiled in a convent charnel-house by the wicked Ambrosio, who subsequently learns to his horror that he has raped his own sister! We are introduced to no less a personage than the Wandering Jew. With pleasure we watch the mob kill the Prioress of St. Clare and we gloat over the sacking of her infamous convent. We are terrified spectators at a meeting of the inner circle of the Inquisition and we are invited to observe an auto-da-fé. The several appearances of Lucifer ("He was a fell, despightful fiend; hell holds none worse in baleful bower below") in different guises, the supernatural machinery, including the magic mirror in its cabalistic frame, enchant the attention and accentuate the beating of the heart. The book, indeed, is written at white heat, with panache, in the grand manner. I will not spoil The Monk for those who have not yet read it by unwinding the extremely intricate plot, but I would ask, with justifiable glee, if you are able to resist the perusal of a tale in which the dread assistant to Lucifer in the accomplishment of his hellish machinations, the female arch-fiend, as vicious a demon as Catulle Mendès's more modern Méphistophéla, in her earthly shape is dubbed Matilda by her creator?

Let us, as is so conveniently possible in this pleasant world of books, look forward fifty years or so, to 1844, when Benjamin Disraeli published Coningsby, a very fashionable novel of its period, in which the author's

avowed intention was "to vindicate the just claims of the
Tory party to be the popular political confederation of
the country." I confess without shame that I blithely
skip the political chapters and the passages dealing with
the Malt Tax, the Reform Bill, and the New Poor Law,
when I read the novel today. The pages that magnetize
my eye deal with the house parties at Beaumanoir, where
lovely ladies in muslin and "rich Indian shawls" arrive in
"whirling britskas" to eat Perigord pie and "pyramids of
strawberries, in bowls colossal enough to hold orange-
trees," or with the ball at Sidonia's palace in Paris, a
wilderness of wild, bronze Negroes, bearing flaming
torches athwart the marble staircases, the ante-rooms
provided with ottomans for the chaperons. Such passages awaken all the quaint, atmospheric charm of the
early Victorian epoch. The young hero, a nineteenth
century moon-calf who falls in love with a manufacturer's
daughter and develops radical political views in opposition
to his grandfather, Lord Monmouth's, wishes, is created
out of solid wood, but Lord Monmouth himself, drawn,
I believe, from the same original model as the Marquis
of Steyne, in some aspects surpasses Thackeray's less
subtle, if more familiar, portrait. The outstanding
figure of the romance is Sidonia, the incomparable Jew,
who apparently knows everything and who stands a little
aloof as he regulates the world by raising his eyebrows.
His rhapsodies on his race should provide Freudians
with a new excuse for hysteria, for Sidonia, of course,
is Disraeli's ideal portrait of himself. This writer's
style, moreover, is warmly redolent of his race, replete
with mystic extravagance, oriental glamour, gorgeous
and grandiose magnificence, with a corresponding lack
of symmetry and proportion. During his season Dis-

[23]

raeli certainly encountered sufficient appreciation, but
it seems to me that his later brilliant career as a states-
man somewhat obscured in the public mind his obvious
gifts as a novelist.

In 1904, or thereabouts, Chatto and Windus issued a
purple volume, with a curious design in blind stamping
on the cover, entitled Hadrian the Seventh. The author's
name is given as Fr. (Frederick, not Father) Rolfe.
The full name of this mad writer, who died in Venice on
October 23, 1913, was Frederick William Serafino Austin
Lewis Mary Rolfe. Baron Corvo was his favourite
pseudonym. Hadrian the Seventh is indescribable in any
of the recognized terms of literary criticism. This account of how George Arthur Rose of England became
Pope is partly autobiographical, partly satirical, partly
malicious, partly baroque, but altogether magnificent
reading if one be in the mood to wrestle with such words
as tygendis and technikrym. They are assuredly, however, part of the fun and colour. Pomp and ceremony
are described with a vocabulary that never falters.
When Hadrian is murdered in the streets of Rome,
Rolfe writes, "How bright the sunlight was on warm grey
stones, on the ripe Roman skins, on vermilion and
lavender, and blue and ermine, and green and gold, on
apostolic whiteness and the rose of blood." The reported
interviews between the Pope, the German Kaiser, and
the Italian King are sufficiently startling. Henry VI
and Mary Queen of Scots are canonized in this book.
So is Joan of Arc, some years before the thing actually
happened. The long, elaborate, pictorial description of
the Papal conclave is bewilderingly effective. Before he
assumed the purple, Rose diverted himself by counting
the split infinitives in the Pall Mall Gazette. An im-

portant character is a cat named Flavio. Edgar Saltus, Barbey d'Aurevilly, and Joris Huysmans in collaboration, with the aid of absinthe and ether, might have produced an approximation of this book.

It is doubtless my limitation, but it is nevertheless certainly true, that the lesser figures in art have always succeeded in arousing my interest to a higher degree than the greater figures. I am quite willing to subscribe to the superior genius of Beethoven and Milton, but I prefer to listen to Scarlatti and to read the slighter works of Thomas Love Peacock. It is the odd, the charming, the glamorous, often the old-fashioned, volume which has the compelling power with me. I am aware of the importance of Joseph Conrad, but while others read Lord Jim I find a warmer pleasure in rambling through formal literary gardens, no longer popular, in strolling along deserted auctorial shores, as I have wandered through those dead villages which during their proper season have been frequented by so many fashionable feet. Anatole France has told us that "the good critic is one who narrates the adventures of his own mind among masterpieces." [3] I would add one word to this aphorism so that it would read *minor* masterpieces. Now, blindfold, I pick a chance volume of France's own Vie Littéraire from the shelves and run my eye down the table des matières. What great names do I discover? Paul Arène, Paul Bourget, Léon Hennique, Gabriel

[3] Edward Thomas in a letter to W. H. Hudson, published in the London Mercury, August 1920, page 434, asserts: "You are unjust about the critical faculty, which seems to be neither more nor less than the capacity for freshly and profoundly enjoying many and widely different things—the more and more widely different the greater the critical faculty."

[25]

## Fashionable Places

Vicaire, Baron Denon, Maurice Spronck, the three Tisseurs, Maurice Bouchor, Joséphin Péladin, Edouard Rod, J. H. Rosny, Auguste Vacquerie, and Octave Feuillet.

Collectors of books are assiduous followers of fashions. Today they are hot after first editions of Walt Whitman, Lafcadio Hearn, George Moore, and Max Beerbohm. How pleasant it is for me, in face of these preferences, to search out the works of Cunninghame Graham, Marmaduke Pickthall, Sheridan Le Fanu, and Brockden Brown, who some day, perhaps, may be as fashionable with collectors as any of the others.

*January 14, 1921.*

## A Note on Philip Thicknesse

### I

What a melancholy fate pursues a library when its master dies! Even the penniless widow and her children, the bereaved pets, cats, dogs, monkeys, and parrots, are more likely to adjust themselves to the new conditions than the beloved books which remain to mourn their erstwhile possessor. Edmond de Goncourt perpended this problem and left the following solution of it in his will: "My wish is that my drawings, my prints, my curiosities, my books—in a word, these things of art which have been the joy of my life—shall not be consigned to the cold tomb of a museum and subjected to the stupid glance of the careless passerby; but I require that they shall be dispersed under the hammer of the auctioneer, so that the pleasure which the acquirement of each one of them has given me shall be given again in each case to some inheritor of my own tastes." Goncourt, apparently, was certain that each of his treasures would reach the man who loved it best. Personally, I feel some doubt on this point. I cannot bear the thought of sending my cats or my books to the auction block. My first edition of Oscar Wilde's Salome, with its faded silver and purple cover, printed in the Rue du Dragon in Paris, and now bound in white vellum by Vittorio de Toldo in Venice, would surely find an admirer or two. So would Champfleury's Les Chats, the most sympathetic

and profound of all the volumes on felines, embellished
with a great number of fascinating illustrations, including several by the Japanese Hokusai, and a curious
Russian drawing depicting gleeful rats and mice bearing
a dead puss on a cart to her grave, and even more important than these, an etching of a cat among flowers by
Manet, who also designed the poster employed to ad-
vertise this book, in which a superb black carl-cat is
paying attention to a white queen on a chimney-potted
roof, while their tails are flaunted in the face of the
rising moon. Examples of this poster are now more
difficult to come by than copies of the first edition of
Sister Carrie. . . . Nor have I anxiety over the ultimate
lot of the first edition of A Story Teller's Holiday, nor
over that of several of George Moore's earlier works,
originally the property of James Huneker who, as was his
wont, has plentifully supplied the margins with ribald
commentary, scribbled in pencil. On the other hand,
there are books on my shelves whose mere titles will convey nothing to the stolid bidder in the auction room.
Who, for instance, will be sensible enough to purchase
my copy of Frank L. Boyden's Popular American Composers, unless some one, fifty or sixty years from now
when I die, may remember to have read my account of
it in The Merry-Go-Round? [1] Who will bid for my copy
of Harry, by the author of Mrs. Jerningham's Journal,
also in my possession? These long narrative poems of
the seventies, written perhaps in imitation of Nothing to
Wear, are worth their weight in platinum to me, and yet
I picked them up for five and ten cents respectively, and
very probably at an auction sale they would go for less.

[1] This paper, entitled The Authoritative Work on American Music,
has since been reprinted in Red.

## Philip Thicknesse

However, if a prospective purchaser turns to page 62 of my copy of Harry, his eye will light on the following marked passage:

> "O, women have no temptations at all;
> They have only to keep their white lives white;
> But men are so tempted, that men must fall—
> O wonderful Harry who stands upright!"

and if he further flips the leaves I think he will desire to call the book his slave at whatever price. . . . In other directions, accidents may occur. Suppose some young priest, misled by the title, should carry away Francis Jacox's delightful Bible Music, or suppose that the Hanslick or H. E. Krehbiel of the period should deprive a cutie from the Follies, its rightful owner, of Les petits mystères de l'opéra, with Gavarni's piquant illustrations. Who but a Follies girl could appreciate Laure's daily prayer?

> "Mon cœur de jeune fille, ô Dieu, vers toi s'élance!
> Prends en pitié mes maux et guéris ma souffrance.
> Oh! fais qu'un prince russe ou qu'un milord anglais
> De Londre ou Moscou vienne admirer mes attraits.
> Le fétide marais est mortel à la rose;
> Non, pour la pauvreté je ne suis pas éclose,
> Le fiacre me déplait; l'omnibus me fait mal,
> Ce qu'il me faut c'est un briska—plus un cheval."

Whether or not God was good to Laure, Albéric Second, the author, does not tell us; he hastens on to describe the debris on Lélia's dressing-table:

> "Un citron à demi grignoté;
> Une livre de café rôti;
> Un cornet de tabac à priser;

[29]

Deux tablettes de chocolat;
Cinq ou six bouts de cigares;
Une poignée de haricots secs;
Une croûte de fromage de Gruyères;
Un collier de verroteries;
Deux brioches émiettées;
Un morceau de savon rose;
Une grappe de raisin de Corinthe;
Un petit chat, âgé seulement de quelques semaines;
Un paquet de cartes crasseuses;
Et un pot de pommade, rempli, jusqu'aux bords, d'un épais et
    onctueux raisiné."

I shall not attempt to translate this very charming free
verse of the year 1844. It seems obvious to me, however, that Albéric Second was one of the earliest, if not
the earliest, of the imagistes. . . . There is my copy of
The Baronet and the Butterfly, autographed with
Whistler's butterfly; there is the first edition of the Works
of Max Beerbohm; there is La Cathédrale, bound in
amethyst, and ruby, and emerald leather, into which these
precious stones have been set, until the cover glows with
the effulgence of one of the windows at Chartres that
Huysmans describes; there is Dr. Burney's The Present
State of Music in France and Italy (1773), and nearby,
Aluigi's Storia dell' Abate Pietro Metastasio, printed
at Assisi in 1783; and there is Philip Thicknesse's
Journey through France and a part of Spain, published
for the author in 1776.

## II

Philip Thicknesse was a cultivated, but irascible, English gentleman-adventurer with a kind of genius for ex-

pressing himself. His life, his published writings, an account of his various friendships and quarrels, of his three wives and more children, are of unusual interest to student and casual reader alike; even a superficial examination of them rewards the attention with a quaint picture of eighteenth century manners, with their causes and consequences and essential decorations, for Thicknesse's career was both active and decorative. It was exceedingly rich, for the career of so full-blooded a man, in delicate nuances; in the foreground of the picture our hero struggles with innumerable figures in political, social, artistic, army, and even religious life; while in the background, house-furnishings, clothes, music, and painting contribute to his pleasure and ours. Not the least important of these pleasures was an intense fondness for animals of all sorts, monkeys, birds, dogs, and horses. He was a most personal writer: he wrote only about himself, or about other things or people as they affected him, so that out of his twenty-four books, or out of any two of them, for that matter, one may with no great difficulty reconstruct both period and personality, not in the manner of a cold steel-engraving, but with all the warmth and colour of a painting. Thicknesse was not a phrase-maker, nor was he in any conscious way an artist, but he succeeded so well in transmitting himself, his ideas, his friends and enemies, and the sights he had observed, to paper that his pages still kindle the spark of delighted appreciation. You must not, however, expect to be transported into the elegant, rococo charm of Vernon Lee's Italian eighteenth century, although, to be sure, you will meet with powdered hair, lace coats, red coats trimmed with gold braid, snuff, crimson-velvet breeches, white wigs and plumes, blue silk capuchins,

# Philip Thicknesse

four-wheeled chaises, and coffee-houses. And if the name of Metastasio is lacking, in compensation there are several references to The Beggar's Opera.

Philip Thicknesse was born in 1719 and he died in 1792; he therefore may be said to be representative of the complete span of the eighteenth century. He was the son of a rector of Northamptonshire, according to Sidney Lee's Dictionary of National Biography, and he was sent first to Aynhoe and later to Westminster School. His father then placed him with an apothecary bearing the very eighteenth century name of Marmaduke Tisdall, but Philip's taste for the chemist's calling appears to have been meagre and in 1735, when he was sixteen years old, he embarked for Georgia with General Oglethorpe. Thus his travels and adventures began, travels and adventures which were to continue throughout his long career. The account of his two years in America, related in Memoirs and Anecdotes of Philip Thicknesse (1788), is sufficiently diverting. His distaste for the white settlers in the colony and his sympathy for the Indians led him to seek the settlement of a native king on the Susquehanna River. "In this situation," he informs us, "I wanted nothing but a *female friend* (the quaint eighteenth century use of italics), and I had almost determined to take to wife one of Queen Cenauke's maids of honour. I seriously paid my addresses to her and she in turn honour'd me with the appellation of *Auche* (friend). She had receiv'd a pair of Indian boots, some paint, looking glass, a comb, a pair of scissars, as tokens of my love, and one Buffaloe's skin had certainly held us had not an extraordinary incident arose which determined me to return immediately to England." This incident was a dream in which his mother appeared to

[32]

him, apparently as a departed spirit. The vision was so vivid that he believed it to be the announcement of his mother's death. He therefore returned to England at once (in 1737) only to find the estimable lady alive and in perfect health.

In England he was employed by trustees of the company until he lost Oglethorpe's favour by speaking too plainly in regard to the management of the company's affairs in Georgia. His next adventure carried him to Jamaica where he obtained a lieutenancy in an independent company and where for a time he was engaged in desultory warfare with wild Negroes. The greater part of the first volume of his Memoirs is occupied with this period, together with much controversial matter concerning a certain James MacKittrick. MacKittrick and Thicknesse seem to have indulged in the mud-throwing game with no reservations whatever, without regard for the libel laws. Here is a sample passage from the Memoirs: "I am now arrived at that important period of my life (yet a compleat half century ago) that James MacKittrick, alias Adair, hath charged me with having the sole command of a party of soldiers when in the woods of Jamaica, and falling into an ambush of the wild Negroes; securing my own person by an early retreat, and leaving the battle to be fought by my victorious Sergeant, who brought many of them in prisoners, at the instant that I was boasting of my personal exploits. I will not call this double named doctor a *beast*, a *reptile*, an *assassin*, a *murder-monger*, but the reader will, I am sure, excuse me in saying he is a base libeller, a liar, and a wicked defamer, and has no pretensions to be considered as a gentleman, if he has dared to write, print, and publish such falsehoods."

**[33]**

# Philip Thicknesse

Thicknesse's account of the fight with the wild Negroes, which follows this diatribe, is conspicuously stirring, none the less so because the author to a great extent sympathized with the cause of the blacks. Whether Thicknesse or MacKittrick gives the true report of what happened in Jamaica, this much at least is certain, that Thicknesse disagreed with his brother officers and returned to England. On his homeward journey the ship caught fire, but the blaze was extinguished and the voyage proceeded. In 1744–45 he joined the Mediterranean fleet under the command of Admiral Medley. In February 1753, he procured by purchase the Lieutenant-Governorship of Land Guard Fort, Suffolk, which he held until 1766. His life at the fort was marked by a series of dissensions. His particular enemy, with whom he must have been in almost continuous altercation, was Francis Vernon (afterwards Lord Orwell and Earl of Shipbrooke), then Colonel of the Suffolk militia. As an ultimate ironic act Thicknesse presented the Colonel with a wooden gun, becoming involved thereby in an action for libel, with the result that he was confined three months in the King's Bench Prison and fined £300. Later, he exhibited the wooden gun, labelled with some depreciatory verses, in front of his house at Bath. In a letter to the Lady of Admiral G., in the second volume of his Memoirs, Thicknesse, with admirable humour, recounts the history of the wooden gun at some length. While he frequently quarrelled with those whose station in military or civil life was above his own, his relations with his inferiors appear to have been distinguished by the finest feelings, the most scrupulous propriety. That he was essentially humane the following passage, referring to a deserting sergeant condemned to death, will testify: "It is an easy matter to sentence a man to death, or to inflict a thousand lashes on his back, but it is terrible to endure; during the fourteen years I commanded Land Guard Fort I made the old invalids do their duty like soldiers, and I have a certificate under all their hands that I did so, and that no man during that period had his shirt stript from his body, or a lash upon his back." And note this passage concerning slavery: "I have seen the slavery of the West Indies, and the slavery of the Galleys, but the *veriest slaves* I have ever seen, are the day labourers of England and Ireland, and the *all work* maidservants of London." It is with the American Indian, the African Negro, that Thicknesse sympathized when he visited this continent and the adjacent islands, and later, during the Revolution, he took the part of the colony against England. "Is it probable," asks Thicknesse in 1776, "that all the fleets and armies of Great Britain can conquer America?—England may as well attempt moving that Continent on this side of the Atlantic."

In 1754, walking near Land Guard Fort, he met Thomas Gainsborough and for twenty years thereafter constituted himself patron of this artist, of whose genius he considered himself the discoverer. He wrote, I think, the first life of Gainsborough, a book which has proved valuable to later biographers of the painter. He even induced Gainsborough to move from Ipswich to Bath, but in 1774 the inevitable, if belated, squabble occurred and the friendship was ended.

This misunderstanding, being fully described in The Life of Thomas Gainsborough, is not mentioned in the two volumes of the Memoirs which I have seen (a third was added later), but many others are set down in full. For instance, he explains how and why he beat up Mr.

[35]

Hutton Briggs with a cane at Portsmouth. Two young misses, sent by their wifeless father to join Mr. and Mrs. Thicknesse at Calais, had the misfortune to bring with them a carnivorous dog which straightway devoured Mrs. Thicknesse's favourite paroquet. As a result, the master of the house promptly packed the young ladies off to a convent where their father, having no home for them, permitted them to remain, under lock and key, for three years! In a chapter entitled Anecdote of a Lord, a Monk, and a Fool, Thicknesse relates how the Earl of Coventry desired him to secure from one of the holy men at Montserrat some botanical specimens for which his lordship eventually refused to pay. Even a quarrel with the Archbishop of Canterbury over a weathercock and a guinea is reported in bitter detail.

But perhaps his greatest feud was with England. In 1766 he settled at Welwyn, Hertfordshire, removing thence to Monmouthshire, and in 1768 to Bath, where he purchased a residence in the Crescent. In 1775 his long cherished hope of succeeding to £12,000 from the family of his first wife was destroyed by the result of an unsuccessful appeal to the House of Lords. He regarded this decision as equivalent to a personal insult, and he resolved to abandon his native land and settle in Spain. Accompanied by his wife, two daughters, a manservant, and his monkey, he set out from Calais in his own cabriolet. "He is," writes Havelock Ellis, "the accomplished representative of a certain type of Englishman. The men of this type have, in fact, a passion for exploring the physical world, they are often found outside England, and for some strange reason they seem more themselves, more quintessentially English, when they are out of England. They are gentlemen and

[36]

they are patriots. But they have a natural aptitude for disgust and indignation, and they cannot fail to find ample exercise for that aptitude in the affairs of their own country. So in a moment of passion they shake the dust of England off their feet to rush abroad, where, also, however,—though they are far too intelligent to be inappreciative of what they find,—they meet even more to arouse their disgust and indignation, and in the end they usually come back to England. . . . For the most part the manners and customs of this type of men are only known to us by hearsay which we may refuse to credit. But about Thicknesse there is no manner of doubt; he has written himself down; he is the veridic and positive embodiment of the type. . . . The type is scarcely that of the essential Englishman, yet it is one type, and a notably interesting type, really racy of the soil. Borrow—less of a fine gentleman than Thicknesse, but more of a genius—belonged to the type. Landor, a man cast in a much grander mould, was yet of the same sort, and the story which tells how he threw his Italian cook out of the window, and then exclaimed with sudden compunction, 'Good God! I forgot the violets!' is altogether in the spirit of Thicknesse. Trelawney was a man of this kind, and so was Sir Richard Burton. . . . They are an uncomfortable race of men, but in many ways admirable; we should be proud rather than ashamed of them. Their unreasonableness, their inconsiderateness, their irritability, their singular gleams of insight, their exuberant energy of righteous vituperation, the curious irregularities of their minds,—however personally alien one may happen to find such qualities,—can never fail to interest and delight."

Thicknesse passed through the south of France into

# Philip Thicknesse

Catalonia, where he sojourned for a time at Barcelona, but with the exception of the Monastery of Montserrat, he found Spain even more unbearable than England and was back in Bath within the year. A delightfully discursive book, in two volumes, illustrated with drawings from Thicknesse's own pen, A Year's Journey through France and a part of Spain, a copy of which is in my possession, was the result of this excursion. The long and detailed description of Montserrat, written before the various despoliations suffered by the monastery, gives the book an especial interest for those, and there are many such, to whom the very name of Montserrat offers a unique thrill. There is a catalogue of the jewels of the madonna: "There are four crowns for the head of the Virgin; two of plated gold, richly set with diamonds; two of solid gold, one of which has two thousand five hundred large emeralds in it, and is valued at fifty thousand ducats; the fourth, and richest, is set with one thousand one hundred and twenty-four diamonds, five of which number are valued at five hundred ducats each; eighteen hundred large pearls, of equal size; thirty-eight large emeralds, twenty-one zaphirs, and five rubies; and at the top of this crown is a gold ship, adorned with diamonds of eighteen thousand dollars' value. The gold alone of these crowns weighs twenty-five pounds, and with the jewels and setting, upwards of fifty. These crowns have been made at Montserrat, from the gold and separate jewels presented to the convent from time to time by the crowned heads and princes of Europe." The legend of Juan Guerin and the miraculous founding of the monastery is told in a fascinating folk-spirit style. Alec Trusselby could do no better. Thicknesse climbed to each of the hermitages and he describes them all,

[38]

each hut set on its tiny pinnacle of mountain, overhanging a precipice, overgrown with extravagant floral vegetation. The holy brothers were expressly forbidden to kill meat or to entertain pets in their huts, but one of them evaded the law by meeting his tame birds outside. They nestled in his beard and his garment, and Thicknesse, who had just bought a new fowling-piece at Barcelona, was so moved by the pretty spectacle that he registered a vow never to employ it, a vow which he breaks a few hundred pages later. Most wonderful of all is the account of the blind mule which, laden with baskets, unaccompanied, made the perilous tour of the hermitages once a day, bearing the monks their food.

The casual reader, however, the lover of literature and life, will be more amused and delighted by the ordinary adventures of the day and night, the report of the inns, of people met by the way, of the astonishing monkey who rejects the opportunity of social intercourse with elderly male monkeys encountered on the road, fearing that each may be his father, thus anticipating by a century Samuel Butler's Ernest in The Way of All Flesh. The author is alive to all impressions and he puts everything down indifferently, from his enthusiastic reaction in regard to the Maison-Carrée at Nîmes to an account of his overturning a dish of spinach on a maidservant's head. Thicknesse had previously observed, with amazement and disgust, the preparation of this spinach, in the courtyard of the inn. He philosophizes about the comparative amount of drinking in the countries he visits; he compares the French with the English; he gossips about Madame de Pompadour; he offers advice to young Englishmen about to travel, warning them against women and gambling; he meets a pretty girl sculling across a

**[39]**

French river, asks her what she does in the winter when
the river is frozen, and elicits the reply that she has two
talents, a fact he faithfully records; there are pages relating to the perils that beset the path of the inexpe-
rienced traveller, bandits, card-sharpers, gipsies, wicked
aguaziles; there are more pages devoted to priests, her-
etics, beggars, and grandees; he visits his daughter,
immured as a nun in a convent at Ardres because small-
pox has ravaged her face and, finding that the mother-
superior, through ignorance or cupidity or both, has let
rooms on the parlour floor to two Englishwomen whose
pretensions to respectability he suspects, in some heat he
adjures the holy mother to hustle them out at once, lest
their worldly influence shall corrupt his daughter's peace
of mind;[2] he sees and describes, in horrible detail, the
more excruciating because he tries to evade the experience but cannot push through the crowd, an execution:
a man is broken on the wheel and the executioner's aged
mother, not without relish, assists him in his noisome
job; he avoids the coronation of Louis XVI at Rheims

---

[2] That Thicknesse had ground for his suspicions we may readily
believe after reading what Mrs. Emily James Putnam has to say in
The Lady about eighteenth century French convents: "Many convents
received ladies from the world as transient guests and these inmates
brought the world with them. Madame de Genlis, shortly after her
marriage, sojourned in a convent while her husband was absent on
military duty. She enjoyed herself thoroughly. The abbess used to
invite men to dinner in her apartment; at the carnival, Madame de
Genlis was allowed to give in the convent-parlour two balls a week
attended by nuns and school-girls; when these amusements were insufficient she would sometimes rise at midnight, run down the corridor
in the costume of the devil and wake the nuns in their cells. When
she found a sister very sound asleep she would paint her cheeks and
affix a mouche or two. The little girls were often allowed free access
to the lady-boarders and listened with round eyes to their tales of
life in the world."

and tells us why; he is mistreated by Messrs. Curtoys and Wombwell, who refuse to recognize his English bank notes in Barcelona, and he sets down the minutiae of the transaction, together with his unflattering opinions of the gentlemen in question; he paints a picture of the fandango and even prints the music to which it may be danced; in fact, he gossips and chats and scolds and praises in the loosest and freest manner, probably without ever considering himself consciously in any professional sense a writer, and yet skill of the most acute kind has seldom produced so entertaining a book of travel. Indeed, I ramble through the two musty old volumes, sprinkled with obsolete and mistaken spellings and S's like F's with much the same pleasure that I would derive from rambling through the same scenes with a sympathetic companion.

In 1784 Thicknesse erected in his private grounds at the Hermitage the first monument raised in England to Chatterton's memory. Five years later this restless spirit purchased a barn at Sandgate near Hytte, and converted it into a dwelling place, from which he might gaze on the shores of France into which country he made another excursion in 1791, visiting Paris during the early days of the Revolution. The following year he was back in Bath, but he again departed for the continent and died November 19, 1792 in a coach near Boulogne on his way to Paris with his wife. He was buried in the Protestant Cemetery at Boulogne.

He was married three times. In 1742 he married Maria, only daughter of John Lanove of Southampton, a French refugee. She died early in 1749 and on November 10 of the same year he married Elizabeth Touchet, eldest daughter of the Earl of Castlehaven. Her sister,

## Philip Thicknesse

Lady Mary Touchet, met the Pretender at a ball in Paris in 1745. Attracted by her personal charm, he asked her to dance with him, communicated to her the details of his expedition, even ripped the star from his breast and gave it to her. . . . She died at the age of twenty. Elizabeth Touchet Thicknesse died March 28, 1762, leaving three sons and three daughters. The eldest son succeeded to the Barony of Audley. His father hated him and in his will desired that his right hand be cut off and sent to Lord Audley, "to remind him of his duty to God, after having so long abandoned the duty he owed to his father." There is a further reminiscence of this family feud in the complete title of his last book which reads, Memoirs and Anecdotes of Philip Thicknesse, late Lieutenant Governor of Land Guard Fort, and unfortunately father to George Touchet, Baron Audley. The disagreement with George, which seems to have been about money, eventually extended to another son, Philip. . . . Thicknesse married his third wife, Anne (1737–1824), daughter of Thomas Ford, September 27, 1762. She was a musician, playing the guitar, the viola da gamba, and the musical glasses, and singing Handel and old Italian airs. She even gave concerts in London. The customs inspector at Cette, on the way to Spain, found "a bass viol, two guittars, a fiddle, and some other musical instruments" in Thicknesse's luggage. The third Mrs. Thicknesse also employed the pen; she wrote sketches of the lives and literature of the ladies of France.

Twenty-four books by Thicknesse are listed, although none of them is easy to procure nowadays. Perhaps the most important are: Observations on the customs and manners of the French nation (1766; second edition, 1779; third edition, 1789); Useful hints to those who make the tour of France (1768); Sketches and characters of the most eminent and singular persons now living (1770); A Treatise on the art of decyphering and writing in cypher, with an harmonic alphabet (1772); A Year's Journey through France and a part of Spain (1777; second edition, 1778; third edition, 1789); Queries to Lord Audley (1782); A Sketch of the Life and Paintings of Thomas Gainsborough (1788) and the Memoirs (1788–91).

At one time in his life he became interested in the subject of gall-stones. He wrote a book on their exorcism entitled The Valetudinarian's Bath Guide and, to cure Lord Thurlow, with whom, of course, he afterwards broke off relations, he prescribed a trotting horse, "to render the externals of the gall-stones perfectly smooth." He recurs to the subject, which must have obsessed him for a score of years, in his Memoirs and also therein discusses other bladder complaints with some freedom.

There is a further chapter in this fantastic chronicle about Mrs. Mary Tuft of Godalming, who asserted that she gave birth to rabbits, delivering fifteen in a batch, and a few ironic paragraphs are aimed at St. Andre, the anatomist, who wrote a pamphlet to prove that rabbits were preternatural human fœtuses in the form of quadrupeds. At the end of the first volume, in lieu of the listed errors, usual in books printed at this period, one finds the following statement: "Errata for *both* volumes. The author is in his Seventieth Year and never pretended to be an accurate writer," and in the extensive catalogue of patrons it seems very pleasant to meet the names of David Garrick and Thomas Gainsborough.

[43]

# Philip Thicknesse

## III

I should find little difficulty in hitting upon a future owner for my Philip Thicknesse. Indeed, I have few friends who would not cherish this book. Doubtless, the ideal way to dispose of a library is to give each volume by deed of testament to the friend best fitted to receive it, but there are valid objections to this procedure. Perhaps, when I die, Peter Whiffle,[3] who now ardently desires my set of Lafcadio Hearn, may be browsing in other fields; perhaps he may have acquired a set of his own. Noël Haddon assured me but the other day that she would be willing to see me expire if I would leave in her hands my Petronius, bound in old rose and quaintly tooled with golden fruit, but in a few weeks Noël will have satisfied her curiosity in regard to Petronius and will turn her roving but envious attention to my shelfful of Catulle Mendès's works, bound in gay Florentine wall-papers.

Nor could I leave all my books to one person, unless I added to the bequest a sum sufficient for their upkeep, for who is there who desires to possess all of another man's books? Who is there, indeed, who wants half of another man's books?

Still studying the problem, I stood before my shelves, flipping open the covers of this and that beloved volume, bestowing admiration and approval while yet I might, sometimes on the contents, sometimes on the printing, sometimes on the binding, sometimes, even, on the illustrations, and I cast about in my mind for a decent method of disposal, for I could not tolerate the idea of sending my books to the auction block. I have loved them in this

[3] Written in 1918; Peter Whiffle died December 15, 1919.

life and I determined they must rest safely after my death. Days and days have I spent in dusty and splendid bookshops (although, alas, I never knew Arthur Symons's Holywell Street), conning the shelves, always to find some new treasure, some new delight, for it is my fortune that I can never retire empty-handed from a bookshop. And even the most tattered volume assumes its dignity and importance once it is dusted and placed in its correct position on my stately shelves.

Pondering thus, I found a satisfactory solution. When I am dead, my books shall be cleaned and laid out for burial in bronze chests made to harbour them. Not a single volume is to be excluded. The chests are then to be hermetically sealed and buried in a secret place, which only one shall know, and it may be that I shall cause the chests to be sunk, like another Atlantis, to the bottom of the sea, or they may be hidden in caves, or interred five fathoms deep in the soil, or they may be conveyed across rivers and oceans and continents to the mouth of an extinct volcano and there deposited in the crater, but wherever they are concealed only one shall know.

And after several centuries (perhaps, indeed, my chests will escape sacking for as long a time as the Egyptian tombs) some fellow, digging, if they be entombed in land, will uncover my chests. Or, if they be consigned to the sea, they may be found by some diver, or perhaps the course of the waters will again be altered and what is now wet will then be dry. At any rate, sooner or later my chests will be discovered and pried open, and great, at first, will be the disappointment of the man who brings them to light, for will he not count on a treasure? His first thought will be, Surely these heavy chests so carefully sealed contain shivering handfuls of rubies and emeralds, or malachite goblets, or perhaps they enclose bars of clean yellow gold or plates of tarnished silver. Metal surely—their weight portends that; weapons, perhaps: daggers, with curiously contrived hilts, Florentine stilettos, rapiers, crossbows, or pistols of Toledo work.

Then, after he has pondered over these matters for some time, as a woman caresses an unopened letter, wondering who the writer may be, he will open the chests with implements of iron. Disappointment will succeed astonishment, but in the end he will brighten with joy. For the veriest dolt of a peasant, the veriest zany of a manufacturer's son, will presently realize the extent of his good fortune. The private and personal library of a gentleman of the twentieth century! he will exclaim, and his enthusiasm will be justifiable, for the period, nay several periods, may be readily reconstructed from these poor bones. And if he be peasant he will sell his find to some collector and if he be collector he will seek vehicles to bear his find to some city where he may display it on fine shelves builded for the purpose, and the books will be the joy of scholar and dilettante for a generation, as they strive to puzzle out the strange words of the twentieth century. It is agreeable to fancy that when my chests are unearthed most of the books therein will have disappeared from other collections, even from the libraries, and the titles and names of the authors on the backs will find a new lease of fame, a new and wiser glory, for which one of us can predict with any certainty which of these books will best please the taste of the fortieth century?

*November 30, 1918.*

[46]

## Ouida

Many of my literary liaisons have been belated. A number of my favourite books have been other men's mistresses before they have become mine. More than once I have blushed for my comfortable failure to keep up with the times, even the old times, although, occasionally, I remind myself with some pride that I read Daudet's Sapho before the prescribed age of twenty.[1] This, however, was an exceptional performance. I can always look back and discover a new face. At ninety I expect to sit before my fire, dallying amorously with some overlooked masterpiece.

Sometimes (and with what delight!), I hit upon an entirely new name. That is a real experience in a wanton career of bibliophilic amours. More often, however, not only have I long been aware of the existence of the future beguiler of my intimate moments but also a volume or two by this author has snoozed patiently on my shelves, silently waiting the magic hour when its pages may begin to call to me with the voice of seduction. Certainly I cannot say that I remember ever having been ignorant of Ouida, but in some hazy way her work was associated in my mind with that of the Duchess, Laura Jean Libbey, and Bertha M. Clay. Little by little, however, I became conscious that this name fell frequently from the lips of intelligent people. It was borne in upon me, in-

[1] The reference here, of course, is to Daudet's dedication. See infra, page 275.

sistently if slowly, that I had missed something, just what was not too apparent, but something important beyond any manner of doubt. Joseph Hergesheimer had read Ouida; Max Beerbohm had read Ouida, and not only devoted an essay to her but also invented his most celebrated dedication in her honour; [2] Edgar Fawcett [3] had read Ouida; so had Stephen Crane, Vernon Lee, G. S. Street,[4] and Arthur Symons. Wilfred Scawen Blunt and Auberon Herbert read and admired her. G. K. Chesterton, reader for Fisher Unwin in 1899, wrote in his report of The Waters of Edera, "Though it is impossible not to smile at Ouida, it is equally impossible not to read her."

In the course of time, my curiosity was aroused. It behooved me, I began to believe, to follow in the footsteps of this illustrious, if somewhat incongruous, company. My mood was excellent for the enterprise. I was weary of modern fiction, tainted with Freud and Fabre, weary of James Joyce and Dorothy Richardson and D. H. Lawrence, weary of Romain Rolland and his quest for a perfect world; what better opportunity to sample the simpler diversions of a novelist who had given as much pleasure to ingenuous chambermaids as she had to the recondite author of The Happy Hypocrite? I sought a guide to this bewildering forest (the bibliography lists forty-seven titles) and was referred to a long

[2] To his More. See infra, page 284. Norman Douglas's first book, Unprofessional Tales, published under the pseudonym of Normyx by Fisher Unwin in 1901, and now very rare, is also dedicated to Ouida.

[3] His paper, The Truth about Ouida, is to be found in Agnosticism; Belford, Clarke and Co.; 1889.

[4] See An Appreciation of Ouida on page 167 of The Yellow Book for July 1895. Republished in Quales Ego; John Lane; 1896. There should also be reference here to Chapter XXII (How Heroes Smoke) of J. M. Barrie's My Lady Nicotine.

paper, in the Atlantic Monthly for July 1886, by Harriet Waters Preston, who seems to have been the first critic to inquire seriously into the causes of Ouida's popularity, but I found her admiration rather tepid. My second choice in ciceroni was more fortunate; it was Elizabeth Lee's Memoir, a fortuitous accident, for Ouida's life explains her work and gives it an intricacy of design that is not entirely obvious to those unacquainted with Mademoiselle de la Ramée [5] herself. Then I began to read the novels . . .

Now those who have preceded me in this adventure, I discover, applaud Ouida for qualities she undoubtedly possesses: her passionate hatred of injustice, her love for animals, her feeling for beauty, and her skill in evoking the atmosphere of Italy. Indubitably, she assimilated and reproduced in a remarkable manner the spirit of this country. Even Henry James has given his grudging admiration to her handling of the Italian scene. Her sympathy for the peasant is responsible for many a nice piece of prose. In her review of the work of F. Marion Crawford, for example, she contradicts his assertion that the Italians are lacking in imagination: "This is but partially true; I am not sure that it is true at all. Their modern poetry is beautiful, more beautiful than that of any other nation. Their popular songs are poetic and impassioned as those of no other nation are, and one may hear among their peasantry expressions of singular beauty of sentiment and phrase. A woman of middle age, a contadina, said to me once, 'So long as

---

[5] Ramé is the spelling adopted by Elizabeth Lee and I have followed it in The Blind Bow-Boy. As I can discover no other authority for this arbitrary dropping of an e, I am returning to the more popular form.

one's mother lives, one's youth is never quite gone, for
there is always somebody for whom one is young.' A
rough, rude man, a day-labourer, who knew not a letter
and spent all his life bent over his spade or plough,
said to me once, one lovely night in spring, as he looked
up at the full moon, 'How beautiful she is! But she
has no heart. She sees us toiling and groaning and suffering down here, and she is always fair and calm, and
never weeps!' Another said once, when a tree was hard
to fell, 'He is sorry to come away, it has been his field
so long.' And when a flock of solan geese flew over
our land, going from the marshes to the mountains on
their homeward way, and descended to rest, the peasants
did not touch them: 'They are tired, poor souls,' said
one of the women; 'one must not grudge them the soil
for their lodging!'" Her humanitarianism included a
horror of war, oppressive taxation of the poor, vivisec-
tion, Joseph Chamberlain, and the German Emperor.
She was a warm admirer of Georges Darien, the French
anti-militarist novelist, the Barbusse, the John Dos Pas-
sos of the Franco-Prussian war. She deplored the dese-
cration of the Tuscan country-side and the vandalism
prevailing in Italian cities. While I am by no means
blind to these æsthetic and moral virtues in her well-
rounded work, I lay my wreath on another altar. My
joy in Ouida is more akin to that of the chambermaid:
I take an unfeigned delight in her reports of the pleasant
lives of the idle rich.

Readers of the Memoir, which might have been entitled A Novel Without a Hero, will learn that Ouida
was a snob. She was also vain, capricious, obstinate, and
foolishly proud. She believed that her place in history
would be with Semiramis, Aspasia, Cleopatra, and

# Ouida

Madame de Staël. Pilgrims to the Villa Farinola or hostesses who had the daring to attempt her entertainment, were certain to be snubbed, unless they knelt abjectly before her.[6] Queens and Duchesses alone, perhaps, were spared this dishonour and, in her critical papers and her letters, she even permitted herself the privilege of scoffing at royalty (vide the scandalous verses addressed to Victoria, her arraignment of the Italian Royal Family, and her remarks, in her letters to the Baron Tauchnitz, concerning the Kaiser). In her novels this snobbishness assumed a still more curious form. The social climber in real life, the spendthrift, who sent to Worth in Paris for white, or pale-blue, or mouse-coloured satin and velvet gowns, with skirts short enough to expose her trim ankles, to wear driving on the

[6] W. H. Mallock, to whom Ouida dedicated Views and Opinions in 1895, writes (in Memoirs of Life and Literature): "Ouida lived largely in a world of her own creation, peopled with foreign princesses, mysterious dukes—masters of untold millions, and of fabulous English guardsmen whose bedrooms in Knightsbridge Barracks were inlaid with silver and tortoise-shell. And yet such was her genius that she invested this phantom world with a certain semblance of life, and very often with a certain poetry also. In some respects she was even more striking than her books. In her dress and in her manner of life she was an attempted exaggeration of her own female characters. For many years she occupied a large villa near Florence. During that time she visited London once. There it was that I met her. She depicted herself to herself as a personage of European influence, and imagined herself charged with a mission to secure the appointment of Lord Lytton as British Ambassador in Paris. With this purpose in view she called one day on Lady Salisbury, who, never having seen her before, was much amazed by her entrance, and was still more amazed when Ouida, in confidential tones, said, 'I have come to tell you that the one man for Paris is Robert.' Lady Salisbury's answer was not very encouraging. It consisted of the question, 'And pray, if you please, who is Robert?' In a general way, however, she received considerable attention, and might have received more if it had not been for her reckless ignorance of the London world. In whatever company she might

# Ouida

dusty Tuscan roads, sitting in her little victoria, drawn
by the chestnut ponies, Mascherino and Birichini, with
bunches of pheasant feathers stuck in their harness, once
she took pen in hand, was uncompromising in her attitude
towards luxury. She described the homes of the rich
to the last marble staircase and the Aubusson carpeted
pavilion where the guests indulged in wicked merrymak-
ing; she counted every pearl on the throat of her adventuress and, having added them, poured them over her
pages, prodigally, by the bucketful. Exotic flowers,
priceless jewels, orphic baubles, elaborate toilets, and
unparalleled foods are carted past the eye until the vision
is surfeited, but it is only for the purpose, Ouida almost convinced herself, of showing the reader how empty
is the life of the very rich. She has not convinced one
reader. Ouida wrote of a life she hungered to enjoy,
she catalogued precious stones she wanted to wear, she
painted portraits of men she desired to embrace. Nor
was this merely the unintelligent envy of the outsider.

be in, her first anxiety was to ingratiate herself with the most important members of it, but she was constantly making mistakes as to
who the most important members were. Thus, as one of her enter-
tainers—'Violet Fane'—told me, Ouida was sitting after dinner between
Mrs. ——, the mistress of one of the greatest houses in London, and a
vulgar little Irish peeress who was only present on sufferance. Ouida
treated the former with the coldest and most condescending inattention,
and devoted every smile in her possession to an intimate worship of
the latter. Among the ladies to whom she had been introduced in
London was Winifred, Lady Howard of Glossop. A year or so later
Ouida wrote me a letter from Florence, saying, 'Your name has just
been recalled to me by seeing in the Morning Post that you were
dining the other night with Lady Howard of Glossop, one of my
oldest friends.' This is an example of the way in which her imagination enabled her to live in a fabric of misplaced facts, for the person
through whom she became acquainted with Lady Howard was none
other than myself."

# *Ouida*

She was enough on the inside to observe the objects of her jealous attention at close range and she has set down their existence with an idealization of its power and fascination which, even when she most moralizes over its fatal rottenness, has almost persuaded me that the life of the idle English is the life for me.

Unrequited affection was another subject which obsessed her. Readers of the Memoir will again understand. At the age of fourteen Ouida began to fall in love with any man who treated her with ordinary politeness and believed him to be equally in love with her. Later, in her womanhood, an Italian Marchese became the embarrassed object of her attentions, and there is circumstantial evidence that she even felt amorously inclined towards Mario, for she always kept a picture of the tenor on her desk in her villa at Scandicci, and she tenderly represented him as Corrèze in her novel, Moths.[7]

---

[7] W. H. Mallock gives another example of this trait. He paid a visit one summer to Robert, the second Lord Lytton, at Knebworth. "On the day of my arrival one of the first topics discussed was Ouida, who at that time was in England, and had been staying at Knebworth only the week before. Ouida's view of life was nothing if not romantic. Lytton, during the previous spring, had been spending some weeks in Florence. He was quite alone; and Ouida, who, apart from her affectations, was a remarkable woman, had had no difficulty in securing his frequent company at her villa, where she fed him at an incredible price with precociously ripe strawberries. On her memory of these tender proceedings she had built up a belief that his nature had been emptied of everything except one great passion for herself, and she had actually come to Knebworth convinced that a single word from her would tear him from the bosom of his family and make him hers alone. The magic word was said. The expected results, however, had failed to follow—perhaps because the word, or words, had not been very happily chosen. They had been these: 'Why don't you leave this bourgeois man-and-wife milieu behind you and prove in some Sicilian palace what life may really mean for people like you and I?' "

# Ouida

Never, however, was her affection for a man reciprocated. In Ariadnê, she depicts the real artist as always unhappy, always suffering, unless he can give himself wholly to his art and eschew human love.

It has long been a contention of mine that middle-class life is as dull in art as it is in reality. Ouida, seemingly, agreed with me. Her novels deal with the aristocracy or the peasantry or the artist class, never with the middle-classes, except in the guise of nouveaux riches, whom she was never weary of ridiculing (classic examples are the Masserenes and Fuchsia Leach in Moths). In her report of the world that interested her, her imagination and her vitality were unflagging.[8] There is something Homeric in her sweep and carrying power, something almost Balzacian, or at least Sandian, in the superb manner in which she crowded a stupendous canvas with figures. Max Beerbohm, indeed, has asserted that Mr. Meredith was "the only living novelist in England who rivals Ouida in sheer vitality." I like to think of her, attired in a Worth velvet gown, her hair loose and flying down her back (so she wore it on all occasions long past middle age), superbly ugly in her eccentric splendour, surrounded by her dogs which, Henry G. Huntington informs us, had none too clean habits, dashing off in her broad hand, which wrote, perhaps, sixty words to the page, her ecstatic romances. The unnumbered sheets were permitted to flutter to the floor. Later they were pieced together. Correction was deemed supererogatory; verification of references, unheard

[8] Would it were possible, I sometimes sigh, to recreate the novel along these free romantic lines! The forerunners of this renaissance should stick to high life and fundamental emotions and their slogan might be: Back to Ouida!

of. Has any other creator ever worked like this, directly from the imagination, save such geniuses as Gautier and Balzac and George Sand? "Her prodigality," Ambrose Bierce once wrote (and whatever one may say of the author of The Devil's Dictionary, one cannot deny that he was a judge of intellect), "was seen chiefly in her expenditure of intellectual force, of which she wasted enough to have made a half-hundred better novelists than herself. Almost any contemporary worker at her trade would have profited as a dog under her intellectual table."

Never, except in some of her shorter stories, did Ouida rid herself entirely of her vice of redundancy. Her method of composition was largely responsible for this flaw. But how delightful to read an author that one may skip occasionally! How fatigued one becomes, in perusing the closely packed pages of The Wings of the Dove, in focusing one's eyes not only on the lines but on the spaces between the lines as well!

Mademoiselle de la Ramée struck her pace in her first novel, Granville de Vigne, or Held in Bondage. Other of her romances, possibly, are written with more care and with more art, but, with Max Beerbohm, I agree that Ouida was always Ouida. True lovers of this novelist will not concur with the hesitant and belated opinions of those who suddenly and condescendingly discovered the importance of the change in her style and manner with the publication of The Masserenes, which Ouida herself admitted was "worth 10,000 Trilbys." The change in style and manner are certainly to be noted, but the congenital frenzied glamour which made her what she was that day, just as certainly was apparent in Granville de Vigne. For some, perhaps, there may be too much glamour, but as Mr. Street has sensibly remarked, "You must allow the convention—the convention between you and the temperament of your author."

In Granville de Vigne, Ouida introduces us to the first of her daring, intrepid, ultra-raffiné, wasp-waisted guardsmen, the fascinating Vivian Sabretasche: "They said he was deucedly dangerous to women, and one could hardly wonder if he was. A gallant soldier in the field, a charming companion in a club or mess-room, accomplished in music, painting, sculpture, as in the hardier arts of rifle and rod, speaking eight continental languages with equal facility, his manners exquisitely tender and gentle, his voice soft as the Italian he loved best to speak, his. face and form of unusual beauty, and to back him, all that subtler art that is only acquired in the eleusinia of the boudoir—no marvel if women, his pet playthings, did go down before Vivian Sabretasche." It is from this book, too, that I have culled what is, perhaps, all things considered, my favourite passage in all fiction, that descriptive of Constance Trefusis, the first of Ouida's wicked, wicked women: "Magnificent she looked in some geranium-hued dress, as light and brilliant as summer clouds, with the rose tint of sunset on them, and large white water-lilies in her massive raven hair, turned back à l'impératrice off her low brow, under which her eyes shot such Parthian glances. One could hardly wonder that De Vigne offended past redemption the Duchess of Margoldwurzel, ruined himself for life with his aunt, the Marchioness of Marqueterie, annoyed beyond hope of pardon the Countess of Ormolu, the five baronesses, all the ladies in their own right, all the great heiresses, all the county princesses-royal, all the archery-party beauties, and, careless of rank, right, or comment, opened the ball with—the Trefusis."

If, among this prolific writer's books, there is one for which I hold a particular affection, it is, I fancy, Idalia, that romance of a rich and powerful superwoman, patriot, and revolutionist, the devastating Countess Vassilis who, in her implications, occasionally reminds one of both Sandra Belloni and the Princess Casamassima. This novel vividly suggests an opera to me, with Mary Garden as Idalia, "the lady of his dreams," as Ouida would have called the book but for the intervention of Harrison Ainsworth, editor of the New Monthly Magazine, in which the story first appeared; it is easy to imagine Mary Garden in her torn domino, having been forcibly dragged from the masked ball, confined in the monastery, confronting with chaste contempt the vicious Monsignore Villaflor. As a matter of fact, the novel was dramatized almost immediately after publication and the play seems to have met with success in London, but either in opera or drama it is impossible to dream of a satisfactory embodiment of the brave and beautiful Sir Fulke Erceldoune.

In one of his letters Flaubert asserts, "Very great men often write very badly, and so much the better for them." Many sermons might be preached from this text. A convenient, if somewhat arbitrary, manner of dividing creators of fiction is to classify them as geniuses and artists. Dostoevsky, for example, was a genius, and Turgeniev, an artist. The comparison may be conveyed into the realm of painting: Whistler was an artist, Cézanne, a genius. It was Cézanne's avowed ambition to paint like Ingres, an ambition he never quite realized. To carry this discussion into the field of music is more difficult for, in this art, form and idea are identical, but, even here, there are exceptions, for Musorgsky was assuredly more genius than artist; so, conceivably, were Stephen Foster and Ethelbert Nevin. It is possible, of course, to be both, but the combination is rare and in most cases arguable. What, for instance, would George Moore be without his art? What, Theodore Dreiser, without his genius? In the case of Ouida, there can be no dispute. Ouida was not an artist, but just as surely she was a genius.

Remy de Gourmont once remarked, "Le style, c'est de sentir, de voir, de penser, et rien plus." If this be true, Ouida assuredly has style. She feels her characters; she has observed their milieu. Indeed, it is one of her most typical faults that she has too much feeling. Friendship, that roman a clef which relates her side (was there another?) of her eccentric love affair with the Marchese Lotteringhi Della Stufa, whom Ouida met in 1871 and for whom she conceived the one grand passion of her life, would have benefited by the exercise of a colder pen. The background, however, here as elsewhere, is carefully studied. Street caught the truth when he remarked that the essentials are there and Max Beerbohm has pointed out that Ouida's lavish descriptions of interiors are not clichés, in the manner, say, of Mrs. Alexander McVeigh Miller; [9] they are actuated by her real love of beauty and are meticulously observed and recreated. Baudelaire exclaimed of Théophile Gautier, "Homme heureux! homme digne d'envie! il n'a jamais aimé que le Beau!" This apostrophe might just as reasonably have been addressed to Ouida.

[9] Authoress of The Bride of the Tomb; or, Lancelot Darling's Betrothed.

## Ouida

"In writing Patience, Gilbert thought he was copying Oscar Wilde, whereas he was drawing Willie Yeats out of the womb of Time," Mr. George Moore once declared. When Dickens created Harold Skimpole in Bleak House, the world and Leigh Hunt himself thought that Leigh Hunt had been intended, but Dickens was really drawing Oscar Wilde out of the womb of Time. "The best appreciation of Bernard Shaw is that written some twenty years before he was born: I refer to Carlyle's Sartor Resartus," avers Herbert Skimpole. "Shaw is an embodiment of Diogenes Teufelsdröckh, the Philosopher of Clothes." Shaw himself has said, "I have noticed that when a certain type appears in painting and is greatly admired, it presently becomes common in nature." Charles Dudley Warner was aware of this phenomenon. He blamed the feeble, underbred literature of America for the herds of feeble, underbred Americans. Even "Nature herself seems readily to fall into imitation. It was noticed by the friends of nature that when the peculiar coal-tar colours were discovered, the same faded, æsthetic and sometimes sickly colours began to appear in the ornamental flower-beds and masses of foliage plants," and Warner also reminds us of the effect of Werther, of Childe Harold, and of Don Juan on an impressionable populace, the result of the painting of Rossetti, which popularized red hair and clinging robes of "dirty-greens." In Moby Dick, Herman Melville writes, "The Brahmins maintain that in the almost endless sculptures of this immemorial pagoda (the famous cavern-pagoda of Elephanta in India) all the trades and pursuits, every conceivable avocation of man, were prefigured before any of them actually came into being." In the thirty-second chapter of The Adventures of Philip,

# Ouida

Thackeray speaks of Beethoven's Dream of St. Jerome, which is not mentioned in any catalogue of Beethoven's works. There were, however, so many requests for this opus after Thackeray's reference to it, that in due time it appeared and now it may be purchased at any respectable music-dealer's. Eliphas Levi says that the wise man cannot lie because nature will accommodate herself to his statement. Oscar Wilde embroidered the theme: "Life imitates art far more than art imitates life. A great artist invents a type, and life tries to copy it, to reproduce it in a popular form, like an enterprising publisher. Schopenhauer has analyzed the pessimism that characterizes modern thought, but Hamlet invented it. The Nihilist, that strange martyr who has no faith, who goes to the stake without enthusiasm, and dies for what he does not believe in, is a purely literary product. He was invented by Turgeniev, and completed by Dostoevsky. Robespierre came out of the pages of Rousseau as surely as the People's Palace rose out of the debris of a novel. Literature always anticipates life." [10]

[10] Since this paper was written I have found additional evidence attesting the truth of this theory in Marcel Proust's Le Côté de Guermantes (II, 19): "Les gens de goût nous disent aujourd'hui que Renoir est un grand peintre du XVIII e siècle. Mais en disant cela ils oublient le Temps et qu'il en a fallu beaucoup, même en plein XIXe, pour que Renoir fût salué grand artiste. Pour réussir à être ainsi reconnus, le peintre original, l'artiste original procèdent à la façon des oculistes. Le traitement par leur peinture, par leur prose, n'est pas toujours agréable. Quand il est terminé, le practicien nous dit: Maintenant regardez. Et voici que le monde (qui n'a pas été créé une fois, mais aussi souvent qu'un artiste original est survenu) nous apparaît entièrement différent de l'ancien, mais parfaitement clair. Des femmes passent dans la rue, différentes de celles d'autrefois, puisque ce sont des Renoir, ces Renoir où nous nous refusions jadis à voir des femmes. Les voitures aussi sont des Renoir, et l'eau, et le ciel: nous avons envie de nous promener dans la forêt pareille à celle qui le premier jour nous semblait tout excepté une forêt, et par exemple une tapisserie

# Ouida

In her report of the world, then, Ouida may have been a trifle inaccurate, but she found no difficulty in creating a world of her own, a world which, to some extent at least, has existed since she created it. Ouida's society is a little wickeder, a little gayer, a little richer than the real thing, but heaven knows that society since her day has done its best to live up to her specifications. Lanky guardsmen with their wasp-waists, the vampire of the silver screen, these we owe to Ouida's imagination.

There is still another phase of Ouida's talent that deserves a passing reference, her essays in criticism. Ouida was an excellent critic, clear-sighted, unshackled, fearless. She formed independent judgments and said what she thought. Naturally, however, her opinions were frequently deeply coloured by her ferocious prejudices. At the age of eleven we find her recording in her diary that she preferred Florian to La Fontaine, "although this gentleman is such a favourite with the public." Sydney C. Cockerell visited Tolstoy in 1903 and was full of enthusiasm for the Russian as a thinker and a writer. Ouida was not impressed. "To me," she wrote to Cockerell, "Tolstoy has not much intellect. Many of his doctrines are absolutely foolish. He has little judgment of literature, and not much, surely, of men. His admiration of Dickens proves the non-intellectual fibre of his mind; and his morality and monogamy are against common sense and nature." Again, "Thanks for the Tolstoys. But I know all his views and arguments. When he says that 'any rational being requires to be-

aux nuances nombreuses mais où manquaient justement les nuances propres aux forêts. Tel est l'univers nouveau et périssable qui vient d'être créé. Il durera jusqu'à la prochaine catastrophe géologique que déchaîneront un nouveau peintre ou un nouvel écrivain originaux."

[61]

lieve in a god,' he shows how limited his mind is. Probably if he had not been a Russian he would have been a much greater man. In many ways he is absolutely silly. In vulgar parlance, his doctrines 'will not wash.' Observe, too, how he ignores the fact that fighting is *natural* to man. See a little child's rage before it can speak; its angry gestures, its inflamed face, its dumb fury. Men would not live in peace together if armies were abolished. Tolstoy does not realize that man is a very rudimentary, imperfect creature, occupying a very small space in an immense and unknown universe." Of patriotism, she declared, "Patriotism is not what we want in Europe and America. It is a much wider, finer, more impersonal feeling." Of the Oscar Wilde trial, she wrote to her friend, Mrs. Huntington, "It may be very immoral of me, but I do not think the law should meddle with these offences. The publicity aroused does much more harm than the offence itself." She described Wilde as a successful poseur and a plagiarist. Perhaps she thought he owed something to her. I shall always believe that the author of Lady Windermere's Fan caught the trick of smart comedy dialogue from the talk of Lady Cardiff (a portrait of Ouida's friend, Lady Orford), in Friendship. Wilde, it is on record, called on Ouida at the Hotel Langham in London in 1887.

Ouida's study of D'Annunzio, the first to appear in England, is rather remarkable, and stands up well today, even when it is compared with Henry James's criticism of the Italian writer. It is a pity that she did not turn her attention more frequently to this branch of writing. Critical Studies, although it contains her diatribe against Joseph Chamberlain and papers on subjects dear to her heart such as the ugliness of modern life, humanitarianism, and the decadence of the Latin races, is made up for the most part of essays on the novel, or essays on novelists, in which she often expresses her views on the writing of fiction. It is entirely characteristic of this lady that she frequently saw in others the faults she never saw in herself. In her essay on D'Annunzio, she writes, "The tendency of redundancy is not his fault alone; it is that of his time." In this paper she continues to be unconsciously brutal to herself: "There is unhappily an absolute absence of wit, of mirth, of humour." Ouida was gifted with a certain type of wit, but she was entirely lacking in humour. "He does not trust enough to the power of suggestion," is another of her boomerangs, and she takes Bourget to task for using foreign words! In Ariadnê there is a eulogy of Shakespeare which does the author's sensibility much credit; she finds in the poet's work "never a drop of envy or spleen." This from the malicious author of Friendship, a novel which cost her her position in English society in Florence. In Frescoes may be found her celebrated paper on Romance and Realism, which contains her cri de cœur: she asks her readers to remember that the passion-flower is as real as the potato. She seems to have held the opinion that realism was a matter of subject and not of method. A comparison of Laura Pearl in Puck with Zola's Nana will prove that even passion-flowers may be dealt with in two distinct manners.

As I have remarked earlier in this paper, everybody reads Ouida, but only such men as Joseph Hergesheimer and Max Beerbohm are not ashamed to admit it. G. S. Street observes, "Her faults, which are obvious, have brought it about that she is placed, in the general estimation of critics, below writers without a tenth of her ability." "The world takes its revenge on us for having despised it," she wailed to Wilfred Scawen Blunt. I think that some of the inhibitions of the world and its critics in regard to Ouida are due to the printing and binding of her novels. In America, their most elaborate dress is the red or green volumes stamped with gold, issued by Lippincott in Philadelphia. The reprints of Chatto and Windus in London are even worse, bound in tomato red and printed in small type from carious plates. Indubitably, a new edition of Ouida, on good paper, handsomely printed and bound, with prefaces by a few of her more illustrious admirers, would do much to dispel the current illusion which has it that in reading Ouida one is descending to the depths of English literature. I suspect, indeed, that if Ouida were suitably printed and bound she would begin to rank not very much below Dickens and Thackeray and considerably above the turgid George Eliot. Personally, however, I must confess that I nourish a fancy for the old bindings. It is a pleasure for me to read Ouida in the form in which she is most easily procurable. A certain old-fashioned artlessness clings to the battered volumes which at present occupy more than a yard of shelf on my garret walls. When her works are reissued in stately large-paper reprints, with introductions by Edmund Gosse and J. Middleton Murry, I shall still remain faithful to the set I have collected with so much pains.

*December 29, 1921*

## The Later Work of Herman Melville

Among the writers of England, those, perhaps, who most completely satisfy me are the restless fellows who, enraged beyond solace by the customs and habits of their native island, shake the Albion soil from their boots and embark on great ships. Once abroad, they are prone to find as much fault with other countries as they had found in the past with their own and eventually, in a passive state of contented despair, they return to the wave-ruling motherland.[1] Philip Thicknesse, Walter Savage Landor, James J. Morier, George Borrow, and Richard Burton, and perhaps, at any rate to some degree, Cunninghame Graham, Marmaduke Pickthall and W. H. Hudson, all belong to this class and each of these men has written books which are oftener peeped into than most of the other volumes on my garret shelves. The type is by no means rare in England; every generation, it will be perceived, produces at least one outstanding example. In America, on the other hand, this type is almost non-existent. A single figure, as a matter of fact, can be brought forward as a claimant for the distinction. The figure of Herman Melville, however, is sufficiently imposing to rank with the loftiest names in the English list.

Recently many attempts have been made—and they have been to a surprising degree successful—to drag this author out of his semi-obscurity, to refurbish his faded reputation, and to re-establish him in a place of

[1] The reader will perceive that this is an echo of a passage by Havelock Ellis, quoted on page 36.

honour in our literary hierarchy. These efforts, carried
through under mighty auspices, have not been half-
hearted or niggardly, but almost without exception they
have been made with reservations. The author of
Typee, Omoo, and Moby Dick is assuredly a world
genius, contemporary critics on both sides of the Atlantic
inform us, but the author of Pierre, Mardi, and The
Confidence Man is awarded the same scant courtesy he
received in the forties and fifties. It is apparent that
Melville himself foresaw his future fate when he wrote
to Hawthorne: "What 'reputation' H. M. has is horrible. Think of it! To go down to posterity is bad
enough anyway; but to go down as 'a man who lived
among the cannibals!'" When he dispatched the letter,
from which this is a celebrated excerpt, to the author
of The Ma·ble Faun, Melville had written and published
Mardi, and from the reviews of this book, the first in
which he had implied more than was set down on the
printed page, he was able to cast his melancholy horo-
scope. In another bitter passage in this identical letter
he refers to the compromise which appeared to be demanded of him: "What I feel most moved to write,
that is banned,—it will not pay. Yet, altogether, write
the other way, I cannot. So the product is a final hash,
and all my books are botches." As the particular
botch on which he was then engaged was Moby Dick, I
cannot regard as pertinent the argument used by those
of the critical gentry who try to twist this remark into
a forecast of the failure of Melville's subsequent output.
Ban or no ban, he continued to write what he felt most
moved to write.

His other early books (for it must not be forgotten
that Mardi was his third published work, although for

a reason, hereinafter to be stated, it falls into place quite naturally with the output of his second period), Typee, Omoo, Redburn, and White Jacket, his sea and island tales, were greeted with contemporary applause on both sides of the ocean. To no other American has higher praise been accorded by London. These, indubitably, are lovely romances, replete with languorous and lively descriptions, sparkling with a sophisticated and cosmopolitan humour. It is certain, however, that no metaphysical overtones, no "ontological heroics" hover over these stories. No shadows of meanings lurk in the curves of the sentences. All is pleasantly plain. As a matter of fact, in his preface to Omoo, Melville parades this very clarity (he was, I am convinced, the conscious artist in his every undertaking): "In no respect does the author make pretensions to philosophic research. In a familiar way, he has merely described what he has seen; and if reflections are occasionally indulged in, they are spontaneous, and such as would, very probably, suggest themselves to the most casual observer."

It is not to be wondered at that the naïve admirers of Typee and Omoo, admittedly charming and delightful books, should have been perturbed, embarrassed, and a little angry when they read the two volumes of Mardi, which are as acrid as wormwood, as subtle as a deep-sea pearl, and as chaotically imaginative as creative genius can be at its wildest. The American reviewers staggered helplessly before this performance, but found refuge in the conviction that the work exposed the pernicious influence of a misunderstanding of the benignant philosophy of Emerson; the French dragged Rabelais into the discussion; while the English blamed Carlyle and Sir Thomas Browne. In the two books succeeding

[67]

# The Later Work

Mardi, Melville, it appeared, had reverted to his earlier, comfortable, human ways, but in Moby Dick once more he consorted with the stars. Again, excoriation was his lot. A coeval writer in The Spectator whines over The Whale: "Such a groundwork is hardly natural enough for a regular-built novel, though it might form a tale, if properly managed. But Mr. Melville's mysteries provoke wonder at the author rather than terror at the creation; the soliloquies and dialogues of Ahab, in which the author attempts delineating the wild imaginings of monomania, and exhibiting some profoundly speculative views of things in general, induce weariness or skipping; while the whole scheme mars the nautical continuity of the story." In 1851, Pierre, or the Ambiguities, followed, the morbid, transcendental pessimism of which caused the critics to spill more ugly ink. Doubtless Pierre seemed a mad piece of business in the fifties, but what would the fifties have made of The Golden Bowl, or Women in Love, or Mr. James Joyce's Ulysses? According to one of Melville's obituary notices his withdrawal from literary life was occasioned by the unfavourable manner in which Pierre had been received. Whatever the cause (and a more plausible, if startling, one has been hinted at), he wrote no more novels [2] after The Confidence Man in 1857, although he published two volumes of verse, a department in which he was a vastly inferior performer, and two privately printed pamphlets.[3]

[2] At the time this paper was written I was unaware of the existence of the posthumous Billy Budd, since included in Constable's Standard Edition.
[3] Twenty-five copies of each were issued. Of John Marr, and other sailors, with some sea-pieces; New York; The De Vinne Press; 1888, I possess the author's presentation copy to Richard Henry Stoddard, with corrections and alterations in Melville's hand. Of Timoleon; New

## of Herman Melville

Let us examine some of the contemporary reviews of Mardi and Pierre. Here is a passage from a criticism of Mardi which appeared in the Dublin University Magazine for January 1856: "We are once more introduced to the lovely and mysterious isles of the vast Pacific, and their half-civilized, or, in some cases, yet heathen and barbarous aborigines." As a matter of fact, we are introduced to nothing of the sort, as any intelligent reader may discover for himself by reading five pages at random. To continue, with such patience as we are able to muster: "The reader who takes up the book, and reads the first half of volume one, will be delighted and enthralled by the original and exceedingly powerful pictures of sea-life, of a novel and exciting nature, but woeful will be his disappointment as he reads on. We hardly know how to characterize the rest of the book. It consists of the wildest, the most improbable, nay, impossible series of adventures among the natives, which would be little better than insane ravings, were it not that we dimly (sic) feel conscious that the writer intended to introduce a species of biting, political satire, under grotesque and incredibly extravagant disguises. Moreover, the language is throughout gorgeously poetical, full of energy, replete with the most beautiful metaphors and crowded with the most brilliant fancies and majestic and melodiously sonorous sentences. But all the author's powers of diction, all his wealth of fancy, all his exuberance of imagination, all his pathos, vigour, and exquisite graces of style, cannot prevent the judicious reader from laying down the book with a weary sigh, and an inward

York; the Caxton Press; 1891, I possess the copy presented to Arthur Stedman by Mrs. Melville. An autograph signature of Herman Melville is inserted.

[69]

pang of regret that so much rare and lofty talent has been wilfully wasted on a theme, which not anybody can fully understand, and which will inevitably repulse nine readers out of ten, by its total loss of human interest and sympathy. It is, in our estimation, one of the saddest, most melancholy, most deplorable, and humiliating perversions of genius of a high order in the English language." With almost equal justice, these words might stand for a review of Anatole France's l'Ile des pingouins or James Branch Cabell's Figures of Earth, works which, in certain respects, resemble Mardi.

The contemporary reviews of Pierre are even more abusive. In Putnam's Magazine for February 1853, Fitz-James O'Brien wrote: "It is no easy matter to pronounce which of Mr. Melville's books is the best. All of them (and he has published a goodly number, for so young an author) have had their own share of success, and their own peculiar merits, always saving and excepting Pierre—wild, inflated, repulsive that it is. . . . In his latest work he transcended even the jargon of Paracelsus and his followers. The Rosetta Stone gave up its secret, but we believe that to the end of time Pierre will remain an ambiguity. . . . Thought staggers through each page like one poisoned. Language is drunken and reeling. Style is antipodal and marches on its head."

From 1860 on, with the exception of the ineffective and modest publicity which his death in 1891 afforded him, the name of Melville appears to have been almost forgotten, so nearly forgotten, indeed, that Barrett Wendell in A Literary History of America could write: "Herman Melville, with his books about the South Seas, which Robert Louis Stevenson is said to have declared the best ever written, and his novels of maritime adventures, began a career of literary promise, which never came to fruition." This is all he finds to remark about one of the greatest writers that America has yet produced. To show how very complete was the oblivion into which Melville had fallen, it is only necessary to adduce the fact that when Viola Meynell's famous paper appeared in the Dublin Review in 1920 even Moby Dick was out of print!

The renaissance has begun, however. Typee, Omoo, White Jacket, and Redburn are again admired. Moby Dick, at last, has been moved up to the place of prominence at the very top of the list which undoubtedly it deserves, being, indeed, not only Melville's most significant achievement, but one of the most significant achievements in the record of modern letters. To the merits of the later novels, however, the new critics are as blind as their forefathers. Mardi, Pierre, Israel Potter, and The Confidence Man have been rejected as unanimously as they were in the fifties. This may be considered as particularly unfortunate because they have not been reprinted [4] along with the others and unless a prospective reader is lucky enough to meet with one of the early editions—a matter of considerable difficulty at present when Melville is being assiduously collected —he cannot form his own judgment in regard to them.

Viola Meynell seems to believe that Mardi was written *after* Moby Dick, for she says, "On its inventive side Moby Dick is superior, at any rate to ordinary understanding, to the later books, Mardi and Pierre, or the Ambiguities, and others. It will not surprise readers of Moby Dick to think that after it was written, its author

[4] True in 1921 when this paper was written. Now they are all readily procurable.

passed from them in a sense." Carl Van Doren asserts
that "Pierre is hopelessly frantic, the work of a mad
Meredith raving over moral ambiguities," and he is satisfied to hit off Mardi as "one of the strangest, maddest
books ever composed by an American." [5]

In spite of the detractors, I think it highly probable
that the day may come when there will be those who will
prefer the later Melville just as there are those who
prefer the later James, those who will care more for the
metaphysical, the riotously shapeless, and at the same
time more self-revealing works, than for the less subtle
and more straightforward tales. It is possible that the
delay in appreciation of the later works has been occasioned by the fact that in Melville's day, and long
after it, the public was not ripe for the richer under-
currents inherent therein. These books cannot be in-
vestigated by the aid of the critical jargon ordinarily ap-
plicable to works of art: they are the man himself. Moby
Dick is neither a sea story nor the account of the hunting
of a monster whale: it is a window which opens on the
harassed and mystic soul of the author. Of the three
major later novels it may, roughly speaking, be said
that they form a kind of tragic triptych: Mardi is a
tragedy of the intellect, Moby Dick a tragedy of the
spirit, and Pierre, a tragedy of the flesh; Mardi is a
tragedy of heaven, Moby Dick, a tragedy of hell, and
Pierre, a tragedy of the world we live in.

The work of Melville cannot be divided into periods

[5] In The American Novel; 1921. In this book, Mr. Van Doren,
no ungenerous admirer of Melville's genius, the inspiration, indeed,
of Mr. Weaver's biography, devotes but eight pages to Melville at
the end of a chapter entitled Romances of Adventure, while William
Dean Howells is honoured with twenty-four pages and James Fenimore
Cooper with an entire chapter.

with the ease, say, that one divides the operas of Verdi. The progression is somewhat irregular and has proved a stumbling block to earnest biographers and critics. The satiric and philosophic Mardi, for example, precedes, chronologically, the simple sea tales, Redburn and White Jacket. The fact is that Melville was only making sketches in Typee and Omoo, assembling his background, so to speak. The milieu of these plain-spoken narratives furnishes the décor for Mardi, ostensibly laid in the same environment. Following Mardi, Melville wrote two *objective* stories of the sea, Redburn and White Jacket, in turn followed by Moby Dick, which utilizes the newly assembled scenery subjectively.[6] Thereafter he never reverted to purely objective writing, save, perhaps, in a short story or two. Let no one, therefore, interested in Melville the man (and who can read him at all that is not so interested, for all his work is autobiographical in one sense or another, "an indelicate probing into his own consciousness," as one writer nicely puts it) consign, without reading, Pierre, The Confidence Man, and Israel Potter to limbo.

With the above explanation in mind, it will be easy to permit Mardi, Melville's third published work, to slip into its proper place among the later novels. This book is a social-political-medical-economic-artistic-religious satire, more polite, and, at the same time, more subtle, than most satires, more allegorical than others, perhaps, in its framework. The irony is suave and mystic and the bitterness comes in the aftertaste. Out of the swill-barrel of contemporary abuse poured on the work it is

[6] This statement cannot be taken entirely literally, because Melville had recorded his whaling, as well as his South Sea island, experiences in Typee and Omoo.

pleasant to dig out two reviews, the authors of which, in a sense at least, comprehended the intention of the creator, that of Philarète Chasles, the Frenchman,[7] and that of an anonymous journalist in the Democratic Review (July 1849). The latter critic says, in part: "Typee and Omoo were written for the multitude and consequently had no deep philosophy. . . . The man who expects and asks for loaf sugar will not be satisfied with marble, though it be built into a palace. . . . The fact that Mardi is an allegory that mirrors the world has thus far escaped the critics who do notices for the book-table on a large scale. Pilgrim's Progress and Gulliver's Travels were written so long ago that they seem to have dropped through the meshes of the memory of the critics, and they have ceased to think any reproduction or improvement of that sort of thing possible in the future, because they have forgotten its existence in the past." But even this sapient fellow ends on a moronic note: "Mr. Melville seems to lack the absolute faith that God had a purpose in creating the world." He also views with chagrin the author's obvious disposition to drink and smoke.

Nevertheless, he must be given credit for his perspicacity in the dark ages. Mardi is no more obscure than Gulliver's Travels, l'Ile des pengouins, Erewhon, Candide, The New Republic, or Alice in Wonderland, with all of which masterpieces it can claim a certain kinship and to most of which it can claim precedence. It glows with rich humour; it is sophisticated and gentlemanly. Its more obscure passages were written to befog the bourgeoisie and to cheer the intelligentsia. The mystical

---

[7] Etudes sur la littérature et les mœurs des Anglo-Américains aux XIXe siècle; Paris; 1850.

philosopher, Babbalanji, remarks somewhere in the book, "Meditate as much as you will but say little aloud, unless in a merry and mythical way." Certainly Melville said more aloud than any one else dared to say in the America of 1847. The opening chapters, recounting the adventures of sailors adrift at sea, are the old Melville, open and above-board. This disarming introduction requires no footnotes. It may be mentioned, however, that these chapters contain some of the author's finest descriptive writing. I especially recommend to the reader's attention the chapter entitled, The Sea on Fire, with its vivid picture of the sperm whales spouting phosphorescent spray in the darkness, a strange pyrotechnical effect not frequently to be met with in nature. Presently, Melville rescues the lovely Yillah who, like the Blue Bird, represents Happiness, from the clutches of the priests, who are attempting to conceal her, and descends on the mythical island of Mardi. Here he abides in a state of perfect content with the ethereal Yillah, until she is again torn from his side by the clergy. Melville rather had it in for the ecclesiastics since they had challenged the accuracy of his derogatory references to the missionaries in Omoo. They had conveniently dubbed him a Mariolatrist and had suggested to their congregations that a fellow with his self-confessed record of island amours was no man to be trusted in other respects.

In search of Yillah and pursued by Hautia (Passion), Melville, accompanied by Babbalanji, the philosopher, Mohi, the historian, Yoomy, the poet, and Media, the representative of the law, take a turn around the world, visiting England, France, Scotland, Ireland, Germany, Spain, and America, all disguised as outer islands of the archipelago.  Naturally, there is much conversation and speculation.  It is disheartening to note that there has always been an Irish question.  The chapter on Ireland, indeed, might have been written today or tomorrow.  "Isle, whose future is in its past.  Hearthstone from which its children run," philosophizes Babbalanji.  "I cannot read thy chronicles for blood," murmurs Mohi, and presently Babbalanji continues:  "Verdanna's worst evils are her own, not of another's giving.  Her own hand is her own undoer.  She stabs herself with bigotry, superstition, divided councils, domestic feuds, ignorance, temerity; she wills, but does not; her East is one black storm-cloud that never bursts; her utmost fight is a defiance; she showers reproaches, where she should rain down blows.  She stands a mastiff baying at the moon."

Nor did Melville spare America:

"The canoes drew near.

" 'Lo! what inscription is that?' cried Media, 'there, chiseled over the arch?'

"Studying those immense hieroglyphics awhile, antiquarian Mohi still eying them, said slowly:—

" 'In-this-re-publi-can-land-all-men-are-born-free-and-equal.'

" 'False!' said Media.

" 'And how long stay they so?' said Babbalanji.

" 'But look lower, old man,' cried Media, 'methinks there's a small hieroglyphic or two hidden away in yonder angle.—Interpret them, old man.'

"After much screwing of his eyes, for those characters were very minute, Champollion Mohi thus spoke—'Except-the-tribe-of-Hamo.' "

Here is a masterpiece of humour:  "They were a fine young tribe, like strong wine they worked violently in becoming clear. Time, perhaps, would make them all right." Thus is the boasting, tobacco-chewing, tooth-picking nation summed up. Later Babbalanji comments, "There's not so much freedom here as these freemen think. I laugh and admire." Media affixes a scroll to a palm-tree. The opening lines read: "Sovereign-kings of Vivenza! it is fit you should listen to wisdom. But well aware that you give ear to little wisdom except your own; and that as freemen, you are free to hunt down him who dissents from your majesties; I deem it proper to address you anonymously." Would that Eugene Debs and Jim Larkin had heeded this warning. Later, the scroll continues: "For, mostly, monarchs are as gemmed bridles upon the world, checking the plunging of a steed from the Pampas. And republics are vast reservoirs draining down all streams to one level; and so, breeding a fulness which cannot remain full, without overflowing." Still further along: "He who hated oppressors, is become an oppressor himself. . . It is not the prime end, and chief blessing, to be politically free. And freedom is only good as a means; is no end in itself! . . . Freedom is the name for a thing that is *not* freedom; this, a lesson never learned in an hour or an age. By some tribes it will never be learned. . . . It is not, who rules the state, but who rules me. Better be secure under one king than exposed to violence under twenty million monarchs, though oneself be of the number."

Philarète Chasles was astonished to discover so gascon an American, but he admired him. A cosmopolitan, a sly humorist, a great creative genius, what must his American contemporaries have thought of this man who ballyhooed for a drunkard's heaven, flaunted his dally-ings with South Sea cuties, proclaimed that there was no such things as truth, coupled "Russian serfs and Republican slaves," and intimated that a thief in jail was as honourable as General George Washington?

After Melville has visited and criticized Europe and America, judging even Alma and Serenia (Christ and his Kingdom) to be uninhabitable, he betakes himself to that metaphysical mistland where he is most content to dwell. Yillah is lost for ever. During the course of this fantastic journey the author discusses any subject that occurs to him and throws the pepper of doubt into the reader's eyes. There are chapters on religion, chapters on the dispensation of justice, chapters on war, which remind one a little of the later battles between Tweedledum and Tweedledee, chapters on the gay world, on Italian art, on Spanish etiquette and French nobility. The use of teeth as money on the island of Mardi is a hint to nations with a deflated currency. The doctors are trampled on; Spinoza, Hegel, and Lombardi all rear their heads. The book is a magnificent and witty jumble of all the current philosophies. "Fancy Daphnis and Chloë dancing I know not what strange gavotte with Aristotle and Spinoza, escorted by Gargantua and Gargamelle!" exclaimed the critic of the Revue de Deux Mondes, after reading Mardi. The language is extravagant, the thought still more so. Why not? one asks, and remembers that the early critics praised Shakespeare's character drawing and his knowledge of the human heart while they shook their heads deprecatingly over the extravagance of his diction. A wild and brilliant work of the imagination, such as Mardi, demands more extravagant expression, certainly, than a style like the solemner moments of Walter Pater. One of the best of the social satires, Mardi probably means a little less and also a little more than is ordinarily believed. As Babbalanji avers, "In many points the works of our great poet Vavona, now dead a thousand moons, still remain a mystery. Some called him a mystic, but wherein he seems obscure it is perhaps we that are in fault." Jean Cocteau paraphrased this dictum in 1918: "Lorsqu'une œuvre semble en avance sur son époque, c'est simplement que son époque est en retard sur elle."

So much for Mardi. For reasons already set down I sweep lightly past Redburn and White Jacket. As for Moby Dick, so much has been written about this great book (perhaps not enough, but surely enough for the present) that it seems unnecessary to pause very long even here. I may say, however, that I have scant patience with those who consider Moby Dick only a tale of the sea. One man, indeed, a well-known critic of literature, recently informed me that he had not read the book because he did not care for stories of adventure. Equally pertinently he might have stated that he could not read Hamlet because he did not care for plays about Danes. Moby Dick *is* a story of adventure in the sense that Hamlet is, in the sense that Dante's Divine Comedy is. It is the narrative of man's great struggle against the natural and the supernatural and man's final defeat. It is assuredly Melville's greatest book, assuredly one of the great books of the world. Its threads, however, in the curious fabric I am weaving are so obvious that this mere suggestion is quite sufficient to give the reader his guide to my design.

From this time on, until he stopped writing entirely, Melville devoted himself to subjective rather than ob-

[79]

jective creation, and from this time on he lost credit with public and critics alike. His very next work, indeed, Pierre, or the Ambiguities, infuriated the reviewers and drove them to devastating tongue-lashings. The clergy and the one hundred per-cent Americans assisted at the lynching. It may be said, in extenuation of the actions of these naïve folk, that the performance was strange enough, even from the writer of Mardi, to wring astonishment from stout hearts. Yet I cannot help believing that had Pierre been written today by James Joyce or D. H. Lawrence its reception would have been far different. Either, with certain personal alterations, might have conceived the book. The subject, indeed, would have delighted the soul of Henry James, had he hit upon it.

In its consideration, the subtitle must be stressed. Ambiguity is Melville's theme. Pierre, a happy son, living with his widowed mother and betrothed to Lucy Tartan whom, apparently, he dearly loves, learns, or thinks he learns, that he has an illegitimate sister. On the instant (indeed, a little before, for his first strange encounter with Isabel is anonymous), he is filled with adoration for this new demi-kinswoman, an adoration the nature of which to the reader certainly appears to be sexual, but which to Pierre himself is always equivocal. His instinct at first demands a public recognition of the girl, a tardy restitution of her problematical rights, but more sober reflection convinces him that his mother will never consent to receive this symbol of the bar sinister, of whose very existence she is quite unaware. Further, it is necessary to consider his dead father's good name, entirely unbefouled so far as public scandal goes. In his perplexity this insane hero lights on the mad expedient of a white marriage. During the ceremony, "the surplice-like napkin dropped from the clergyman's bosom, showing a minute but exquisitely cut cameo brooch, representing the allegorical union of the serpent and dove." Pierre bids his Lucy farewell and is turned from his home by his priggish mother whom he never sees again. Dying within a few months, she disowns him by testament, leaving her property to his cousin, Glen Stanley, also in love with Lucy. Pierre and Isabel go to New York, where he tries to make a living as a novelist. In the meantime, Lucy, having, through some mystic visitation, embraced the belief that Pierre has behaved quixotically but nobly (she is entirely unacquainted with the reasons for this behaviour) insists on joining the possibly incestuous pair. Glen and her brother fail in an attempt to drag her away. So does her mother. Nunlike, she occupies an adjoining chamber to that of the guilty (?) couple. The ensuing chapters are blood-curdling in their implications. There are passages which seem to suggest that this amazing marriage was truly consummated. There are passages which seem to suggest that Lucy . . . but let the author speak: "As a statue, planted on a revolving pedestal, shows now this limb, now that; now front, now back, now side; continually changing, too, its general profile; so does the pivoted soul of man, when turned by the hand of truth. Lies only never vary; look for no invariableness in Pierre. *Nor does any canting showman here stand by to announce his phases as he revolves. Catch his phases as your insight may.*"

The plot hastens towards its catastrophe, in which Pierre's novel is rejected as Voltairean and atheistic, and in which, stirred by insult, he kills Glen in a street brawl. Led to prison, he is visited by Isabel and Lucy. The sister-wife drinks poison and Pierre and Lucy drain the bottle. The three ambiguous corpses clutter the stage as the curtain falls swiftly on this Webster and Tourneur melodrama with its ingeniously subtle theme. Towards the close, a curious scene is introduced in which the very evidence that Pierre had urged to make himself believe that Isabel was his sister is discovered to be worse than circumstantial. The book, indeed, is a study of a man of ideals who is able to commit an ignoble act by convincing himself that he is committing a noble one. The dangers of idealization are freely exhibited. Pierre is so difficult to come by at present (only the first edition exists [8] and that was largely depleted by a fire at the Harpers' in the early fifties) that it is by no means as well-known or as much admired as it would be, were it reprinted. Whoever republishes it should send advance copies to Drs. Freud and Brill and to Mr. D. H. Lawrence and Miss May Sinclair. They will be entranced.[9] I prophesy that a new cartload of Freudian literature will grow up around this book, the peripeteia of which occurs in a dream.

In regard to both Pierre and in Moby Dick, certain critics have protested against the author's use of Gothic dialogue. I think there can be no question but that this was a perfectly conscious device on Melville's part, for when he wished, as in Bartleby, he could be as convincingly colloquial as the next man. Melville utilized the device for the same reason that Shaw rejected it in Cæsar and Cleopatra. Shaw wished to endow his play

---

[8] This is no longer true.

[9] This interest may be enhanced, perhaps, by Mr. Weaver's statement, not unsubstantiated, that the work contains portraits of Melville's father and mother and also of Melville himself.

with contemporary feeling. Melville desired these novels to lack that feeling. This Gothic dialogue serves to remove Captain Ahab and Pierre from any particular environment or period. It creates a strange atmosphere of nowhere, no place, very apposite to his general purpose in the construction of these works.[10]

Pierre appeared in 1851. Three years elapsed before Israel Potter was published, three years, at the beginning of which Melville was execrated, at the end, forgotten. This novel, then, is Melville's satiric dart at Fame, a lady at whom he had already aimed many derogatory epithets. I have already quoted the passage from his letter to Hawthorne. In another letter he declares, "Though I wrote the gospel in this century, I should die in the gutter." In Mardi, doubtless furious at those who thought of him only as an ethnologist among cannibals, he has Babbalanji say, "Not seldom to be famous, is to be widely known for what you are not, says Alla-Malolla. Whence it comes, as old Bardianna has it, that for years a man may move unnoticed among his fellows; but all at once, by some chance attitude foreign to his habit, become a trumpetful for fools; though, in himself, the same as ever. Nor has he shown himself yet; for the entire merit of a man can never be made known; nor the sum of his demerits, if he have them. We are only known by our names; as letters

[10] Padraic Colum's pronouncement that Moby Dick is an epic ("It is a mistake, I think . . . to approach Moby Dick as a novel") in rhythmic and polyphonic prose serves further to explain this peculiarity. This paper was published in the Measure for March 1922. There are many readers who gag at Melville's tortured style who swallow that of Meredith, a writer with whom Melville shares many points of resemblance.

[83]

sealed up, we but read each other's superscriptions." [11]
From Pierre I have culled the following: "In the inferior instances of an immediate literary success, in very
young writers, it will be almost invariably observable,
that for that instant success they are chiefly indebted to
some rich and peculiar experience in life, embodied in a
book, which because, for that cause, containing original
matter, the author himself, forsooth, is to be considered
original." This may be regarded in a sense, as a rather
bitter criticism of his own Typee. "Many, many souls
are in me," Melville cries in Mardi, and E. L. Grant-
Watson [12] has attempted to prove that each character in
Moby Dick represents a different phase of its fascinating and many-sided author.

Ostensibly a historical novel, Israel Potter [13] really is
the forlorn record of a man who has given everything
and received nothing. The last chapter, relating to
Israel's melancholy return to America after his forty
years' exile, of which Raymond M. Weaver [14] writes,
"The unnecessary degradation of the hero with which
the book closes is utterly inexcusable both in art and in

[11] This refrain runs through Melville's work to the end. The
following is from John Marr:

> "Where is Ap Catesby? The fights fought of yore
> Famed him, and laced him with epaulets, and more.
> But fame is a wake that after-wakes cross,
> And the waters wallow all, and laugh *Where's the loss?*"

[12] Moby Dick: The London Mercury; Vol. III, page 180.

[13] This novel is based on a pamphlet entitled, Life and remarkable
adventures of Israel R. Potter, who was a soldier in the Revolutionary
War and took a distinguished part in the Battle of Bunker Hill, etc.;
Providence; 1824.

[14] This paper was written before Raymond Weaver's biography of
Melville had appeared. The quotation here is from Mr. Weaver's
article, The Centennial of Herman Melville, published in the Nation
for August 2, 1919.

probability," may be more readily condoned if it be regarded as a symbol for Melville's return to the field of literature, searching vainly for his fame. While Potter, in the Revolutionary War, braves every danger and suffers every privation, Dr. Franklin, Ethan Allen, and Paul Jones reap the rewards. Thus might Melville have summed up his own career which Barrett Wendell, in carefully chosen words, informs us, "never came to fruition." A bitter book with a bitter dedication to the Bunker Hill monument. I cannot understand why it has been passed by so slightingly by the commentators, none of whom tosses it more than a contemptuous line, for aside from its autobiographical interest, it boasts passages of great charm, and there is a description of a sea-fight in Melville's best manner. Personally, however, it is the figure of Dr. Franklin, the eccentric American Minister to France, which most enchants me. This old gentleman, preaching prohibition and economy, warning Israel to beware of the wiles of the lascivious and Fragonardesque chambermaid, and removing bottles of cologne from the young fellow's bedroom, is an extremely diverting character. Curiously enough, Gothic dialogue is eschewed in this historical romance. Between this book and Moby Dick there can be, of course, but one possible choice, but had I to choose between Israel Potter and Typee, my preference would go to the former.

A year later, Melville published a volume of fugitive pieces, The Piazza Tales, the title of which, as well as the prologue, may have been suggested by Tanglewood Tales, just as I have sometimes thought it possible that Pierre may have been Melville's emotional reaction to The Scarlet Letter. Of these sketches, the first two, Bartleby, with its recurrent and memorable refrain, "I prefer not to," and Benito Cereno, a sea story which should be better than it is, are worth reading. The Bell Tower is a fairly good horror story in the manner of Poe and the rest are essays rather than stories. There is more uncollected material of this nature.[15]

We get an interesting portrait of our subject at this period from Hawthorne. In 1856, Melville, on his way to Constantinople, turned up at Liverpool, where Hawthorne was then living, and the author of Our Old Home noted in his diary: "He looked much the same as he used to do; a little paler, perhaps, and a little sadder, and with his characteristic gravity and reserve of manner. I felt awkward at first, for this is the first time I have met him since my ineffectual attempt to get him a consular appointment from General Pierce. However, I failed only from real lack of power to serve him; so there was no reason to be ashamed, and we soon found ourselves on pretty much the former terms of sociability and confidence. Melville has not been well of late; he has been affected with neuralgic complaints, and no doubt has suffered from too constant literary occupation, pursued without much success latterly; and his writings, for a long time past, have indicated a morbid state of mind. So he left his place in Pittsfield, and has come to the Old World. He informed me that he has 'pretty much made up his mind to be annihilated'; but still he does not seem to rest in that anticipation, and I think will never rest until he gets hold of some definite belief. It is strange how he persists—and has persisted ever since I knew him and probably long before—in wandering to

[15] Since published by the Princeton Press under the title of The Apple-Tree Table and other sketches, and by Constable, in volume XIII of the Standard Edition, under the title of Billy Budd and other prose pieces. Cock-a-doodle-doo! is well worthy of examination.

and fro over these deserts, as dismal and monotonous as the sandhills amidst which we were sitting. He can neither believe, nor be comfortable in his unbelief; and he is too honest and courageous not to try to do one or the other. If he were a religious man, he would be one of the most truly religious and reverential; he is a very high and noble nature, and better worth immortality than most of us." Readers of Mardi will remark that this search for "some definite belief" began very early. The characters of this satire search for religious consolation as avidly as they search for happiness.

Let us bear in mind Melville's struggle for faith and the apparent collapse of his career as we approach The Confidence Man, his last extended work in prose. It is not a novel, nor is it, as Frank Mather Jewett ingenuously suggests, a series of "middle-western sketches." Melville simply carried Brook Farm to the deck of a Mississippi steamboat, as in Mardi he had carried Europe to the South Seas. Emerson is the confidence man, Emerson who preached being good, not doing good, behaviour rather than service. Why no one heretofore has recognized Melville's purpose in writing this book, I cannot profess to understand. Perhaps some one has, but I can find no record of the discovery. Probably dozens of critics have been influenced by the misleading comments of their forebears into not reading the book at all. At any rate, here Melville has his revenge on those who accused him earlier in his career of transcendental leanings. This is the great transcendental satire. The work assumes the form of a series of ironic dialogues, somewhat after the manner of W. H. Mallock's The New Republic, between the representatives of theory and practice, transcendentalism and reality, with the devil's advocate winning the victory. Emerson's essay on Friendship is required preparatory reading for this book. "If a drunkard in a sober fit is the dullest of mortals, an enthusiast in a reason-fit is not the most lively," is a good summing up of Ralph Waldo's "lofty and enthralling circus." Hawthorne may have been secretly pleased with The Confidence Man, if he understood it, because Emerson confessedly had never been able to finish a volume by the worthy Nathaniel. There is no evidence on this suggestive point. A recent commentator, H. M. Tomlinson,[16] is content to say of it, in an otherwise glowing account of the genius of its creator, "The Confidence Man is almost unreadable."

This was the end. The Battle Pieces followed and, after an Asiatic tour, the fabulous Clarel, but these are in verse, and wherever else I can follow Herman Melville, I find I cannot follow his excursions into poetry. He settled down to twenty-eight years of silence and seclusion in New York, erecting a monument to himself by refusing to become a charter-member of the Authors' Club and otherwise comporting himself with dignity and circumspection. Like George Borrow, and for a similar reason, he was forgotten. Most people did not know how good his work had been; those who did no longer remembered it, and he made no effort to awaken dead enthusiasm. Readers who are satisfied to stop with Moby Dick will not understand his later life, but those who go on through Israel Potter and The Confidence Man will get a clearer picture of his bitterness and unhappy striving.

*November 15, 1921.*

[16] A Clue to Moby Dick: The Literary Review of the New York Evening Post for November 5, 1921.

[88]

## Edgar Saltus

Two phenomena, frequently recurring, are to be noted in the unfathomable chronicle of American letters: one, the irrational effect produced by comets whose effulgence for the time being completely eclipses the perdurable literary milky way in the eyes of the public and the critics; the other, the careless attitude assumed by these gentry towards certain fixed stars. It frequently happens that true luminaries are not observed at all until they have been shining for two or three decades. When, indeed, they are examined condescendingly by their contemporaries it is only that they may be excoriated for possessing the impertinence to pretend to shine. To make this argument concrete it is only necessary to adduce the names of Edgar Allan Poe, Herman Melville, Walt Whitman, Ambrose Bierce, and Edgar Saltus, men of unequal merit, but each in his way more important than two or three of his more highly acclaimed coevals.

Edgar Saltus, born in 1858, accomplished some of his best work in the eighties and the nineties, in the days of mutton-legged sleeves, bustles, whatnots, Rogers groups, cat-tails, peacock feathers, Japanese fans, musk-mellon seed collars, and big-wheel bicycles. He has written history, fiction, poetry, literary criticism, and philosophy, and to all of these forms, at least in some degree, he has brought sympathy, erudition, an intelligent point of view, and a personal style. He enjoys an imagination and he understands the potent art of arranging facts in

[89]

# Edgar Saltus

kaleidoscopic patterns so that they may attract and not repel the reader. Yet this man, who is still alive,[1] has been permitted, in his auctorial capacity, to drift into comparative oblivion. Even his early reviewers shoved him impatiently aside or ignored him altogether; a writer in Belford's Magazine for July 1888, asseverates, "Edgar Saltus should have his name changed to Edgar Assaulted." Soon he became a literary leper. The doctors and professors would have none of him. To most of them to-day, I suppose, he is only a name. Many of them have never read any of his books. He is not so much as mentioned in Katharine Lee Bates's American Literature (1898), Barrett Wendell's A History of American Literature (1901), A Reader's History of American Literature, by Thomas Wentworth Higginson and Henry Walcott Boynton (1903), A Manual of American Literature, edited by Theodore Stanton (1909), William Edward Simonds's A Student's History of American Literature (1909), William B. Cairns's A History of American Literature (1912), John Macy's The Spirit of American Literature (1913), Fred Lewis Pattee's A History of American Literature Since 1870 (1915), or William Lyon Phelps's The Advance of the English Novel (1916). The third volume of The Cambridge History of American Literature, bringing the subject up to 1900, has not yet appeared, but I shall be amazed if the editors decide to include Saltus therein.[2]  His name, quaintly invoked, lurks on page 117 of Vance Thompson's French Portraits. James Huneker has referred to him several times in pass-

[1] He died July 31, 1921 and was buried in Sleepy Hollow Cemetery at Tarrytown, next to his half-brother Frank and in the same plot with Mrs. Saltus's dog, Toto. Under the name, Edgar Saltus, the single word, eternamente, is carved on the tombstone.

[2] They did not.

# Edgar Saltus

ing.[3]   There are three such references (pages 214, 269, and 273) in Unicorns (1917).   His bibliography, up to Madam Sapphira, is included in Herbert Stuart Stone's First Editions of American Authors (1893) and, quite expectedly, Percival Pollard has a good deal to say about him in Their Day in Court (1909).   In 1903, G. F. Monkshood and George Gamble arranged a compilation from Saltus's work which they entitled Wit and Wisdom from Edgar Saltus (Greenwood and Co., London), but the job is done without sense or sensitiveness and the prefatory essay is without salt or flavour.   Curiously enough, he is mentioned in Oscar Fay Adams's A Dictionary of American Authors (1901 edition), and, of all places, I have discovered citations in two books [4] by Agnes Repplier.[5]

[3] When this paper originally appeared in The Merry-Go-Round, James Huneker wrote me: "Twenty years ago, Vance Thompson and I promised ourselves the pleasure of writing a definitive article on Edgar—and we didn't. Now you have done it and beautifully . . . Edgar is a genius. George Moore once told me that Walt Whitman and Saltus were the only two Americans he read." Let Mr. Moore, in a letter to me, speak for himself: "I was especially interested in your review of Edgar Saltus, for it has always been a puzzle to me why he did not achieve a really memorable piece of work. I attach much importance to the writer's name; some people think undue importance. However that may be, Edgar Saltus seems at first sight an inspiring name, yet it did not inspire the owner. Edgar Saltus is cultivated and possessed by a brain and style—the equipment is perfect and we sit agape when we think of him." Huneker introduced Edgar Saltus as a character in his novel, Painted Veils (1920).

[4] Books and Men (1888), pages 102, 163–4; In the Dozy Hours (1894), page 142.

[5] Carl Van Doren devoted two pages to Saltus in Contemporary American Novelists (1922). Pascal Covici in Chicago has issued (1925) Edgar Saltus: The Man, by Mrs. Marie Saltus. This book, although sloppily written and occasionally inaccurate, offers a convincing portrait of its subject and fully explains the causes of his comparative obscurity.

# Edgar Saltus

You will find few papers about the man or his work in current or anterior periodicals. There is, to be sure, the article by Ramsay Colles, entitled A Publicist: Edgar Saltus, which appeared in the Westminster Magazine for October 1904, but this paper could have won our author no adherents. If any one had the courage to wade through its muddy paragraphs, he doubtless emerged vowing never to read Saltus. Besides, only the novels are touched on. An anonymous writer in Current Literature for July 1897 asks plaintively why this author has been permitted to remain in obscurity and quotes some of the reviews of his work. In the Philistine for October 1907, Elbert Hubbard takes a hand in the game. He avers, "Edgar Saltus is the best writer in America —with a few insignificant exceptions," but he deplores the fact that Saltus is not attentive to the cows and chickens; only ancient cities and gods appear to interest him. Still, there is some atmosphere in this study, devoted to one book: The Lords of the Ghostland.[6]

The events of Saltus's life, for the most part, remain shrouded in mystery. His comings and goings are not reported in the newspapers; [7] he does not make public

[6] Since this paper appeared in The Merry-Go-Round, Arthur Symons has published his essay on Saltus in Vanity Fair (March 1920), later included in the volume entitled Dramatis Personæ. The Limbo of American Literature, by Gorham B. Munson, in Broom (June 1922), and The Edgar Saltus I Knew, by Sadakichi Hartmann, in the Bookman (September 1923) should also be noted. The latter drew forth a violent letter of protest from Marie Giles Saltus, published in the Bookman for January 1924.

[7] I have since discovered that his name appeared only too frequently in the newspapers and Town Topics during the nineties. His third wife ascribes his subsequent dislike for publicity to this fact. In my paper, Edgar Saltus: an Epitaph, published in the Double Dealer for October 1921, and afterwards included, without my permission, in a nondescript volume called Et Cetera, I wrote of him: "He was an

# Edgar Saltus

speeches; and his name is seldom, if ever, mentioned "among those present." He was a recluse. In one of his books he perpends this problem: "For a thinking man . . . what is there except solitude?" In another he remarks: "To be enjoyable solitude should not be coupled with suspense; in that case it is uneasiness magnified by the infinite." I feel certain that Saltus's solitude was coupled with suspense. However that may be, he consistently maintained it. May we not herein find some

egoist, seldom with a good word for another author, sensitive, bitter, cynical and at times, perhaps, even malicious. In the nineties he had known such men as Oscar Wilde, Edgar Fawcett, J. K. Huysmans, Vance Thompson, and James Huneker. For the past twenty years, however, he had withdrawn from the world. He had few, if any, friends. Huneker told me in 1920 that he had not seen him for ten years. He appeared pretty regularly at the Manhattan Club in Madison Square for his mail and for a whisky and soda, until prohibition deprived him even of this comfort. The Manhattan Club was the only address he ever gave to me.

"He was a strangely distinguished figure, something of a dandy, handsome in his youth, if one can judge from his pictures, and later, while more massive, still inspiring, short, but with the head of a personage. He really *looked* like a man of letters. He is the only author I have ever seen who did.

"There may have been reasons for his bitterness. I have heard that he suffered reverses of fortune in Wall Street which necessitated alterations in his mode of living. Then, while he carefully and tenderly carved out his jewelled miniatures, he watched the glory often go to his inferiors. Galling enough, no doubt. More than all, he stuttered, a physical affliction which cuts many harder personalities away from social intercourse.

"I have set down a few plausible excuses for the unpleasant impression his manner and his conversation created when I finally met him, but all the same, I do not think he had changed. In the early nineties, he was the same acidulous cynic, the same caustic wit. In 1891, his first wife divorced him. In an interview, published in a newspaper of the period, Saltus is quoted as saying of his father-in-law, whom he blamed for the action: 'I shall not forget Mr. Read. He shall have a divorce from my bed and board, the alimony for which he asked as well. Now that the charges he made are with-

[93]

small explanation for his apparent neglect? Many thousands of lesser men have lifted themselves to prominence by blowing their own tubas and striking their own crotals. Even in the case of Bernard Shaw we may be permitted to doubt if he would be so well known had he not taken the pains to erect monuments to himself on every possible occasion in every possible location. Fame is a quaint, old-fashioned lady who loves to be pursued by the living. She seldom, if ever, runs after anybody save in her favourite rôle of necrophile.

drawn I can refuse him nothing. I have put him down in my will. He is a member of the Society for the Protection of Animals, and in recognition of his affection for beasts, I have left him a mirror—with reversion to his charming representatives at the bar.' It must also be remembered, in any consideration of his character, that The Philosophy of Disenchantment, The Anatomy of Negation (even the titles of which are revealing), Mr. Incoul's Misadventure, and The Truth about Tristrem Varick were all published in the eighties. Nevertheless, it seems that this professional misogynist married three times!"

Elmer Brennecke, in the New York World for August 28, 1921, writes of "his carefully waxed moustache, immaculate and correctly pressed clothes, dark, romantic eyes, and small feet, almost too delicate to tread the thorny paths of erotic literature."

This is Sadakichi Hartmann's description: "Saltus was always extremely courteous, and his gestures were like hieroglyphics made with his finger-tips. In his dress he was neither loud nor eccentric, but rather up to date with the latest fashion, tailor-made, immaculate. With his boutonnière and the traditional triangle of a silk handkerchief always visible, with white socks, gloves, stovepipe and walking stick, he impressed one as a dandy of the McAllister era. He was picturesque without being conspicuous. His face in later years had peculiarly deep lines about the nose and mouth, only partly hidden by a heavy brown moustache—the colour no doubt was due to some generous process of rejuvenation, as the author was near sixty when I saw 'him last."

Mr. Hartmann contradicts himself. Mr. Saltus really resembled a "dandy of the McAllister era," but that is a very different thing from being "up to date with the latest fashion." The man, as a personality, impressed me as a paradoxical combination of Beau Brummel, Don Juan, and Saint Francis of Assisi.

# Edgar Saltus

Edgar Evertson Saltus was born in New York City, June 8, 1858.[8] He is a lineal descendant of Admiral Kornelis Evertson, the commander of the Dutch fleet, who captured New York from the English, August 9, 1673. Francis Saltus,[9] the poet, was his half-brother. Edgar's first wife was Helen Read, the daughter of Mr. William G. Read, "a rich and prominent New Yorker," a banker, who lived at 1 East Forty-eighth Street. In her suit for divorce, filed in December 1889, Mrs. Saltus named two co-respondents. In May 1891 she amended this complaint, making the co-respondent "a woman unknown to this plaintiff." The decree was signed by Judge O'Brien on June 18, 1891. According to the New York Herald, Saltus was willing to give his wife a divorce, but refused to permit "two innocent girls to be compromised," and he and his lawyers fought until the complaint was amended.

Edgar Saltus's second wife was Elsie Welsh Smith of Philadelphia, granddaughter of John Welsh, at one time United States Minister to London. He married her in Paris in 1895. In 1901, she secured a separation from him and a long fight followed for the possession of their

[8] According to Who's Who. Mrs. Saltus gives the correct date as October 8, 1855. She adduces the Saltus family Bible record as evidence.

[9] Francis S. Saltus born in New York City in 1849, died at Tarrytown, June 24, 1889. Educated at Columbia, he spent many years abroad. He knew something of ten languages and wrote many poems in French, German, and Italian. Some of his contributions to magazines were signed Cupid Jones. At his death he left a formidable mass of manuscript, not only poetry, but also lives of Rossini and Donizetti, monographs on Bellini and Mercadante, etc. He also left comic histories of France, Greece, Germany, England, and Rome. After his death a number of his poems were collected and published by his father. The best known volume is entitled The Bayadere. Honey and Gall was published by Lippincott in Philadelphia in 1873.

only child, Elsie Welsh Saltus, which Mrs. Saltus finally won. Miss Saltus married J. Theus Munds and is at present living in New York.

The second Mrs. Saltus died in 1909 and in 1911 Edgar Saltus married Marie Florence Giles.[10] These are the salient facts of his extensive career as a yokemate.[11]

Saltus enjoyed a cosmopolitan education which may be regarded as an important factor in the development of his tastes and ideas. From St. Paul's School in Concord he migrated to the Sorbonne in Paris, and thence to Heidelberg and Munich, where he bathed in the current of German philosophy. Finally, he took a course of law at Columbia University. Beginning, quite possibly, as a disciple of Emerson in New England, he fell under the spell of Victor Hugo in Paris, of Arthur Schopenhauer and Eduard von Hartmann in Germany. His knowledge of languages made it easy for him to drink deeply at many fountain heads. Essentially, however, he was the son of Victor Hugo by Schopenhauer. Strange bedfellows these! Their marital antics resulted in strange children. Gautier and d'Aurevilly also influenced him. He annexed the horrors of Hugo, the exotic, flamboyant style of Gautier, the snobbism of d'Aurevilly, and the pessimism of Schopenhauer. For a few tricks he was indebted to Balzac, an early admiration. If Oscar Wilde found his chief inspiration in Huysmans's *A Rebours*, it is certain that Saltus also quaffed intoxicating draughts

---

[10] Marie Florence Giles has been an author herself. She published at least three books: The End of the Journey; Dillingham; 1897; The Game of Consequences; Dillingham; 1898; Though Your Sins Be as Scarlet; F. Tennyson Neely; 1899. The dates are approximate.

[11] In the first issue of Who's Who in America (1899–1900), it is stated that Saltus married Elsie Welsh Smith. In subsequent issues of this work there is no reference made to any marriage.

at this source.  His kinship with these writers is apparent, but through this mixed blood run strains inherited from the early pagans, the mediæval monks, and the London of the nineties (although Saltus is not mentioned in Holbrook Jackson's history of the yellow decade); another literary relative was an American, Edgar Allan Poe, who bequeathed him a garretful of curious odds and ends.

A prevalent theory has it that great art is always provincial, never cosmopolitan; that only provincial art is universal in its appeal.  The flaw in this theory lies in the fact that it fails to take account of the fantastic.  The fantastic in literature, in art of any kind, can never be provincial.  The work of Poe is not provincial; nor is that of Gustave Moreau, an artist with whom Edgar Saltus may very readily be compared.  If you have visited the Musée Moreau at Paris where, in the studio of the dead painter, is gathered together the most complete collection of his canvases, which lend themselves to endless inspection, you may, in a sense, reconstruct for yourself an idea of the works of Edgar Saltus.  One discovers therein the same unicorns, the same hippogryphs, the same virgins on the rocks, the same exotic and undreamed of flora and fauna, the same mystic paganism, the same exquisitely jewelled workmanship.  On the other hand, Saltus's style may be said to possess American characteristics.  It is dashing and rapid, as clear as the water in southern seas.  The fellow has a penchant for short and nervous sentences which explode like so many firecrackers and remind one of the great national holiday.  Nevertheless, Edgar Saltus should have been born in France.

His essays, whether they deal with literary criticism,

[97]

history, religion (almost an obsession with this writer), devil-worship, or cooking, are pervaded by that rare quality charm. Somewhere he quotes the French aphorism:

"Etre riche n'est pas l'affaire,
Toute l'affaire est de charmer,"

which might be applied to his own work. There is a deep and beneficent guile in the simplicity of his style, as limpid as a brook, and yet, as over a brook, in its overtones hover a myriad of sparkling dragon-flies and butterflies; in its depths lie a plethora of trout. He deals with the most obstruse and abstract subjects with such ease and grace, without for one moment laying aside the badge of authority, that they assume a mysterious fascination to catch the eye of the passerby. In his fictions he has sometimes cultivated a more bizarre manner, but that in itself constitutes a plausible excuse for the reader's infatuation. Scarcely a word but evokes an image, often a complication of images. He is never afraid of the colloquial, never afraid of slang even, and he frequently weaves lovely patterns with the aid of obsolete or technical words. These lines, in which Saltus paid tribute to Gautier, he might, with equal justice, have employed to describe himself: "No one could torment a fancy more delicately than he; and he had the gift of adjective; he scented a new one afar like a truffle; and from the Morgue of the dictionary he dragged forgotten beauties. He dowered the language of his day with every tint of dawn and every convulsion of sunset; he invented metaphors that were worth a king's ransom, and figures of speech that deserve the Prix Montyon. Then, reviewing his work, he formulated an axiom which

[98]

will go down with a nimbus through time: Whomsoever a thought however complex, a vision however apocalyptic, surprises without words to convey it, is not a writer. The inexpressible does not exist." It is scarcely fair to taste at this man's table. One must eat the whole dinner to appreciate its opulence. Still I may offer a few olives, a branch or two of succulent celery to those not yet initiated to the feast itself. One of his ladies walks the Avenue in a gown the "colour of fried smelts." Such figurative phrases as "Her eyes were of that green-grey which is caught in an icicle held over grass," "The sand is as fine as face powder, nuance Rachel, packed hard," "Death, it may be, is not merely a law but a place, perhaps a garage which the traveller reaches on a demolished motor, but whence none can proceed until all old scores are paid," "The ocean resembled nothing so much as an immense blue syrup," "She was a pale, freckled girl, with hair the shade of Bavarian beer," "The sun rose from the ocean like an indolent girl from her bath," "Night, that queen who reigns only when she falls, shook out the shroud she wears for gown," are scattered on every page. Certain phrases sound good to him and are re-used: "Disappearances are deceptive," "ruedelapaixian" (to describe a dress), "the kiss of flutes," "toilet of the ring" (lifted from the bull-fight in Mr. Incoul's Misadventure to do service in an account of the arena games under Nero in Imperial Purple), but repetition of this kind is infrequent in his work. Ideas and phrases, endless chains of them, spurt from the point of his ardent pen. He never wrote from his heart; he seldom, indeed, wrote from his brain; he wrote with his nerves.

From the beginning, his style has attracted the attention of the few, and no one, I feel sure, has ever written a three-line review of a book by Saltus without referring to it either in derogation or appreciation. Amélie Rives has quoted Oscar Wilde as saying to her one night at dinner, "In the work of Edgar Saltus passion struggles with grammar on every page!" It might, indeed, be said of him, in the words with which Léon Bloy described Huysmans, that "he drags his images by the heels or the hair up and down the worm-eaten staircase of terrified syntax." Percival Pollard pictured Saltus as "an author drunken with his own phrases," even a "prose paranoiac," and Elbert Hubbard thus summed him up: "He writes so well that he grows enamoured of his own style and is subdued like the dyer's hand; he becomes intoxicated on the lure of lines and the roll of phrases. He is woozy with words—locoed by syntax and prosody. The libation he pours is flavoured with euphues. It is all like a cherry in a morning Martini." An epithet which Remy de Gourmont employs to describe Villiers de l'Isle Adam might be applied with equal success to the author of The Lords of the Ghostland: "L'idéalisme de Villiers était un véritable idéalisme verbal, c'est-à-dire qu'il croyait vraiment à la puissance évocatrice des mots, à leur vertu magique." And we may listen to Saltus's own testimony: "It may be noted that in literature only three things count, style, style polished, style repolished; these imagination and the art of transition aid, but do not enhance. As for style, it may be defined as the sorcery of syllables, the fall of sentences, the use of the exact term, the pursuit of a repetition even unto the thirtieth and fortieth line. Grammar is an adjunct but not an obligation. No grammarian ever wrote a thing that was fit to read." It is also well to recall

## Edgar Saltus

that Vernon Lee once remarked sapiently, "He who creates a style becomes its slave."

At his worst—and his worst can be monstrous—garbed fantastically in purple patches and gaudy rags, Saltus wallows in muddy puddles of Burgundy and gold dust. His women have eyes which are purple pools, their lips are scarlet threads. Even the names of his characters, Roanoke Raritan, Ruis Ixar, Tancred Ennever, Erastus Varick, Gulian Verplank, Melancthon Orr, Justine Dunnellen, Roland Mistrial, Giselle Oppensheim, Yoda Jones, Stella Sixmuth, Violet Silverstairs, Sallie Malakoff, Shane Wyvell, Dugald Maule, Eden Menemon (it will be observed that he cherishes a persistent, balefully procacious, perhaps, indeed, Freudian, predilection for the letters U, V, and X) [12] are grotesque and, occasionally, ridiculous. Some of his work, in which incredible characters enact extravagant fables in towers of painted velvet words, almost approaches the burlesque. He lacked, it may be admitted, all signs of a sense of humour, but he was by no means deficient in a sense of wit.

Always the snob (somewhere he defends the snob in an essay), rich food ("half-mourning" [artichoke hearts and truffles], "filet of reindeer," a cygnet in its plumage, bearing an orchid in its beak, "heron's eggs whipped with wine into an amber foam," "mashed grasshoppers baked in saffron," "sows' breasts with Lybian truffles; dormice baked in poppies and honey, peacock-tongues flavoured with cinnamon, sea-wolves from the Baltic, fig-peckers from Samos, African snails, polar bears in pink lard, and

[12] You will find an account of Balzac's interesting theory regarding names and letters, which may well have had a direct influence on Edgar Saltus, in Saltus's Balzac, page 29 et seq. For a precisely contrary theory turn to The Naming of Streets in Max Beerbohm's Yet Again.

[101]

## Edgar Saltus

a yellow pig cooked after the Trojan fashion, from which, when carved, hot sausages fell and live thrushes flew"), rich clothes, rich people, alone serve to awaken his interest. There is no poverty in his fictions. His creatures do not toil. Usually, they cut coupons off bonds. Sometimes they write or paint, but for the most part they are free to devote themselves exclusively to the pursuit of emotional experience, eating, drinking, reading, and travelling the while. When they have finished dining they are wont to dry their hands, wetted in a golden bowl, in the blond curls of a tiny serving boy. A character in Madam Sapphira explains this tendency: "A writer, if he happens to be worth his syndicate, never chooses a subject. The subject chooses him. He writes what he must, not what he might. That's the thing the public can't understand."

There is always a preoccupation with ancient life, sometimes freely expressed, as in Imperial Purple, but more often suggested by plot, phrase, or scene. He kills more characters than Caligula destroyed during the whole course of his bloody reign. Murders, suicides, and other forms of sudden death flash their sensations across his pages. Webster and the other Elizabethans never steeped themselves so deeply in gore. In almost every novel there is an orgy of death, and he has been ingenious in varying its agonies. The poisons of rafflesia, muscarine, and orsere are introduced in his fictions; somewhere he devotes an essay to toxicology. Daggers with blades like needles, pistols, drownings, asphyxiations, play their torturing rôles. In one book there is a crucifixion!

Again I discover that Mr. Saltus has said his word on

the subject: "In fiction as in history it is the shudder that tells. Hugo could find no higher compliment for Baudelaire than to announce that the latter had discovered a new one. For new shudders are as rare as new vices; antiquity has made them all seem trite. The apt commingling of the horrible and the trivial, pathos and ferocity, is yet the one secret of enduring work—a secret, parenthetically, which Hugo knew as no one else."

His fables depend in most instances upon sexual aberrations, curious coincidences, unparalleled happenings. Rapes and incests decorate his pages. He does not ask us to believe his monstrous stories; he compels us to. He carries us, by means of the careless expenditure of many passages of somewhat ribald beauty, along with him, captive to his pervasive charm. We are constantly reminded, in endless, almost wearisome, imagery, of gold and purple, foreign languages, forgotten philosophies, foods, the names of which strike the ear as graciously as they themselves might strike the tongue. All our senses are lured. Words are often used for their own sakes to evoke parenthetical concepts, colour smears the page, fills in, indeed, the outline of each line. We taste, we smell, we see, we hear, we touch. There is a suggestion of the pomp and circumstance of the Roman Catholic ritual, stealthily confused with mythical monsters, singing flowers, and blooming women. Scarlet and mulberry threads form the woof of this tapestry, threads pulled with infinite pains from the art of the past. There is, in much of his work, an undercurrent of subtle, sensuous corruption.

He is always obsessed by the mysteries of love and

death, the veils of Isis, the secrets of Moses.[13]   While
others were delving in the American soil his soul sped
afar; he is not merely cosmopolitan; he is concretely a
Greek, a Brahmin, a worshipper of Istar.   There is a
prodigal display of vitality in his work, savannahs of epigrams [14] (many of them unspeakable), forests of ideas
(many of them borrowed), phrases enough to fill the
ocean.   There is sufficient material in the romances of
Edgar Saltus to furnish all the cinema companies in
America with scenarios [15] for a twelvemonth.

Early in the eighties a writer in the Argus referred to
him as "the prose laureate of pessimism."   His philosophy may be summed up in a few phrases:   Nothing matters, Whatever will be, is, and Since, unfortunately we live
today, let us make the best of it and live in Paris.
Through all of Saltus's books, as a pendent to the rapes
and murders, the religious, philosophical, and social discussions, like a persistent refrain, rings Cherubino's still
unanswered question, Che cosa è amor?

To guide the reader, as yet uninformed in Saltus, into
this literary museum I have prepared a short catalogue
by the aid of which he may pilot himself through the

[13] Towards the end of his life, at the behest of the third Mrs.
Saltus, he became a theosophist, a religion he adopted the more will-
ingly, perhaps, because of his love for animals. Cats in particular
were his passion. It is reasonable to suppose, indeed, that they
awakened the warmest side of his nature.

[14] Wit and Wisdom from Edgar Saltus, by G. F. Monkshood and
George Gamble, and The Cynic's Posy, a collection of epigrams, the
majority of which were culled from Saltus, may be brought forward
in evidence.

[15] At least two of his books, subsequent to the original appearance
of this paper, have been made into moving pictures: Daughters of
the Rich, with Miriam Cooper, and the Paliser Case, in which Pauline
Frederick was the featured player.

collection. I have also added a list of publishers, together with the dates of publication, although I cannot, in some instances, be altogether certain that these are the first editions. It may be noted that almost all of this author's books have been reprinted in England.[16]

Balzac,[17] signed Edgar Evertson Saltus (for a time he used his full name) is such good literary criticism and such good biography, of the personal variety, in spite of the fact that he accepts the Balzac legend at its face value, that one wishes the author had experimented further with this form. He did not, save in the prefaces to his translations, his essay on Victor Hugo,[18] and his short study of Oscar Wilde. In miniature, for the book is slight, Balzac ranks with James Huneker's Chopin, Auguste Ehrhard's Fanny Elssler, and Frank Harris's Oscar Wilde. In style it is perhaps superior to any of these. A very pretty performance, indeed, for a début. The two most interesting chapters, largely anecdotal but continuously illuminating, are entitled The Vagaries of Genius, wherein one may find an infinitude of details concerning the manner in which Balzac worked, and The Chase for Gold, but tucked in somewhere else is a charming digression dealing with the subject of realism in

---

[16] Certain books by Edgar Saltus have been announced from time to time but have never appeared. This apocryphal list includes: Annochiatura, Immortal Greece, Our Lady of Beauty, Cimmeria, Daughters of Dream, Scaffolds and Altars, Prince Charming, and The Crimson Curtain, this last, possibly, a projected translation of d'Aurevilly's Le rideau cramoisi.

[17] Houghton, Mifflin and Co.; 1884. Reprinted 1887 and 1890. Saltus has informed me, indeed, that this book was still in print at the time this paper appeared. His royalties therefrom for the year 1917 were approximately four dollars.

[18] The Forum; June 1912.

[105]

fiction. The bibliography may be outmoded by now.

The Philosophy of Disenchantment [19] is an ingratiating account of the pessimism of Schopenhauer, a philosophy with which, it would seem, Saltus is in complete accord. Two-thirds of the book are allotted to Schopenhauer, while the remainder is devoted to an exposition of the teachings of von Hartmann and a final essay, Is Life an Affliction?, a query which the author seems to answer in the affirmative. The Philosophy of Disenchantment is written in a clear, translucent style, with none of the baroque embellishment of Saltus's later manner.

After-Dinner Stories from Balzac, done into English by Myndart Verelst (obviously E. S.), with an introduction by Edgar Saltus,[20] contains four of the Frenchman's tales, The Red Inn, Madame Firmiani, The Grand Bretèche, and Madame de Beauséant. The introduction, Saltus at his most beguiling, may be referred to as one of the most readable short essays on Balzac extant.

The Anatomy of Negation [21] is Saltus's masterpiece in his earlier manner, which is as free from flamboyancy as early Gothic. This manual is a history of antitheism from Kapila to Leconte de Lisle and, while Saltus in a brief prefatory notice disavows all responsibility for the opinions of others expressed therein, it can readily be felt that the book represents love's labour, that the author's sympathy lies with the iconoclasts throughout the centuries. The chapter entitled, The Convulsions of the Church, a tabloid history of Christianity, is one of the most coruscant passages to be found in any of the

[19] Houghton, Mifflin and Co.; 1885. Reprinted by the Belford Co.
[20] George J. Coombes; 1886. Reprinted by Brentano's.
[21] Scribner and Welford; 1887. Revised edition, Belford, Clarke and Co.; 1889. Reprinted in 1925 by Brentano's.

works of this brilliant writer. Indeed, if you are searching for the soul of Saltus, you can do no better than turn to this chapter. Of Jesus he says, "He was the most entrancing of nihilists but no innovator." Here is another excerpt: "Paganism was not dead; it had merely fallen asleep. Isis gave way to Mary; apotheosis was replaced by canonization; the divinities were succeeded by saints; and, Africa aiding, the Church surged from mythology with the Trinity for tiara." Again: "Satan was Jew from horn to hoof. The registry of his birth is contained in the evolution of Hebraic thought." Never was any book, so full of erudition and ideas, written by a true sceptic, so easy to read. Following the Baedeker system, so amusingly adopted by Henry T. Finck in his Songs and Song Writers, The Anatomy of Negation should be triple-starred.

Tales Before Supper, from Théophile Gautier and Prosper Mérimée, told in English by Myndart Verelst and delayed with a proem by Edgar Saltus.[22] Translation again. The stories are Avatar and The Venus of Ille. The preface is charming.

Mr. Incoul's Misadventure,[23] Saltus's first novel, is also superior to any of his later fiction. It, too, should be triple-starred. In it will be found, fastidiously distilled, the very essence of all the personal qualities of this writer. Mr. Incoul is composed with fine reserve; the fable holds the attention; the characters are unusually well observed, felt, and expressed. A mocking irony grins between the lines and the final cadence includes a murder and a suicide. For the former, bromide of potassium and gas are employed in combination; for

[22] Brentano's; 1887.
[23] Benjamin and Bell; 1887. Republished by Brentano's in 1925.

# Edgar Saltus

the latter, laudanum, injected hypodermically, suffices. There are scenes in Biarritz and northern Spain, with a thrilling account of a bull-fight. There is a fascinating glimpse of the Paris Opéra. There is a catalogue of an epithymetic library which embraces many forbidden titles (how that "baron of moral endeavour . . . the professional hound of heaven," Anthony Comstock, would have gloated over these shelves!), a vibrant passage about Goya, and another about a Thibetan cat. Much evidence might be cited to prove that Saltus loves the fireside sphinx. Mr. Incoul himself presents one with a very exact idea of how inhuman a just man can be. I cannot discover a single slip in the skilful dilineation of this monster. The beautiful heroine vaguely shambles into a tapestried background. She is moyen age in her appealing weakness. On the other hand the jeune premier, Lenox Leigh, is well drawn and lighted. The pages are permeated with suspense, horror, information, cynicism, and an icy charm, about evenly distributed, all of which qualities are suggested by the astounding title.

The Truth about Tristrem Varick [24] is composed with the same restraint that informs the style of Mr. Incoul's Misadventure, a restraint seldom to be encountered in Saltus's later fictions. The book is a history of the pursuit of the ideal which lands the pursuer in the electric chair. It might profitably be compared with Herman Melville's Pierre, an experiment with the same theme. One of the angles of the plot, in which an irate father attempts to suppress a marriage by suggesting incest, bobs up at least twice again in Saltus's romances. Irony is the keynote of the work, a keynote sounded in

[24] Belford Co.; 1888.

[108]

the dedication, "To my master, the philosopher of the unconscious, Eduard von Hartmann, this attempt in ornamental disenchantment is dutifully inscribed." The heroine, as so frequently happens with the heroines of this writer, is veiled with the mysteries of Isis; we do not see the workings of her mind and so we can sympathize with Varick who accords her arduous devotion and persistent misunderstanding through two hundred and forty pages, attributing her lack of response to his father's unfounded charge that she is his half-sister. Learning that she has borne a child, he suspects rape and, with a needle-like dagger that leaves no sign, he kills the man he credits with the action. Thereafter he approaches the lady to accept her gratitude, only to inform himself that he has killed the man she loved. Varick gives himself into the hands of the police, confesses, and is delivered to justice, the lady gloating. This pessimistic tale is most excellently written. La Cenerentola and Lucrezia Borgia are mentioned in passing. Saltus has (or had) an exuberant admiration for Donizetti and Rossini. Give Tristrem Varick at least two stars.

Eden,[25] the third of Saltus's fictions, marks a decided decline in his powers. Eden is the name of the heroine. Her husband is almost too noble, but nevertheless, appearances are against him until he explains that the lady with whom he has been seen in a cab is his daughter by a former marriage, while the young man paying ambiguous attentions to Eden is his son. Characteristic of Saltus is the use of the Spanish word for nightingale. There are no deaths, no suicides, no murders to be discovered herein: a very eunuch of a book! A motto

[25] Belford, Clarke and Co.; 1888.

from Tasso, "Perdute è tutto il tempo che in amor non si spende," adorns the title page.

With The Pace that Kills,[26] Saltus doffs his old coat and dons a new and gaudier garment. A hard, brilliant glitter informs the surface of this sordid melodrama. Abortion sets the pace at the beginning and the race ends with a drop from a bridge into the icy East River. The strangulation of a baby is averted and for the second time in a Saltus opus a dying millionaire bequeaths his fortune to the St. Nicholas Hospital. Was the author ballyhooing for this institution? The hero is a modern Don Giovanni. Alphabet Jones appears occasionally, as he does in many of the other novels. This Balzacian trick obsessed Saltus for a time. The morbid motto of The Pace that Kills is a quotation from Rabusson: "Pourquoi la mort? Dites, plutôt, pourquoi la vie?"

In A Transaction in Hearts,[27] the Reverend Christopher Gonfallon confesses a guilty love for his wife's sister. A New England Countess, a subsidiary figure, suggests d'Aurevilly. This story was originally published in Lippincott's Magazine and the editor who accepted it was dismissed. A year or so later a new incumbent of the job accepted The Picture of Dorian Gray. Saltus tells me that still later he met Oscar Wilde in London, and the latter inquired about the new editor. "He's quite well," Saltus informed him. Wilde did not appear to be pleased: "When your story came out the editor was removed; when they published mine I supposed he would be hanged. Now you tell me he is quite well. It is most disheartening."

[26] Belford Co.; 1889.
[27] Belford Co.; 1889. Mrs. Saltus states that this novel is to some extent autobiographical.

# Edgar Saltus

A Transient Guest and Other Episodes [28] contains three short tales, in addition to the title story: The Grand Duke's Riches, an account of an ingenious robbery at the Brevoort, A Maid of Athens, and Fausta, a romance of love, revenge, and death, laid in Cuba. If the peroration of this volume is a dagger thrust, the prelude is a subtle poison, rafflesia, a Sumatran plant, intended for the hero, Tancred Ennever, but consumed with fatal results by his faithful fox terrier, Zut Alors.

The slender pamphlet entitled Love and Lore [29] assembles a series of slight papers, interrupted by slighter sonnets, on subjects which, for the most part, Saltus has treated at greater length and with greater effect elsewhere. He makes a whimsical plea for a modern revival of the Court of Love and he derides that Puritanism in American letters whose dark scourge H. L. Mencken still attacks with a cat-o'-nine-tails and a handgrenade. He gives us a fantastic set of rules for a novelist which, happily, he has ignored in his own fictions. The most interesting and personal chapter, palpably derived from The Philosophy of Disenchantment, is that entitled What Pessimism Is Not; here again we are in the heart of the author's philosophy. Those who like to read about the Iberian Peninsula will probably enjoy Fabulous Andalucia, in which an able brief for the race of Othello is presented: "Under the Moors, Cordova surpassed Baghdad. They wrote more poetry than all the other nations put together. It was they who invented rhyme; they wrote everything in it, contracts, challenges, treaties, treatises, diplomatic notes, and messages of love. From the earliest khalyf down to Boabdil, the courts of

[28] Belford, Clarke and Co.; 1889.
[29] Belford Co.; 1890.

# Edgar Saltus

Granada, of Cordova, and of Seville were peopled with poets, or, as they were termed, with makers of Ghazels. It was they who gave us the dulcimer, the hautbois, and the guitar; it was they who invented the serenade. We are indebted to them for algebra and for the canons of chivalry as well. . . . It was from them that came the first threads of light which preceded the Renaissance. Throughout mediæval Europe they were the only people that thought." Love and Lore is dedicated to Edgar Fawcett, "perfect poet—perfect friend," and is embellished with a portrait of its author.

The Story Without a Name,[30] a translation of Une histoire sans nom, of Barbey d'Aurevilly, is preceded by one of Saltus's atmospheric prefaces, one of the best papers on d'Aurevilly to be found in English. When this book was published, Mr. Saltus informs me, a reviewer, "who contrived to be both amusing and complimentary," announced that Barbey d'Aurevilly was a fictitious personage and that this vile story was Saltus's own vile work!

Mary Magdalen,[31] on the whole, is disappointing. The opening chapters, like Oscar Wilde's Salome (published two years later than Mary Magdalen), owe much to Flaubert's Hérodias. The dance on the hands is a detail from Flaubert,[32] a detail which Tissot followed in

[30] Belford Co.; 1891. In 1919, Brentano's issued this translation in the Lotus Library. For this edition Saltus provided a new preface.

[31] Belford Co.; 1891. Reprinted by Mitchell Kennerley; 1906, and later by Brentano's.

[32] Flaubert did not invent this detail. In illuminated manuscripts of the fourteenth century and in windows of stained glass, Salome walks on her hands before Herod, to his delight and to the amazement of his guests. The inspiration for this posture is to be found in an old version of the New Testament in which it is said that Salome "vaulted" before Herod.

his painting of Salome. From the later chapters it is possible that Paul Heyse filched an idea. The turning point of his drama, Maria von Magdala, hinges on Judas's love for Mary and his jealousy of Jesus. Saltus develops precisely this situation. Heyse's play appeared in 1899, eight years after Saltus's novel. Saltus, however, has protested to me that it is an idea that might have occurred to any one. "I put it in," he added, "to make the action more nervous." The book begins well with a description of Herod's court and Rome in Judea, but the glamour of the opening scenes is not maintained. Once the plot is under way Saltus seems to lose interest. He lazily quotes dialogue from the Bible, a pitfall George Moore cannily avoided in The L ook Kerith. The early chapters suggest Imperial Purple, published a year later, on which the author may well have been working at this time. There is a foreshadowing, too, of the thesis expanded in The Lords of the Ghostland in a cynical passage in which Mary as a child listens while Sephorah the Sorceress relates the legends and myths of Assyria and Egypt. Mary interrupts with "Why you mean Moses! You mean Noah!", just as a child of today, confronted with the situations in the Greek dramas might attribute them to Hauptmann or Ibsen. Saltus is too much of a scholar to find much novelty in Christianity. Aside from this passage, however, Mary Magdalen oddly enough lacks cynicism, a quality which makes another story on a cognate theme, Le procurateur de Judée, one of the great short stories in any language. Mary's sins, unforgivably, are quickly brushed aside and we come almost immediately to her conversion. Herod Antipas, with his "fan-shaped beard," and vacillating Pilate, quite comparable in his conception to a modern politician, are

[113]

the most human and best-realized characters in a book which should have been better than it is. Mary Magdalen is dedicated to Henry James.

The Facts in the Curious Case of H. Hyrtl, Esq.,[33] is a slight yarn in the mellow Stevenson manner, with a kindly old gentleman as the messenger of the supernatural who provides the wherewithal for a marriage between an impoverished artist, engaged in painting Heliogabalus's feast of roses, and his sweet young thing. Quite a radical (and by no means welcome) departure this from the usual Saltus manner; nevertheless, there are two deaths, one by shock, the other in a railway accident. The plot depends on as many impossible entrances and exits as a Palais Royal farce and the reader is requested to credit many coincidences. H. Hyrtl is dedicated to Lorillard Ronalds who, the author explains in a few French phrases, had asked him to write something, "de très pure et de très chaste, pour une jeunesse, sans doute." He adds that the story is a rewriting of a tale which had appeared twenty years earlier.

[33] P. F. Collier; 1892; "Written especially for Once a Week Library." Saltus at one time and another did a vast amount of hackwork. For a period he contributed either a column or the entire editorial page to Collier's Weekly. He also supplied "supplementary chapters on recent events" for a reissue of the following volumes in the Nations of the World Series: Russia (two volumes); 1898; India (two volumes); 1899; Persia (two volumes); Germany (four volumes); n. d. His crowning effort in this direction was an incredible compilation entitled: The Lovers of the World, a chronicle of the sensational dramas, enchanting romances, tragical histories, pathetic trials, fierce passions, and pure hearts of all who have lived and loved from the earliest times to the present day, with faithful descriptions of the virtues and charms which inspired them and the joys and disasters which they caused; profusely illustrated; three volumes; Peter Fenelon Cooper; New York; n. d. (circa 1895). The Lovers of the World begins with Helen of Troy and ends with Queen Victoria. Altogether about fifty pairs of lovers are considered. Charles Honce also lists

# Edgar Saltus

Imperial Purple [34] marks the high-tide of Edgar Saltus's peculiar and limited genius. The emperors of Rome in its glory and its decadence are led by the chains of art behind the chariot wheels of the poet: Julius Cæsar, whom Cato called "that woman," Augustus, Tiberius, Caligula, the wicked Agrippina, who endowed Agnes Repplier's cat with her name, Claudius, Nero, Hadrian, Vespasian, down to the incredible Heliogabalus. Saltus, who spreads freely on the record the unsavoury and noisome details of the careers of the boy emperor's predecessors, seemingly falters before this name, but only seemingly. More can be found about Heliogabalus in Lombard's l'Agonie and in Franz Blei's The Powder Puff, but Saltus, although brief, creates an intended impression. The catastrophe is theatrically casual: "One day this little painted girl, who had prepared several devices for a unique and splendid suicide, was taken unawares and tossed in the latrinæ."

The sheer lyric throb of this book has remained unsurpassed by its author. Indeed, its peculiar sensational swing is rare in all literature. The man writes with invention, with sap, with urge. Our eyes are not delayed by footnotes and references. It is plain that Saltus has delved in the Scriptores Historiæ Augustæ, that he has devoured Lampridus, Suetonius, and the other historians, but he does not strive to make us aware of this fact. Clio has at last found a poet to carry her banner. Blood flows across the pages; gore and booty and lust

The Battles of all Nations; two volumes; P. Fenelon Collier; 1899. This book is signed Archibald Wilberforce. Spain and Her Colonies (Peter Fenelon Cooper; 1898) is also "compiled from the best authorities by Archibald Wilberforce."

[34] Morrill, Higgins and Co.; 1893. Reprinted by Mitchell Kennerley; 1906, and later by Brentano's.

are the principal themes; yet Beauty struts supreme through the horror. The author's sympathy is his password, a sympathy he occasionally exposes, for he is not above pinning his heart to his sleeve, as, for example, when he asserts: "Triremes have foundered; litters are out of date; painted elephants are no more; the sky has changed, climates with it; there are colours, as there are arts, that have gone from us forever; there are desolate plains, where green and yellow was; the shriek of steam where gods have strayed; advertisements in sacred groves; Baedekers in ruins that never heard an atheist's voice; solitudes where there were splendours; the snarl of jackals where once were birds and bees." Here is a detailed picture of squalid Rome: "In the subura, where at night women sat in high chairs, ogling the passer with painted eyes, there was still plenty of brick; tall tenements, soiled linen, the odour of Whitechapel and St. Giles. The streets were noisy with match-pedlars, with vendors of cake and tripe and coke; there were touts there too, altars to unimportant divinities, lying Jews who dealt in old clothes, in obscene pictures, and unmentionable wares; at the crossings there were thimble-riggers, clowns, and jugglers, who made glass balls appear and disappear surprisingly; there were doorways decorated with curious invitations, gossipy barber shops, where, through the liberality of politicians, the scum of a great city was shaved, curled, and painted free; and there were public houses, where vagabond slaves and sexless priests drank the mulled wine of Crete, supped on the flesh of beasts slaughtered in the arena, or watched the Syrian women twist to the click of castanets."

Imperial Purple has undergone curious adventures.

[116]

# Edgar Saltus

Belford, Clarke and Co., who hid their identity behind the "Morrill, Higgins" imprint, failed shortly after the book was published. "Presently," Mr. Saltus writes me, "a Chicago bibliofilou brought it out as the work of some one else and called it The Sins of Nero." In 1906, Greening and Co., issued the book in London. In 1911, Macmillan in London brought out The Amazing Emperor Heliogabalus by the Reverend John Stuart Hay of Oxford. The preface to this volume contains the following acknowledgment: "I have also the permission of Mr. E. E. Saltus of Harvard University (sic) to quote his vivid and beautiful studies on the Roman Empire and her customs. I am also deeply indebted to Mr. Walter Pater, Mr. J. A. Symonds, and Mr. Saltus for many a tournure de phrase and picturesque rendering of Tacitus, Suetonius, Lampridus, and the rest." The holy father certainly partook freely of Imperial Purple. Words, sentences, nay whole paragraphs, reappear without the formality of quotation marks, without any indication, indeed, save these lines in the preface, that they are not a result of Dr. Hay's own imagination, unless one compares them with the style in which the remainder of the book is written. "In one instance," Mr. Saltus writes me, "he gave a paragraph of mine as his own. Later on he added, 'as we have already said,' and repeated the paragraph. The plural struck me as singular."

Madam Sapphira [35] is a vivid study of unchastened womanhood. This novel, as a matter of fact, appears to be Saltus's chivalric version of the circumstances surrounding his first divorce. He has even dragged in his comments in regard to a bequest to his father-in-law,

[35] F. Tennyson Neely; 1893.

[117]

quoted supra, page 93. It is likely that much more of this malicious form of autobiography will be dug up in Saltus's work.

Enthralled, a story of international life setting forth the curious circumstances concerning Lord Cloden and Oswald Quain: [36] an insane phantasmagoria of crime, avarice, and murder. For the second time in this author's novels incest plays a rôle. Oswald Quain is as vile and virulent a villain as any who stalks through the horror fictions of Ann Ker, Eliza Bromley, or Mrs. Radcliffe. A Dr. Jekyll and Mr. Hyde motif is sounded. An ugly man returns from London as a handsome fellow after visits to a surgeon who rearranges the lines of his face. The transformation is effected every day now (some of our prominent actresses are said to have benefited by this operation), but in 1894 the mechanism of the trick must have creaked appallingly. This tale, indeed, borders on the burlesque. The period is subtly evoked by one detail, constantly reiterated in Saltus's early books: ladies and gentlemen when they leave a room "push aside the portieres." Sometimes the "rings jingle." He has in most instances mercifully spared us further descriptions of the interiors of New York houses at this epoch. At a dinner party one of the guests refers to Howells as the "foremost novelist who is never read." Saltus returned to the central theme of Enthralled in The Impostor, published in Ainslie's for May 1917.

When Dreams Come True [37] again brings us in touch with Tancred Ennever, the stupid protagonist of The Transient Guest. In the meantime he has become an

[36] Tudor Press; 1894.
[37] The Transatlantic Publishing Co.; 1895.

almost intolerable prig. It is probable that Saltus meant
more by this fable than he dared let appear. The roar
of the waves on the coast of Lesbos is distinctly audible
for a time and the solution appears to belong to quite
another story. . . . Ennever has turned author. We are
informed that he has completed studies on Huysmans and
Leconte de Lisle; he is also engaged on a Historia Amoris.
An interesting passage relates to the names of great
writers. Alphabet Jones assures us that they are always "in two syllables with the accent on the first. Oyez:
Homer, Sappho, Horace, Dante, Petrarch, Ronsard,
Shakespeare, Hugo, Swinburne . . . Balzac, Flaubert,
Huysmans, Michelet, Renan." The reader is permitted
to add . . . Saltus.

The first two stories in Purple and Fine Women [38] are
French in form. Paul Bourget himself is the hero of one
of them. In The Princess of the Sun we are offered a
revised version of the Coppelia theme. The Dear Departed exposes Saltus in a murderous, amorous mood
again. In The Princess of the Golden Isles a new poison
is introduced, muscarine. Alchemy furnishes the leitmotif
for one tale; the experimenter seeks an alkahest, a human
victim for his crucible. We are left in doubt as to
whether he chooses his wife, who wears a diamond set
in one of her teeth, or a gorilla. Metaphysics and
spiritualism rise like dim vapour out of the melodrama
of this book. There are dramas of dual personality and
of death. There is a duchess who mews like a cat, and
somewhere we are assured that Perchè non posso odiarti
from La Sonnambula is the most beautiful aria in the

[38] Ainslie; 1903. Reissued in 1925, with a preface by W. L. George,
by Pascal Covici.

[119]

Italian repertory.   Here is a true and soul-revealing epigram:   "The best way to master a subject of which you are ignorant is to write it up."

The Perfume of Eros [39] is frenzied fiction again; amnesia, drunkenness, white slavery, sex, are its mingled themes.   Romance and Realism consort lovingly together in these pages.   There is a pretty sketch, recognizable in any smart community, of a witty woman of fashion, and a full-length portrait of a bounder.   An unforgettable passage describes a young man in the act of ridding himself of his mistress.   He interrupts his flow of explanation to hand her a card-case which she promptly hurls out of the window.

" 'That is an agreeable way of getting rid of twelve thousand dollars,' he remarked.

"Yet, however lightly he affected to speak, the action annoyed him.   Like all men of large means he was close. It seemed to him beastly to lose such a sum.   He got up, went to the window and looked down.   He could not see the case and he much wanted to go and look for it.   But that for the moment Marie prevented."

The Pomps of Satan [40] is replete with grace and charm, a quality more valuable to its possessor than juvenility, the author informs us in a chapter concerning the lost elixir of youth.   Neither form nor matter assumes ponderous shape in this volume.   Satan's pomps are varied; the author exhibits his whims, his ideas, images the past, forecasts the future, deplores the present.   There is a chapter on cooking and we learn that Saltus does not care for food prepared in the German style . . . nor yet in

[39] A. Wessels Co.; 1905. Originally published under the title, The Yellow Fay, in Tales from Town Topics for December 1904.
[40] Mitchell Kennerley; 1906. Republished by Brentano's.

the American. He forbids us Pol Roger: "Champagne is not a wine. It is a beverage, lighter indeed than brandy and soda, but, like cologne, fit only for demireps." He seems untrue to himself in a paper condemning the use of perfumes. His own works are heavily scented.[41] Saltus forsakes his previous choice from Bellini to install Tu che a Dio as his favourite Italian opera air. Here is another flash of self-revelation: "Byzance is rumoured to have been the sewer of every sin, yet such was its beauty that it is the canker of our heart we could not have lived there." Always this turning to the far past, this preoccupation with Rosetta Stones and palimpsests, this partiality for the sights and sins of the ancient gods and kings. A chapter on poisons and another on Gille de Retz, which probably owes something to Là-bas, further betray this preference. He playfully suggests that the Academy of Arts and Letters be filled up with young nobodies: "They have, indeed, done nothing yet. But therein is their charm. An academy composed of young people who have done nothing yet would be more alluring than one made up of fossils who are unable to do anything more." Hardly as evenly inspired as Imperial Purple, The Pomps of Satan is more witty. It is also more tired.

In Stella Sixmuth, Vanity Square [42] boasts such a vampire as even Theda Bara is seldom called upon to portray. Not until the final chapter, however, do we discover that this suave adventuress has been poisoning a rich man's wife, with an eye on the husband's hand and

---

[41] Bill Sayers, in The Ghost Girl (Boni and Liveright; 1922), "writes his books as the Moslems build their mosques, mixing musk with mortar, that the whole structure should be perfumed."

[42] J. B. Lippincott Co.; 1906.

purse. Orsere is the slow and subtle drug which leaves no subsequent trace. Thwarted, she is successful in a subsequent attempt. Robert Hichens has utilized this theme in Bella Donna. There is a suicide by pistol. Little more than an exciting story, this novel contains fewer references to the gods and the cæsars than is customary in Saltus. In compensation, he discusses phobias, dual personalities (a girl with six is described), and theories about the life beyond. Vanity Square, he announces, is bounded by Central Park, Madison Avenue, Seventy-second Street, and the Plaza.

It will be recalled that Tancred Ennever was collecting notes for Historia Amoris [43] in 1895,[44] which would seem to indicate that Saltus had begun to sift material for it himself at that time. The title is a literal description of the contents. Such a work might have been made purely anecdotal or scientific, but Saltus's purpose, at once more serious and more graceful, has been to show how the love currents flowed through the centuries, to explain what effect period life had on love and what effect love had on period life. Beginning in Babylon, and passing on through The Song of Songs, we meet Helen of Troy, Scheherazade (though but briefly), Sappho (to whom an entire chapter is devoted), Cleopatra (whom Heine described as "cette reine entretenue"), Mary Magdalen, Héloïse. . . . The Courts of Love are depicted and deductions are drawn concerning the effect of the Renaissance on the Gay Science. Cicisbeism is not treated in extenso, as it should be, and I also missed the fragrant name of Sophie Arnould. Historia Amoris

[43] Mitchell Kennerley; 1907. Republished by Brentano's.
[44] This was about the time that Saltus was working on his compilation, The Lovers of the World.

is concluded by a Schopenhauerian essay on The Law of Attraction. Readers of Love and Lore, The Pomps of Satan, Imperial Purple, and The Lords of the Ghostland will find that much of the material of those books has gone into the making of this History of Love.

In The Lords of the Ghostland, a history of the ideal,[45] Saltus returns to the theme of The Anatomy of Negation. The newer work is both more cynical and more charming. It is, as the title indicates, a comparative history of religions. With Reinach, Saltus holds that Christianity owes a good deal to its ancestors. Brahma, Ormuzd, Amon-Râ, Bel-Marduk, Jehovah, Zeus, Jupiter, and many lesser deities parade before us in defile. Prejudice, intolerance, even tolerance, are lacking from this book. The Lords of the Ghostland is neither reverent nor irreverent, it is unreverent. Mr. Saltus finds joy in writing about the gods, the joy of a poet, and if his chiefest pleasure is to extol the gods of Greece, that is only what might be expected of a truly pagan spirit. Students of comparative theology might learn much from these pages, but they will learn it unwittingly, for the artist supersedes the teacher. Saltus is never professorial. The scientific spirit never obtrudes; there is no marshalling of dull facts for their own sakes. Nevertheless, I suspect that the book contains more absorbing information than any other volume on a similar subject. With a fascinating and guileful style, this divine devil of an author leads us on to the point where he can justifiably state that the only original feature of Christianity is the crucifixion, and even that is foreshadowed in the Hindu legend, in which Krishna dies, nailed by arrows to a tree.

[45] Mitchell Kennerley; 1907. Republished by Brentano's.

# Edgar Saltus

Most of the scenes of Daughters of the Rich [46] are laid in Paris. Some of the action takes place in a house on the Avenue Malakoff, which must have been near the hôtel of the Princesse de Sagan and the apartment occupied by Miss Mary Garden. The plot of this ingenious detective story hinges on mistaken identity. The book begins rather than ends with a murder, but that is because the tale is told backwards. Through lies, deceit, and treachery, Sallie Malakoff betrays the hero into marriage. When he discovers her perfidy he cheerfully cuts her throat from ear to ear and goes to join the lady from whom he has become estranged. She receives him with open arms and suggests wedding bells. No woman, she asserts, could resist a man who has killed another woman for her sake. A fat manufacturer's wife confronts the proposal of a mercenary duke with an epic rejoinder: "Pay a man a million dollars to sleep with my daughter! Never!"

The Monster [47] is fiction, incredible, insane fiction. The beast of the title is incest, in this instance inceste manqué, because it doesn't come off. On the eve of a runaway marriage Leilah Ogsten is informed by her father that the bridegroom is her own brother (he inculpates her mother in the scandal). To put barriers between herself and the object of her love Leilah becomes the bride of another. Verplank pursues. There are two fabulous duels and a chapter in which the hero is mangled by dogs. The stage (for we are always in some extravagant theatre) is frequently set in Paris, and the familiar scenes of the capital are in turn exposed to our view. It is all mad, a kaleidoscope of purple patches

[46] Mitchell Kennerley; 1909. Republished by Brentano's.
[47] Pulitzer Publishing Co.; 1912.

[124]

and crimson splotches. From this novel Mr. Saltus fashioned his only play,[48] The Gates of Life, which he sent to Charles Frohman and which Mr. Frohman returned. The piece has neither been performed nor published.

Last year (1917) the Brothers of the Book in Chicago published privately a limited edition (four hundred and seventy-four copies) of a book by Edgar Saltus entitled Oscar Wilde: An Idler's Impression, which contains only twenty-six pages, but twenty-six extremely evocative pages. Saltus has done nothing better than his description of a strange occurrence in a Regent Street restaurant on a certain night when he was supping with Wilde and Wilde was reading Salome to him: "Apropos of nothing, or rather with what to me at the time was curious irrelevance, Oscar, while tossing off glass after glass of liquor, spoke of Phémé, a goddess rare even in mythology who, after appearing twice in Homer, flashed through a verse of Hesiod and vanished behind a page of Herodotus. In telling of her, suddenly his eyes lifted, his mouth contracted, a spasm of pain—or was it dread?—had gripped him. A moment only. His face relaxed. It had gone.

"I have since wondered, could he have evoked the goddess then? For Phémé typified what modern occultism terms the impact—the premonition that surges and warns. It was Wilde's fate to die three times—to die in the dock, to die in prison, and to die all along the boulevards of Paris. Often since I have wondered could the goddess have been lifting, however slightly, some fringe of the crimson curtain, behind which, in all its horror, his destiny crouched. If so, he braved it.

[48] If one excepts After the Ball, a one-act play published in the Smart Set for March 1922.

# Edgar Saltus

"I had looked away. I looked again. Before me was a fat pauper, florid and over-dressed, who, in the voice of an immortal, was reading the fantasies of the damned. In his hand was a 'manuscript and we were supping on Salome."

Edgar Saltus began with Balzac in 1884 and he has arrived at Oscar Wilde in 1917.[49] His other literary

[49] Since this paper was published several more volumes have appeared. At my first meeting with Mr. Saltus he asked me to take the manuscript of The Paliser Case, on which he was then working, to Mr. Knopf. Later at the Manhattan Club he handed me the manuscript. After I had read it, I returned it to him with the assurance that it would not appeal to Mr. Knopf. I never saw Mr. Saltus again. In 1919, The Paliser Case was published by Boni and Liveright. In my review of this book, in the Chicago Daily News (April 16, 1919), I wrote, "The careless rapture of his earlier frenzied fiction is somewhat lacking in this, his longest novel, and admirers of Saltus would wish that those who had not previously read his better work would not first make this author's acquaintance through The Paliser Case." Saltus also wrote prefaces for two volumes in the Modern Library, issued during 1919 by Boni and Liveright. These are A Bed of Roses, by W. L. George, and Salome, The Importance of Being Earnest, and Lady Windermere's Fan, by Oscar Wilde. In 1920 Boni and Liveright issued The Imperial Orgy, one of Saltus's most considerable books. I prefer the author's original title, Imperial Sables, for this history of the Romanoffs. In this work he deliberately shut his eyes to all extenuating circumstances. It reeks of gore. It is a lithograph painted in blood. Also in 1920, the Pennell Club published The Gardens of Aphrodite, an essay of twenty-eight pages, limited to sixty-eight numbered copies. In 1922, Boni and Liveright published The Ghost Girl, a mystery novel. Written shortly before the author's death, while he was suffering from dyspepsia and other acute complaints, bitter, disappointed, lying in seclusion like a wounded animal, he constructed this work according to his most flippant formula. Parnassians Personally Encountered was published by the Torch Press, Cedar Rapids, Iowa, in 1923, in an edition of two hundred copies. In 1925, Pascal Covici issued Uplands of Dream, a volume of hitherto uncollected papers from the Cosmopolitan and the Smart Set. The book is limited to seven hundred and fifty numbered copies and contains a preface and bibliography by Charles Honce. Other posthu-

papers, on Gautier and Mérimée in Tales before Supper, on Barbey d'Aurevilly in The Story Without a Name, and on Victor Hugo, all exhibit the superior qualities of his talent. They are clairvoyant and illuminating, more than that arresting. They should be collected in one volume, the more especially as they are now, for the most part, inaccessible.

It is, you may perceive, as an essayist, a historian, an amateur philosopher that Saltus excels, but his fiction should not be underrated on that account. His novels, indeed, are half essays. Even the worst of them contains charming pages, delightful and unexpected digressions. His series of fables suggests a vast Comédie Inhumaine, but this statement must not be regarded as dispraise: it is an exact description of his morbid, erotic art, often inspiring dread and amazement, but never pity. Saltus was sufficiently inhuman so that he found himself incapable of creating a human character. All his figures are the inventions of an errant fancy; scarcely one of them has the lineaments of a living being, but they are none the less creations of art.

In these strange tales we pass through the conventional haunts of metropolitan life, but the creatures are bewilderingly unfamiliar. They have horns and hoofs, halos and wings, or fins and tails. An esoteric band of fabulous monsters these: harpies and vampires take tea at Sherry's; succubi and incubi are observed buying emerald rings at Tiffany's; fairies, angels, dwarfs, and elves, bearing branches of asphodel, trip lightly down Waverly Place; peris, amshaspahands, aesir, izeds, and goblins sleep at the Brevoort; seraphim and cherubim decorate drawing-

mous works are promised, including an unfinished novel, for which Mrs. Saltus has agreed to supply the conclusion.

## Edgar Saltus

rooms on Irving Place; griffins, chimeras, and sphinxes take courses in philosophy at Harvard; willis and sylphs sing airs from Lucia di Lammermoor and Le Nozze di Figaro; naiads and mermaids embark on the Cunard Line; centaurs and amazons romp in the Florentine Cascine; kobolds, gnomes, and trolls stab, shoot, and poison one another; and a satyr encounters the martichoras in Gramercy Park. No such pictures of eccentric, diverting, sensual existence may be found elsewhere, save on the canvases of Arnold Böcklin, Franz von Stuck, and Gustave Moreau. If he had done nothing more, Edgar Saltus should be celebrated for having given New York a mythology of its own.

*January 12, 1918.*

## Henry Blake Fuller

### I

In spite of the depressing consistency of my experience in this regard, I still wax melancholy when I recall how many literary reputations lie buried in America, a country which seems to derive a perverse pleasure from indulgence in necrophilic auctorial amours [1]—the longer the bones have bleached the better. With my own hands I have exhumed the skeleton of Edgar Saltus, arranging its fantastic contours in a corner of my museum, with the satisfactory result that the author of The Anatomy of Negation has become a favourite with "collectors," and is even read belatedly by a few adventurous spirits. I was present at the excavation of Ambrose Bierce, although I did not handle a spade, and I discovered three or four ribs of Herman Melville which had escaped the attention of earlier investigators. At this moment I have in mind a man who is perhaps not the greatest of living American novelists, but certainly one of the most original and distinguished. There are those who would assert with some reason that he is the most distinguished. He possesses none of the pessimistic and inverted wit of Edgar Saltus, none of the bitter, acrimonious gall of Ambrose Bierce, none of the poetic glamour and untrammelled imaginative force of Herman Melville. If, indeed, one must perforce

---

[1] "Il faut être un homme vivant et un artiste posthume," as Jean Cocteau has it.

compare the work of Henry B. Fuller with that of another American, the only suitable name that occurs to me is that of Henry James.

Since, under the pseudonym of Stanton Page, he published The Chevalier of Pensieri-Vani in 1890, the books of Henry B. Fuller have followed each other every few years with reasonable regularity. The latest, dated 1919, is the twelfth.[2] As the critics do not bestir[3] themselves, as his books do not sell, I take it for granted that his group of readers is small. In Chicago, where he has spent most of his life, and whose historian he has constituted himself to an extent that can be claimed for no other novelist, he is possibly less known and less appreciated than elsewhere. A critic on one of the Chicago newspapers asserted, in response to a query of mine, that he knew Fuller very well; "a charming person, not very talkative," was his condescending phrase. This fellow admitted that, although The Chevalier had slumbered on his shelves for many years, he had never read it. He seemed somewhat bewildered when I advised him to repair this omission, as if the idea of reading a book by Fuller had never occurred to him. I asked him if it would be possible for me to meet Fuller. I was informed, apologetically, that he seldom went out, that he was a recluse, that he dreaded "encounters."[4] Perhaps, just here, we have found a clue to the solution of the mystery; perhaps, to get on in America, one must trumpet one's

[2] Fuller wrote me in June 1922: "No further novels likely: too much effort and too little return—often none."

[3] Such men as Percival Pollard, James Huneker, and H. L. Mencken have always been valiant appreciators.

[4] Later, through the courtesy of Robert Morss Lovett, I was introduced to him.

own performances.[5]   It is significant, at any rate, that
Saltus, Bierce, and Melville were all hermits in their several ways.   It is equally significant that Emerson, Whitman, Hawthorne, and Mark Twain were not.   It requires no great powers of vatication, however, to
prophesy that this general neglect of Fuller is both temporary and artificial.

## II

Henry Blake Fuller was born in Chicago, January 9,
1857.  His paternal grandfather, a cousin, it is interesting
to note, of Margaret Fuller, moved from Massachusetts to
Illinois in 1839, when Chicago was still a village over
which hung the shadows cast by a recent Indian raid.
This grandfather, an early capitalist, laid down the first
street-railway in Chicago.   Fuller's father was an official
in a Chicago bank, and after young Fuller had graduated
from the Chicago High School he, too, entered the bank
in some minor capacity.   Later, he made several trips
abroad, at first, apparently, with the intention of studying
music, a project subsequently abandoned, but not before,
one of his early biographers asserts,[6] he had written an
opera or two!   He is also said to have contemplated the
study of architecture.[7]   The Chevalier of Pensieri-Vani

[5] Michael Sadleir, in Excursions in Victorian Bibliography, gives it
as his opinion that the survival of Wilkie Collins's reputation is due to
his intimacy with the chief literary personalities of his time. "There
is no log-rolling so expert, no admiration so mutual, as that existing
among members of the various groups that practise the arts."

[6] Mary Huston Banks in the Bookman:   August-September 1895;
Vol. II., page 15.

[7] Fuller has written me: "I never had any serious thought of a
musical career, though I studied cello, organ, harmony, and orchestra-

[131]

was written in 1886, but publishers did not understand
the book and it lay in manuscript for a long time, finally
appearing under rather obscure auspices in a modest
format, dated Boston, 1890. The years of Fuller's foreign tours have been given as 1879, 1883, 1892, 1894,
and 1897.[8] He returned to Chicago, where, aside from
certain minor and unadvertised excursions (Hamlin Garland [9] gives an amusing account of a trip to Washington),
he seems to have remained for nearly thirty years. There
are probably intrinsic reasons for this prolonged sojourn
in an unsympathetic environment, and it is certain that,
when he dies, Italy will be found inscribed across his
heart. "To Fuller," writes Hamlin Garland, "the town
(Chicago) was a pestilential slough in which he . . .
was inextricably mired." "I would live in Italy if I
could," he once plaintively remarked to Garland, and this
sigh pervades his work. In Lines Long and Short, a
collection of biographies in vers libres, obviously composed under the inspiration of the Spoon River Anthology,
several of the poems appear to wear an autobiographical

tion (all, a little) and improvised freely on the piano from the age
of ten. In the late eighties I wrote the librettos of two romantico-
comic three-act operas and composed the scores for voices and piano.
The high-and-mighty of that day saw, heard, and declined—just as
well, or better.

"As for architecture: my chief friends are architects, and my early
travels were on an architectural basis,—'cathedral towns' in England,
France, Italy, Germany. I have done 'plans and elevations,' not skipping 'specifications and plumbing.'

"In 1902 I had the book page of the Chicago Post and got out
three large 'book numbers.' In 1910–11 I wrote a few thousand
editorials for the Chicago Record-Herald." Mr. Fuller was also a
frequent contributor to the old Dial and his name is often signed to
book-reviews in many contemporary periodicals.

[8] Again in 1924.

[9] A Daughter of the Middle Border.

aspect. Postponement, for example, the history of a man who all his life had planned a trip abroad and had just contrived to arrange for the fulfilment of his desire when the war broke out. Or The Alien, the narrative of an old European woman, whose children grow rich in America. She lived

> "A little in one world,
> A little in another."

More than all, perhaps, that melancholy poem entitled The Day of Danger:

> "More dangerous than birth,
> Or croup or scarlatina,
> Or pubescent perturbations,
> Or wild first love,
> Or earliest venturings in the world of men,
> Are the middle years—
> For one who,
> Jog-trotting faithfully through their long reaches,
> Sees pleasure and rewards fall elsewhere,
> And comes to feel
> That soon the ardent pulse of life
> Must fall, turn cold, expire."

It is characteristic of Fuller to insert a somewhat trivial smile into the midst of this cri de cœur.

Italy, the Italian scene, is the happy environment of the earlier books. Such atmospheric and sympathetic feeling for locality as is exposed in The Chevalier and The Last Refuge is rare in English literature. Later, the theme pulses more bitterly, more trenchantly, as in the story of Eliza Hepburn (Waldo Trench and Others), the elderly American longing to be in Italy, or in New Wine (in the same volume), in which an Italian nobleman, under the tutelage of American friends, changes his mode of living and even submits his villa to alteration, an event which causes an uprising of the peasantry. This story would certainly have delighted Ouida, always the defender of the Italian countryside.

In his early books, it was Mr. Fuller's pleasant formula to introduce a somewhat vulgar (perhaps unsophisticated is a strong enough word) American (George W. Occident in The Chevalier, or Aurelia West in The Chatelaine of la Trinité) as a contrast to the ineffable, glowing wonder and glamour of European life. So, in his Chicago novels, he was wont to reverse this process and to expose the crudeness of his native city by comparing it with some figure who had lived abroad. There is an exception to this general procedure in Abner Joyce's Downfall (Under the Skylights). Abner Joyce, whom Percival Pollard,[10] probably not unreasonably, has identified with Hamlin Garland, is even cruder than Chicago. Chicago, indeed, almost assumes a cosmopolitan air in this tale, the hero of which has written a book which "comprised a dozen short stories—the soil itself spoke, the intimate humble ground; warmed by his own passionate sense of right, it steamed incense-like aloft, and cried to the blue skies for justice. . . . Some of his stories seemed written not so much by the hand as by the fist." Abner Joyce's Downfall is a study, not unsympathetic, of a self-taught writer caught in a comfortless environment in which he develops self-consciousness and rebellion. Earnestness is

[10] Their Day in Court, page 232. Referring to this story and Mr. Garland, Pollard writes: "In artistic attitudinizing there are several sorts. There was the posturing of Oscar Wilde. There was the Top-hat Attitude of the charlatans and the prigs. And there was also, if I may coin a term to cap an opposite, the Sombrero Attitude."

the most obvious quality in his life and art. The town must be reformed. Society sickens him; everything sickens him except his own work. He lacks a sense of humour and believes himself to be the only sincere person alive. He thinks about clubs as "places where the profligate children of Privilege drank improper drinks and told improper stories and kept improper hours. Abner, who was perfectly pure in thought and deed, and always in bed betimes, shrank from a club as from a lazaret." Naturally, he refuses wine at dinner and never wears evening clothes.[11] It is highly typical of Fuller's supple raillery that he should bring this tale to a close with a pretty complete compromise on the part of its intransigent protagonist. Little O'Grady Versus the Grindstone is an amusing contribution to the history of the eternal struggle between artists and business men, and Dr. Gowdy and the Squash [12] is a farcical interpretation of the power of advertising. It might be compared with Melville's Cock-a-doodle-doo! Adrian Bond, "æsthete, yet not without praiseworthy leanings toward the naturalistic," surely Fuller himself, strolls through these stories, and the old Athenæum Building on Van Buren Street (disguised as the Rabbit Warren) and the Fine Arts Building supply their principal backgrounds.

It should not be inferred that in his Chicago novels Fuller has offered his readers samples of the city's crudeness in chunks, or that he has used a muckrake to comb up his material. On the contrary, the picture is fair enough and is painted dispassionately. If the artist's

[11] Hamlin Garland's eventual assumption of the "dress suit" in London is described in A Daughter of the Middle Border.

[12] Mr. Fuller writes me: "Dr. Gowdy was my response to a fortnight of newspaper comment on a lecture I gave—which lecture may be found, in essay form, in the Bookman (1899): Art in America."

# Henry Blake Fuller

brush is dipped in cynicism, it is a smiling cynicism. Such an admirable figure as Mrs. Granger Bates [13] (With the Procession), who cherishes a room done in the old-fashioned manner, in which she seeks relief from the frosty gilt of her salon, gives a human touch to his canvas. This particular novel, obviously created under the influence of Howells, studies the evolution of Chicago from a big town to a great city, in the life of a family; probably Fuller's own family sat for a couple of portraits therein.

In this book and Under the Skylights (I consider The Cliff-Dwellers less successful than these), Fuller's sense of humour is sufficiently delicate, his irony sufficiently polished, to enable him to make quite a considerable effect with comparatively little effort. Mr. Carl Van Doren has complained that Fuller's work is lacking in emphasis.[14] This might be said of him in almost exactly the sense that it might be said of Voltaire. Fuller's touch is like the lifting of an eyebrow, the quick flick of an ash from a cigarette, a gentle tapping of a boot on a not too resounding pavement. A sensitive reader will perhaps react to these peaceful signals more graciously than to the more emphatic outcries of a Theodore Dreiser. Fuller's humour never exacts a great guffaw, or his pathos a flood of tears. He is quietly amusing and gently melancholy.

[13] W. D. Howells presents a sympathetic study of "dear old Sue Bates—sturdy and worthy representative of an earlier Middle West," as Fuller has described her in a letter to me, in Heroines of Fiction; Vol. II, page 246. Harper and Brothers; 1901.

[14] In the Nation, December 21, 1921. Later included in Mr. Van Doren's book, Contemporary American Novelists, page 138. Other recent papers on this author are to be found in The Literary Spotlight, edited by John Farrar; Doran; 1924, and the revised edition of The Men Who Make Our Novels, by Charles C. Baldwin; Dodd, Mead and Co.; 1924.

# Henry Blake Fuller

So, in his Chicago novels, it is perfectly possible that certain Chicagoans—particularly those at whom he aims his bow—may read on, blissfully unconscious that the author is scoffing at them. An unsuspecting reader, indeed, one not intent upon the depths that single, and apparently casual, words may convey, one innocent of an affection for style, may stop reading altogether with a broad yawn. As a typical example of his method, I might offer his manner of presenting the essential quality of Chicago at a fashionable ball by describing one man as wearing a boutonnière in his right lapel, another, one in his left, while a third, wondering which is correct, hardly dares wear one at all!

Readers of With the Procession may recall that the heroine of a casual amorous adventure with Truesdale Marshall in Europe bobs up in Chicago with her blackmailing father. Society is scandalized. To Marshall père, marriage is the only conceivable solution. Truesdale's brother stormily demands this sacrifice. Truesdale is not impressed by their sophistry.

" 'My dear brother,' he began quietly, while Roger beat his foot upon the floor, stung to increased indignation by the conscious artificiality of such an address—'my dear brother,' said Truesdale, 'You don't quite get my position in this trifling episode. Every little conte drôlatique has its Monsieur X, of course—myself, in this instance, and rightfully enough. But is Monsieur X the only gentleman involved? Let us see. Who comes before Monsieur X? Why Monsieur W, to be sure. And who before Monsieur W? Monsieur V, n'est-ce pas? And there is somebody still in front of Monsieur V. And if we go far enough back, we may come at last even to Monsieur A. Now, why are all these worthy gentlemen passed

[137]

over in favour of this cher Monsieur X? Well, perhaps Monsieur W, for example, is a captain of dragoons
and already mated. And maybe Monsieur V is a young
baron whose family won't stand any nonsense about him
—families are different. And as for Monsieur A—well,
let us put him down for a poor devil of a student who
cuts no figure at all. But Monsieur X—ah, that is different! He is pounced upon in the bosom of his family.
It is Monsieur X who has the scrupulous and strait-
laced mother——'

" 'Truesdale!'

" 'And the little coterie of lily-sisters who never——'

" 'Truesdale! For shame!'

" 'And the over-conscientious and supersensitive father
with millions and millions stored away in bursting money-
bags somewhere or other. Oh, those money-bags, those
money-bags, those money-bags!'

" 'Truesdale, what do you mean? Are they ad-
venturers? Are they after blackmail?'

"Truesdale threw back his head, closing his eyes and
twirling his thumbs. . . . 'Complimenti, Roger; you are
ending where I should have expected you to begin.' "

## III

In his essay on Balzac, in Impressions and Opinions,
George Moore writes: "To the nineteenth century, the
abnormal is intolerable, even frank sensuality receives
a better welcome. And as education proceeds, natural
taste, that is to say, individual taste, withers, and man
becomes blinder every day to the charm of the bizarre,
and more intolerant to the exotic. But the abnormal is
found in all great writers, and though not their flesh,

[138]

it is their heart. The abnormal must always be felt, although it may rarely form the subject of picture or poem. To make the abnormal ever visible and obtrusively present is to violate the harmony of Nature; to avoid the abnormal is to introduce a fatal accent of insincerity. . . . Balzac's genius was unquestionably saner than that of any of his contemporaries, if we except Hugo's, and yet Balzac wrote La fille aux yeux d'or, La dernière incarnation de Vautrin, Une passion dans le désert, Séraphita, and Sarrasine. Therefore it may be said that the final achievement of genius is the introduction and artistic use of the abnormal.

"And this for a reason which will not be suspected by the casual student of fiction, and which when first stated will seem like a paradox. But it surely is true, except for those who stand among the highest, that the choice of any but the most ordinary theme will lead into a commonplace. Even in the hands of a man of talent the abnormal slips into sterile eccentricity, which is the dreariest form of commonplace; but let the man of talent choose an ordinary everyday story, and in developing it any originality of mind and vision he may possess will appear to its best advantage."

In Bertram Cope's Year, Henry Fuller selected a subject [15] which is generally taboo in English literature. Indeed, aside from Henry James's The Turn of the Screw I cannot recall a single English or American novel of the first rank that deals with it save in a perfunctory or passing way. Fuller's treatment of this theme is so skilful, so delicate, so studiedly restrained, that it should be no

[15] Fuller had utilized a variation of this theme once before in At St. Judas's in the volume entitled The Puppet Booth. Bertram Cope is ironic comedy. Thomas Mann's Death in Venice is a tragic version of the same subject.

great cause for wonder, considering the fate allotted to his other works, that this, the latest to issue from his pen, should drop from the presses still-born, to meet with absolute silence on the part of the reviewers, and to find itself quickly on sale at the "remainder" tables of the large department stores. If Theodore Dreiser had written this book, it would certainly have been suppressed. If Ben Hecht had written it, he would probably be languishing in jail. I cannot, indeed, name another American writer who could have surveyed the ambiguous depths of the problem presented so thoroughly, and at the same time so discreetly. Bertram Cope's Year deals with the affection felt by a middle-aged man for a young boy, the boy's instinctive rejection of this unwelcome attention, and his acceptance of a certain more plausible affiliation. Around these struggling puppets the author has grouped a typical collection of Chicago women, several of them artists, for Fuller, like James, and probably for a similar reason, has a fondness for employing artists as characters in his tales. The Chicago background is assembled rather more concretely than in any other of the Chicago novels. The story, apparently slow moving, really thrusts forward its emphatic moments on almost every page, but it would probably prove unreadable to one who had no key to its meaning. Once its intention is grasped, however, it becomes one of the most brilliant and glowingly successful of this author's brief series of works.

## IV

In Character and Opinion in the United States, George Santayana writes: "The luckless American who is

# Henry Blake Fuller

drawn to poetic subtlety, pious retreats, oɪ gay passions, nevertheless has the categorical excellence of work, growth, enterprise, reform, and prosperity dinned into his ears: every door is open in this direction and shut in the other; so that he either folds up his heart and withers in a corner—in remote places you sometimes find such a solitary gaunt idealist—or else he flies to Oxford or Florence or Montmartre to save his soul—or perhaps not to save it."

If Henry Fuller had gone to Italy to live, as Henry James went to England, it is entirely possible that his modest genius might have come to a more complete flowering. As matters stand, whether through lack of will or opportunity, he has missed this final experience and his soul, as a consequence, has not been completely saved. He lingers, indeed, in a kind of literary purgatory. How true this is, one may gather from a perusal of his early books, written under the influence of foreign travel. What he might have been able to accomplish ultimately under happier circumstances one might predict with reasonable certainty from the evidence which their pages offer. It is assuredly on these early books, The Chevalier of Pensieri-Vani, The Chatelaine of la Trinité, and The Last Refuge, that his reputation must stand or fall. These slender volumes boast a double virtue: they offer exceedingly delightful pictures respectively of the Italian cities, the Austrian tyrol, and Sicily, and they are an ironic contribution to the discussion of national traits, indeed, of modern traits in general and civilization of whatever kind. They are decorative philosophy, the humour of which is so exquisitely tempered that I fear it will pass over many a head. Indeed, it must already have done so; else, how

[141]

# Henry Blake Fuller

may one account for the comparative lack of fame which has been awarded to these miniature masterpieces?

The Chevalier [16] is a collection of more or less unrelated tales, bound together by the Chevalier himself, the Prorege of Arcopia, who has banished himself from his own domain because his subjects have opposed his desire in the matter of the erection of a row of columns before his royal palace, George W. Occident, the American millionaire, the Seigneur of Hors-Concours, the Margravine of Schwalbach-Schreckenstein, the Duke of Avon, and the Contessa Nullaniuna. This fantastic caravan, as a whole or in sections, moves statelily over Italy, visiting Florence, Pisa, Orvieto, Siena, Rome, Venice, and other less notable localities, in each of which an amusing adventure occurs, the theme of which permits Fuller that free play of slightly satirical comment on the whole range of human nature, for the graceful accomplishment of which he possesses such a supreme talent. The style is ripe, persuasive, the irony, sober, and the memory of the intrigues compels me to pick up the book very often, to reread with delight the episode of the Etruscan crown, or of the début of the opera singer at Pisa, or of the search for the lost Madonna of Perugino, which ends in the discovery of a Sodoma, or of the extraordinary performance on the organ given by Pensieri-Vani at Orvieto, or of the adventure of the iron-pot, or of the Prorege assisting at the excavations of Ostia, or of the pursuit of the Aldines, the discomfiture of the Duke of Avon, and the utter routing of the Contessa. If one is occasionally reminded of Max Beerbohm by this gentle raillery, the fact can scarcely reflect to the discredit of the author, for the earli-

[16] Agnes Repplier early wrote a sympathetic review of this book. See A Byway in Fiction: Essays in Miniature (1892), page 87.

est volume by the incandescent half-brother of Sir Herbert Tree had not yet appeared when Mr. Fuller's book was published.

The general plan of The Chatelaine of la Trinité is similar, although its form is perhaps more perfectly realized, bound together, as it is, by a central situation. The thesis, peculiarly Fullerian, concerns the dauntless efforts of Aurelia West, a young American, to establish the Chatelaine, a perfect example of the aristocrat who has achieved a supreme naturalness in the carelessness of her dress and manner, in a milieu more fitting, according to American ideals, to the habits and customs of nobility. Subservience and class-feeling are demanded of her loyal but familiar subordinates. Liveries and armour are requisitioned and employed. In the end (like the somewhat similar experience of the Chevalier and the Seigneur of Hors-Concours at Pisa, when, in their efforts to create an atmosphere of success for the début of a singer, they overplay their parts to such an extent that the public remains apathetic), this entirely altruistic enterprise oversteps itself and fails, leaving the intrepid American somewhat nonplussed, but leaving the Chatelaine exactly where she was in the beginning.

The Chatelaine is not even so well known as The Chevalier. I do not think it achieved a second edition, while The Chevalier has gone through at least five. It is, nevertheless, quite as charming and distinguished a performance as its predecessor. I have an especial fondness for the superb Tempo-Rubato, acrobat, tarantella dancer, opéra-bouffe singer, and gentleman. For an example of this writer's quality I could offer the reader nothing better than the second chapter of this romance, wherein is described the passage of Aurelia West from

# Henry Blake Fuller

Paris on a train with a travelling theatrical company which she confuses with royalty and its entourage.

The third volume in this series (a series only in manner, not in content), The Last Refuge, seems to have escaped the attention even of those few who profess an interest in Fuller. It is possible that the future will do more justice to this little capolavoro. The fable concerns itself with the pursuit of desire. The Freiherr desires to recapture his youth; the Lady of Quality desires to lose her sense of time; the Painter desires to attain subjectivity, while his companion, the poet, desires to attain objectivity; Monna Chlotilde, the tragic actress, Mam'zelle Hedwig, the Just Man, and others seek outlets for their various thwarted passions. All these pilgrims meet on the road as they journey towards the City of Happiness which, characteristically and symbolically enough, Fuller locates in Sicily (would he could join them!), and they become involved in an amazingly fantastic intrigue, interspersed with discussions on every subject that the author deems worthy of discussion. The Last Refuge is a forerunner of South Wind, and quite comparable to that book in its degree of glamour.

## V

In one of his papers,[17] Mr. Fuller sums up a contemporary writer's ideal of the novel: "Construction, in a novel, is not the art of exciting by means of the connection of incident with incident: it is the art of leaving out, without incoherence, all that does not interest the writer and of putting in all that does." Mr. Fuller weighs this ideal and finds it wanting: " 'Real Art' does

[17] A Plea for Shorter Novels; the Dial, August 30, 1917.

not consist in finding a story in which you can tell what interests you and that only. Such a step indeed makes an advantageous preliminary, and may free one in advance from some of the botherations lying wait—reluctant love-passages, repellent sex-discussions, scenes of violence and bloodshed with which one may have no proper affinity, indelicate 'close-ups' which explore and exploit poor humanity beyond the just bonds of decorum, and such like. 'Real art' is, and will remain, largely a matter of form, of organism, of definition, of boundaries. The artist will express his 'interest'—heaven forbid that he should not; but it must be an interest disciplined by, and within, metes and bounds, an interest which shall result in a unified impression that depends much upon the time-element and in the simple counting of words. Words sometimes darken counsel; and too many of them may becloud and even wreck artistic intention."

A little later, he writes: "Surely a man should know what he is after, and go after it—straight. . . . The novel of today should be required to bant. I believe that a novelist can say his say in 60,000 words, or even in 50,000. . . . Much of the accepted apparatus must, of course, be thrown into the discard. I would be indulgent to the preliminary exposition, but not far beyond it. One should rule out long descriptions of persons—such things are nugatory and vain: with your best effort the reader only sees what he has seen, and figures your personage on the basis of his own experience and recollection. One must abolish set descriptions of places, unless unique, remote, unfamiliar, for the world in these days of easy travel and abundant depiction has come to know itself pretty well. One will banish all 'conversation,' whatever its vraisemblance to life, if it merely fills the page,

[145]

without illuminating it. I would sweep away all laborious
stuff that is dragged in because some one will think it
ought to be there—clichés, conventional scenes and
situations. To prevent sprawl and formlessness I favour
a division into 'books' and a division of the books into
sections. Thus articulation and proportion will be secured, as in the case of an architectural order; and one
will be better able to down the rising head of verbosity."

If I have yielded to the temptation to quote this much,
it is for the excellent reason that Fuller alone, of all
the novelists with whose work I am acquainted, with the
exception of Henry James, Arthur Machen, and one
or two others, has been able to maintain a consistent
affiliation between precept and practice. His novels
are short and they are short because he has obeyed
his own rules. He knows what he is after and he goes
after it straight. His contribution to American fiction
is a certain calm, a repose of manner, a decorative irony,
exquisite in its not too completely hidden implications,
a humour which is informed with abundant subtlety, a
study of human nature at home and abroad as searching
as it is careful, and above all, a delicate, abiding charm.
His novels of Chicago, setting aside for the moment their
unquestioned artistry, fulfil all the requirements of social
and historical documents; his novels and tales of Italy
may be said to represent a search into the restless modern
mind and soul, exposed to a peculiarly refined mode of
treatment. The author's occasional use of an anæsthetic
does not disturb the authenticity of his work.

His writing is by no means free from faults. Sometimes, as in On the Stairs or in The Puppet Booth, his
material runs very thin; sometimes he is precious; sometimes, although rarely, there is a suggestion of provincial-

## *Henry Blake Fuller*

ism. On this latter score, a more perfect artist would have deleted a betraying sentence or two from Bertram Cope's Year. His sweep is never grand. His genre is the miniature. In the words of one of his characters it may justifiably be said of him that he combines "the fortunate moment and the felicitous hand."

*April 28, 1922.*

## Matthew Phipps Shiel

### I

One afternoon in the late winter of 1922–23—it may, I conceive, have been February—Hugh Walpole sat with me in my yellow garret.   The rays of the lowering sun invaded the chamber through a western window, forming strange and effulgent patterns on the Chinese wall-paper and the long rows of books, many of them brightly habited in gay-hued garments, which lined the walls on either side.   Pouring out a portion of makeshift gin from a Venetian glass bottle, I filled my goblet nearly to the brim with ginger beer.   The ginger beer, at any rate, was genuine, I reflected, as I stirred the pleasant mixture with a spoon of orange crystal.   Happy Hugh, a temperate fellow, restricted his refreshment to apples, but how many of these he could eat!   After each of his visits I found it necessary to replenish the blue porcelain bowl which held their rosy rotundity.

Munching the fruit, Hugh gazed about him, giving vent now and again to an exclamation of surprise or pleasure, as his roving eye alighted fortuitously on some volume of which he held a fragrant memory.   The line of his vision took in the row of Herman Melville's works—all of them save only Typee were there, and all of them were firsts; he traced the space, two full shelves including the twelve-volume translation of Casanova, occupied by Arthur Machen; he was amused to discover so long a

series of Ouida novels, and he removed her Critical
Studies from its position to examine the paper on Marion
Crawford, an American author for whom Hugh professes
an interest; the Edgar Saltus collection afforded his attention a new distraction; a little later I offered him a
peep at the orphic romances of Frederick Baron Corvo
and the philosophical, oriental tales of Marmaduke Pickthall; as an additional favour I asked him to look into
my set of Henry B. Fuller, a writer with whose work he
was at that time unfamiliar. Other authors and their
books having, in their turn, sought his scrutiny, at last,
quite abruptly, Hugh turned to me.

"There is not, so far as I have been able to discover,"
he announced, just a trifle triumphantly, "one volume by
M. P. Shiel in this room."

"M. P. Shiel?" The embarrassment of complete
ignorance was apparent in the expression of my voice.
As a matter of fact, I do not believe I had ever heard
the name before this moment.

"M. P. Shiel." Hugh was firm. "I should think," he
went on, nor was there lacking in his tone an impression
of irony, "that you, who pride yourself on a knowledge
of all the byways and crannies of exotic literature, would
know at least a little about a strange fellow like M. P.
Shiel."

"What," I demanded—my humiliation was complete—
"has he written?"

"Stacks of books, rows of them, fat books, very fat
books: one of his novels runs to over seven hundred
pages. His range covers the globe, civilized and un-
civilized; his imagination runs a race with facts and
beats them."

Shortly afterward, having bitten down to the core of

[149]

the final apple, Hugh took his departure. That he had worried me was proved by the fact that when he returned the following week ten volumes by Matthew Phipps Shiel had usurped the particularly visible shelf which hitherto had been the home of the novels of James Morier.

## II

My first impressions of Shiel were rather mixed. I think, indeed, that this might be anybody's experience, unless he happens to be lucky enough to hit first upon one of the better novels, The Lord of the Sea, for example, for the work of this imaginative adept is curiously uneven—not a little of it bearing the mark of undue haste in execution—and its intelligent perusal and appraisement is further complicated by the fact that this author from year to year has varied his "tone," style and form yielding to the mood of the new matter presented. Unfortunately, I did not start out with the best books. I began with Prince Zaleski,[1] published in that same Keynotes Series which originally harboured The Great God Pan and The Three Impostors, and I could honestly

[1] Of this book and its immediate successor, Arthur Machen.has since written me: "For Prince Zaleski and Shapes in the Fire I have the highest admiration, for the latter most of all. It is Poe, perhaps, but Poe with an unearthly radiance." And, reviewing Shapes in the Fire in the London Times, Machen wrote, "Here is a wilder wonderland than Poe ever dreamt of." Shiel's own comment about Prince Zaleski, made thirty years after the fact, is interesting: "Some Poe here!— poh. At seventeen, just as I had begun to smoke, I came across Tales of Mystery, and the mixture of the two smokes drunkened me out to Uranus, where I abode some time. Lately I have reread some Poe, but dully, finding a lack of significance, his kite not 'hitched to any star.'"

say that I liked it, but the next two volumes[2] that I read—I shall not mention their names here—almost caused me to forsake the quest. However, book-sellers whom I had put on the scent continued to dispatch new packages which I automatically opened. I do not recall the exact number of books by Shiel I had examined with mounting enthusiasm before I stumbled upon The Purple Cloud,[3] but I do remember that when, at one sitting, I had finished reading this extremely long novel at four A. M., I cried aloud with the morning stars.

Nevertheless, even if they are lucky enough to begin with one of the better of Shiel's romances, most readers, I fancy, will find it necessary to acquaint themselves with several others before they can appreciate with any exactitude the magic of this writer or can capitulate to his special charm. Any novice in the matter, to be sure, should be perfectly aware at once of the vitality and glamour, the presence of the grand manner, in The Lord of the Sea, but whether he will see further than this, at first, I am not so sure, for Shiel, apparently, to an early reader, is a mere maker of plots, a manufacturer of wild romances in the manner of Jules Verne or of the Dumas of Monte-Cristo. It is only a little later that one perceives that here there is a philosophic consciousness, a

[2] Opinions differ. The first of these H. G. Wells has dubbed "colossal."

[3] Shiel writes of this book: "The comets are the most romantic of the Wanderers because the most far-venturing and lost in solitude; and the Odyssey more romantic than the Iliad. With solitude I was always in love as a theme for painting and poetry; and when an elderly American millionaire, whose ideas were raw, but admirably fresh and strong and manifold, on coming to visit me, suggested to me to write of 'Peary and his family' going to the Pole and coming back to a 'dead world,' I leapt at it, left out 'the family,' and 'Peary,' too, and wrote this."

sophisticated naïveté, an imaginative au delà, of which the plot is only the formal expression.[4] Shiel, I feel convinced, will satisfy any admirer of The Count of Monte-Cristo, but, in the end, he will also satisfy any reader who cares for George Meredith or Herman Melville, two writers, as unlike as the Poles in themselves, with whom the author of The Lord of the Sea has a certain esoteric affinity, and gradually it will further become evident that Shiel may be compared more reasonably with the H. G. Wells of the early romances, and even with W. H. Mallock, than with the creator of Twenty Thousand Leagues Under the Sea.[5]

Shiel's imagination and fancy are boundless [6] and, al-

[4] Shiel himself has written: "And if you would know why the plot stands on so lofty a level, the answer is that, as it only is true to things and to Life, it alone is divine, since the cosmos is a plot, a molecule a plot, the solar rhyming a plot, the story of Life a plot." And again: "A plot is a plat or fabric of facts, in their nature abstract, the statement of which involves a philosophic abstraction."

[5] In my copy of The Lord of the Sea Shiel has written: "To my thinking there have been three supreme wits, all scientists—Galileo, Spencer, and Henry George, George lacking the exact training of the others, but probably born the most penetrating of men: seeing which, I have always felt it my business to discover new demonstrations of his demonstrated theorem: this being one such attempt." Progress and Poverty, then, is the father of The Lord of the Sea! The unwarned reader would not be too much aware of this avowed paternity.

[6] Shiel is an out-and-out romantic. "Since," he has written, "the object of Art is to enlarge (or at least to sharpen, or at the very least to refresh) your consciousness of the truth of things, the question is, which of the two is the truer, realism or romance? Well, there can be no question that realism is true, if it be truly realistic, but the truth is that it is not truly realistic, if it be not romantic, since truth is romantic. With a mood of wistfulness in your eyes you look at the moon one night where, as musing she walks amid the stars, and wish that you were there where she muses; wait: before you go to bed you will be where she muses, if our globe be moving that way, and soon you may be soaring not at all far from where Venus at this hour leads the crowd of the starry orchestra with her crown and

# Matthew Phipps Shiel

though he has informed me that his travels have been
restricted to the West Indies where he was born, to
South Africa,[7] and to Europe, his tales transport the
breathless reader to Persia, Australia, Russia, Japan,
Cuba, the United States, or the North Pole with equal
ease.  When he describes a sea-fight it would be believed
that he had once been an admiral.  Field Marshal Lord
Roberts in the House of Lords once spoke of The
Yellow Danger, which gives a picture of the Chinese
sweeping over Europe, as the prophecy of an expert.  In
Cold Steel [8] and The Man-Stealers, Shiel's only "his-

psaltery. . . . Thus Huck Finn, all hints of stars and darkness, is truly
romantic, for it is truly realistic; and a lot of the Odyssey is truly
realistic in a higher land, its realism being more abstract, as the story
of Circe is realistic, true to life—but highly abstract realism." And,
in another place: "Very curious, in truth, is the resemblance between, say, the modern novel, and the sculptures of Nineveh; nor
could any one to whom it was once pointed out fail to notice it; the
crude, and revolting (because absolute) fidelity to life in the hinder
parts of the winged bulls especially, and the fingers of the kings, is
very instructive. Add to the life-likeness of the bulls the raw instinctive reaction against mere imitation of nature indicated by the
*incoherent* fancy of their *wings*, and you have the modern novel.
It seems, however, that a certain indefinable supremacy of vulgarity
was reserved by the ages for the contemporaries of M. Zola." Shiel
has said that great art depends upon the possession of three qualities,
fancy, imagination, and observation. Music, to him, is the greatest
of the arts, because it depends less than the others on observation.
The best writing, then, aspires towards this ideal. To be a real
creator is to be Godlike; that a writer should create characters as
God creates them, not imitate God's creations, is the foundation stone
of Shiel's literary credo. "He that would be both fictionist and fine-
artist must . . . begin to cast about him for entirely new forms, or,
at least, for characters and incidents of a wholly different kind, very
much less life-like—*equally alive*—very much more artificial, artistic."

[7] Shiel admits that the fantasy of Children of the Wind was somewhat "tamed and depressed" by his knowledge of Africa, "God being
more modest than I."

[8] Of this novel Shiel has written: "The 'historical' novel is like far
music—if it *is* musical, does occur in a world, not necessarily this world.

torical" novels, he has dealt freely with such real figures
as Henry VIII, François I, and the Iron Duke of Welling-
ton, but he is never afraid to deal equally freely with
current history, moulding it to the heart's desire of the
philosophic content of his fable.  The hero of The Yellow
Danger is "of the royal family," but, Shiel writes me,
"the English consider it 'disloyal' to imagine a king as
having brains, and would not listen."  In The Lord of the
Sea, the Prince of Wales (later Edward VII) is a minor
character, and Shiel has not hesitated to establish a
Regency, with his Richard Hogarth as the Regent, at
the expense of Queen Victoria.  Nor in The Dragon
(1913) was it any trouble at all for him to cause the sink-
ing by torpedo from a warship of the Mauretania!

### III

Fortunately, for the further success of this superficial
expedition into the intricacies of this fantastic fellow's
methods, he himself has discussed at some length the
problems of the writer.  The first of his two papers on
this subject, Premier and Maker,[9] in the form of a dialogue, is to be found in Shapes in the Fire.  The second,
entitled On Reading, occupies the place of a preface to
This Knot of Life.  The latter, I may add, is one of the
most fascinating dissertations on the theme with which
I am acquainted, and as a piece of masterly writing,
conceived in a brilliant style, it may be said to surpass
even Shiel's own best in his novels.  In this paper, after

Some one said: 'Your Francis of France has no resemblance to the
real Francis,' and I answered, 'No, but both were dreams, one about
as real as the other.' "

[9] It is in this paper that the theory of artist as Godike creator is
expounded.

defining the distinction between knowledge and consciousness, the author asserts that a real reader conjures up
his consciousness just as a real man of letters writes
from his consciousness. "To think," he adds, "is to be
educated, and to be educated is to be sceptical." The
vital qualities in good writing he sapiently catalogues
under four heads: Matter, Expression, Harmony, and
Tone. The first two need not detain us.[10] Harmony,
naturally, is the correct expression of Matter, the philosophic harmonizing of the plot. For the definition of
Tone I could do no better than append Shiel's own words:
"Now, tone,[11] of course, is thousand-fold: and since the
tone of a whole tome or piece must be so-and-so to suit its
mood, and the tone of each page or part must subtly be
so-and-so to suit *its* mood, and yet the tone of each part or
page be in harmony with the tone of the whole, here once
more, you will see, is a task that only a carle born lucky
to the heart, born with a caul, need attempt to meddle
with. Moreover, in tone, I must advise you, there is invariably in the greatest writers a something, a grain, a

---

[10] But it will do no harm to quote Shiel: "Expression, then: the
power of expressing the inexpressible, and the all but inexpressible—
this is the best arm in the author's armoury."

[11] Shiel writes me: "I am sensitive to changes of tone and change
annually." Describing his ideal writer in Premier and Maker he avers:
"He has no invariable 'style' of his own—and would regard with some
contempt a critic who spoke of his 'style'—for each tale is written in
a different 'literary manner' (itself sometimes an invention, or else
borrowed from some Greek), the manner of all others best suited to
the hue of *that* particular world; nay, one part of one piece is written
this way, another that: for here he is concise as a précis-writer, there
all ordered flowers and fancies, anon he pretends to be bitingly philosophic, and yonder you find him bawling like hell. And the whole
is the complete expression and impression of a new *mood;* that is to
say, does what a piece of music does; and is, in fact, a piece of music;
apparently as perfect, and certainly as unique, as Mars or Venus, a-
singing *their* diverse 'angel-songs.' "

[155]

tone within their tones, which I in my own mind always call naïveté—an element not richly represented in English literature (in Bunyan principally), but very richly in French, in Greek, and in Hebrew literature, and in Heine and Wieland. How a very little savour of it would have saved Poe, Meredith, Milton!"

Shiel then proceeds to explain, by means of an ingenious table, what these qualities in varying combinations indicate. This is his tabular representation:

"Expression + Harmony = 'Magic' (Art).[12]

Matter + Expression = 'Interest' (not Art).

(Compare The French Revolution with Paradise Lost. In The French Revolution, Good Matter + Expression-in-excelsis = much interest. In Paradise Lost, No Matter + Expression-nearly-in-excelsis = no interest.)

Tone + Harmony = 'Charm' (Art).

(Compare Paradise Lost with The French Revolution. In Paradise Lost, Splendid Tone + Harmony-in-excelsis = much charm, and I should have said 'excellent charm,' but that the tone wants *variety,* making it impossible to read more than three pages at one time. In F. R. Fair Tone + no Harmony = no Charm.)

Matter + Expression + Tone = 'Fascination' (not Art).

Matter + Expression + Harmony + Tone = 'Beauty' (Art)."

It would be pleasant for me to continue further this division of the discussion, for Shiel goes on for pages instancing concrete examples and arranging lists of authors in their order of merit under the different heads, in-

[12] "Art, then, is the production by elaborate new contrivance, of intended effects upon intended minds." M. P. Shiel.

# Matthew Phipps Shiel

cidently placing himself third (between Carlyle and Lucretius) under the head of Expression; tenth (between Coleridge and Cicero) under the head of Harmony; and seventh (between Heine and Æschylus) under the head of Tone; [13] but I think it will be of more interest to offer as a peroration to the above, in illustration of the fellow's blinding skill, the following astounding paragraph: [14]

"See me here at this moment composing with a complete, though low, harmoniousness, and with a nearly complete ease—conscious of each consonant and of every (accented) vowel-sound of my outlay; without fail remembering them every one, as the swain bears safe in his brain the faces and tale of his ewes, using an alacrity of consciousness comparable to that of an acrobat or conjuror astonishing some mass of men, of a mathematic (successfully) tackling the job of some very complex problem, wildly well writing and riding this English language with the gallantry and wrist of the charioteer of the Roman amphitheatre as he drove his street-breadth of rebel steeds; and though I speak of 'a nearly complete ease,' understand that that is the result of some thirty years' practice that, applied to the piano or the violin, would certainly have turned me into the most perfect virtuoso that the world has heard; know, too, that I have but a week or two ago completed a harmonious book, but after some months, maybe, if I begin another, harmony will again be to me quite awkward and hard.   Respect

[13] Under the head of Màtter, Shiel writes, after formulating his list, which begins with The Jehovist and ends with Hugo, "Why it is impossible for me to name my place in the list with modesty is, I think, obvious: for I would challenge any critic, in so objective a matter as Matter, to fix his own merits in his own mind with a nice modesty."

[14] It occurs near the close of the paper, On Reading.

me, then. And I have not said all, I have not said half of half. For the violinist's technique, though so far easier than mine, is quite half of his art, while my far harder technique is not nearly half of my art, which far more positively, more insistently, more fruitfully, than his, consists in enlarging your consciousness of the truth of things."

## IV

Of Shiel the man I can tell you comparatively little. He was born of Irish parentage, July 21, 1865, in the West Indies. After receiving a degree at London University, he began to study medicine, but gave this up to teach mathematics. He early essayed to write; his first paper, indeed, was published when he was thirteen. Even today, however, experiments in chemistry and mathematics remain his pastimes. In a letter to me he avows, "I find no little amusement in writing fiction, but like still better mathematics, chemistry, and generally manage to have some sort of laboratory wherever I may be." The range of his interests, indeed, as exhibited in his novels, is broad, and covers, in addition to the above-mentioned sciences, politics, religion, sociology, astronomy, toxicology, and many other abstract topics.

He is, I should judge, almost a fanatic in the matters of health, strength, and youth. His admiration for health, indeed, might be regarded as mystic.[15] He believes that the strong, healthy man in touch with nature

[15] "Genius, as it appears to me, I will furnish you with a definition in one word—nimbleness; in another word—virtue; in another word —vigour; in another word—health; in another word—eyesight; in another word—interest; in another word—consciousness; in another word—life; in another word—bliss: all of which different words, in my dictionary, have scarce a shade of difference in meaning: so if I

[158]

## Matthew Phipps Shiel

virtually achieves a species of divine understanding.[16]
In one of his books he boasts that he has never suffered
a pain. It is still his custom to run several miles before
breakfast and he has a deathless passion for scaling all
the mountains he encounters. This physical vigour
burns with an immarcescible glow through most of his
writing in the guise of literary vitality. It also has had
a distinct influence on his choice of subject and his creation of character.[17] His admiration for the overman—
he repudiates the word superman with its roots from two
languages—pervades his work: hero after hero conquers
the world or a part of it, and it is his unceasingly ex-

think I am a genius, and one wished to know of me for what reason
I think so, my answer would be: because I haven't a club-foot—not
because I have one, since a good man can no more have a bad leg
than a good bedstead can; because, moreover, my mother, seventy-
four years old, has not one hole in any one of her teeth; because I,
over forty years old, can run nine miles with sprightliness, and, stand-
ing on this planet, can with my mind climb the Matterhorns of her
satellite, and scramble through bramble on Saturn." On Reading,
page 69.

[16] "There have been moments in my life when I could not but
recognize in my clothes the most egregious genius and love-child of this
globe (except maybe Leonardo da Vinci) who ever kissed a wife, or
at midnight climbed a piping: instants when the secret of things has
appeared to be but one inch deeper than the wriggling reach of my
middle finger-tip; and though instants so brave and bouyant have been
rare with me since I was a boy, it is but some five months since, that
on a morning of much storm in March, after a run miles long down the
side of the River Loire, I found my being in so nimble an intimacy
with the mountains, the breezes, the stream, so fleet my feet, my eye so
lit, and bright my bliss, that I remembered, I all but remembered, why
ions flock upon electrodes, why waters can't stop laughing, why things
are, and why things are as they are with the stars: in one half-a-moment
I thought I knew, and the moment after I stood deluded." On
Reading, page 22.

[17] It also accounts for most of his faults, for some of his books seem
to be written at a white heat which burns away the cold critical
faculty so essential for the proper revision of a manuscript.

pressed contention that a *wit*, which is his supreme term for genius, can do one thing as well as he can do another. Thus he argues that the inventor of the mono-rail would have made a great man of letters, presumably because the creation of literary masterpieces is of lesser difficulty than that of making scientific discoveries, and Richard Hogarth, Lord of the Sea, has no sooner lost his temporal power than he is acclaimed as the returned Messiah. The concluding paragraph of this book, indeed, is a splendid waving of the most blazing banner of Shiel's philosophy:

"They took him for the Sent of Heaven, nor did the results of his glorious reign gainsay such a notion: the good Loveday, indeed, had the agreeable fancy that our greatest are really One, who eternally runs the circle of incarnation after incarnation from the hoary old ages until now—the Ancient of Days, his hair white like wool, quietly turning up anew when the time yearns, and men are near to yield to the enemy: Proteus his name, and ever the shape he takes is strange, unexpected, yet ever sharing the same three traits of insight, rage and generousness—The Slayer of the Giant—Arthur come back—the Messenger of the Covenant—the genius of our species —Jesus the Oft-Born."

In conclusion, I append a list of the works of Matthew Phipps Shiel:

Prince Zaleski          John Lane (1895)
The Rajah's Sapphire
  (from a plot given Shiel
  viva voce by W. T.
  Stead)          Ward, Lock, and Bowden
                          (1896)

[160]

## Matthew Phipps Shiel

| | |
|---|---|
| Shapes in the Fire | John Lane (1896) |
| The Yellow Danger | Grant Richards (1898) |
| Cold Steel | "        "        (1899) |
| Contraband of War | "        "        (1899) |
| The Man-Stealers | Hutchinson (1900) |
| The Lord of the Sea [18] | Grant Richards (1901) |
| The Purple Cloud | Chatto and Windus (1901) |
| The Weird o' It | Grant Richards (1902) |
| Unto the Third Generation | Chatto and Windus (1903) |
| The Evil that Men Do | Ward and Lock (1904) |
| The Yellow Wave | "      "      "      (1905) |
| The Last Miracle | T. Werner Laurie (1906) |
| The Lost Viol | Ward and Lock (1908) |
| The White Wedding | T. Werner Laurie (n. d.) |
| The Pale Ape | "      "      "      (n. d.) |
| The Isle of Lies | "      "      "      (n. d.) |
| This Knot of Life | Everett (n. d.) |
| The Dragon | Grant Richards (1913) |
| Children of the Wind [19] | "        "        (1923) |

I might mention also Shiel's translation of Charles Henry Schmitt's The Hungarian Revolution: an eyewitness's account of the first five days, a pamphlet published by the Worker's Socialist Federation in London in 1918.

*May 28, 1924.*

[18] Completely revised for Alfred A. Knopf's edition (1924).
[19] Also published by Mr. Knopf in New York.

# Arthur Machen: Dreamer and Mystic

## I

A perdurable source of bewilderment and perplexity
to me (and to any others who consider the matter at
all) arises from the fact that certain authors, more
worthy of attention than many who awaken contemporary
applause, should speak apparently unheard for a long
period, despite the minor apostles and disciples and imitators who chirp feebly concerning the existence of their
masters, but who, unfortunately, are equally inaudible.
Inaudible, that is, until that arbitrary hour when suddenly the deaf hear and the blind see; the silver carillons
at last draw the crowd to the cathedral where light pours
in through every window to illuminate the hidden shrine
and consecrate the secret glory.

It would seem at first thought that there was a satisfactory manner of explaining this phenomenon in the case
of Arthur Machen, obscure for thirty years or more. This
writer is a mystic and it cannot be expected that the man in
the street, the idle bystander, the ecstatic reader of This
Freedom should take with delight to the reading of mystic
books. There are, however, sufficiently compelling reasons for not accepting too readily this superficial interpretation of this immediate problem. First, because
such obviously spagyric tales as The Hill of Dreams
and The House of Souls are written in a beautiful English prose which should have awakened wider enthusiasm

[162]

for its own sake, if for no other. Second, because in such books as The Three Impostors and The Chronicle of Clemendy the inherent mysticism is solely creative. The former is a mystery yarn in the manner of Stevenson's The Dynamiter, quite as good as, probably better than, its more famous prototype. The latter consists of a series of romantic novelle, "nine joyous journeys," in the manner, say, of Boccaccio or Marguerite of Navarre. In any case his books have tardily begun to sell—not, to be sure, to the degree that books by Sinclair Lewis and Mrs. Wharton sell, but certainly within hailing distance of the sales of such men as Max Beerbohm and Walter de la Mare. His name, too, may now be spoken in almost any drawing-room without the speaker's fearing that he will be stared at blankly or beset with questions. *Who* is, etc.? There is, belatedly, beyond doubt, an awareness, on the part of a growing section of the reading public, that an author by the name of Arthur Machen really exists, an awareness which includes, among a few, at any rate, the perception that he is one of the most skilful living writers of English prose, and that he has composed at least one masterpiece which is not likely soon to be forgotten.

The problem is engaging, but it need not detain us. The point on which attention may be focused is that while Machen is indubitably a mystic, in spite of (or because of) this fact, he is no longer an obscurity. His whole conception of literature is mystic, as any one may find out for himself by perusing Hieroglyphics, a volume which offers a test by which one may make the distinction between mere books and books which are works of art. Strangely enough—this correlation is almost unexampled

[163]

in the world of letters—he has been consistent in creating his own works of fiction according to his own defined formula. One subject has always intrigued him, the rending of the veil, and the danger that awaits the adventurer who makes this dread experiment. Further, as he tells us in so many different ways in Far Off Things, his method has invariably been the same, to proceed from the external fact, a house, a mountain, a sunset, or a tree, to the internal, subconscious suggestion. With Hazlitt, he believes that all men of genius relate what they remember of what they knew before they were eighteen.

To the reader unskilled in such mysteries, Far Off Things will appear to be little more than a somewhat disconnected account of certain places, people, and incidents in the author's early life. Nevertheless, even such a reader will not find the book lacking in charm, for the prose is finely distinguished, simple, supple, and stamped with the writer's personality, and the incidents, places, and people described are far from uninteresting in themselves. But to one who comes to this book prepared, so to speak, by a reading of Mr. Machen's other work, every page, every line, in Far Off Things falls into its place as a symmetrical detail in a whole which is only conce ned with a consideration of method in writing, the method of an adept. This is obvious not only when Mr. Machen asserts that he never thought of literature as a career, but only as a destiny; not only when he affirms that he holds a secret doctrine to the effect that in literature no imaginative effects are achieved by logical predetermination; not only when he avers: "I would suggest that the whole matter of imaginative literature depends on this faculty of seeing the universe, from the æonian pebble of the wayside to the raw suburban street, as something new, unheard of, marvellous, finally, miraculous. The good people—amongst whom I naturally class myself—feel that everything is miraculous; they are continually amazed at the strangeness of the proportion of all things. The bad people, or scientists, as they are sometimes called, maintain that nothing is properly an object of awe or wonder since everything can be explained. They are duly punished;" not only when he plans "to invent a story which would recreate those vague impressions of wonder and awe and mystery that I myself had received from the form and shape of the land of my boyhood and youth. . . . Could one describe hills and valleys, woods and rivers, sunrise and sunset, buried temples and mouldering Roman walls, so that a story should be suggested to the reader? Not, of course, a story of material incidents, not a story with a plot in the ordinary sense of the term, but an interior tale of the soul and its emotions; could such a tale be suggested in the way I have indicated?"

It could be, and it has been. Far Off Things is such a tale. From the opening pages in which the author describes his birthplace, at Caerleon-on-Usk in the heart of Gwent on the border of Wales, a country redolent with memories of the Roman occupation, the seat of the romances of Arthur and the Graal and the Round Table, to the end of the book, whether he writes of the Gothic in architecture, apple tarts, Sir Walter Scott, Thomas De Quincey, or the streets of London, the wonder is still there, the strangeness persists. It may be well to inform the intending reader of Machen at this point that this author was first turned towards magic by a paper in Dickens's periodical, Household Words, and that a performance of Les Cloches de Corneville once set him to dreaming. Of such curiously startled dreams is this book compounded.

Somewhere in this volume Machen writes: "I am often made quite envious when I see and hear how a young man, fresh on the town, drops so easily, so pleasantly, so delightfully into a quite distinguished place in literature before he is twenty-five. He enters the world of letters as a perfectly well-bred man enters a room full of great and distinguished company, knowing exactly what to say, and how to say it; every one is charmed to see him; he is at home at once; and almost a classic in a year or two.

"And I, all alone in my little room, friendless, desolate, conscious to my very heart of my stuttering awkwardness whenever I thought of attempting the great speech of literature; wandering, bewildered, in the world of imagination, not knowing whither I went, feeling my way like a blind man, like a blind man striking my head against the wall, for me no help, no friends, no counsel, no comfort."

But it was this solitude which gave the boy his opportunity to dream his dreams, and the leisure to acquire the skill to learn how to interpret them.

*November 16, 1922.*

## II

Things Near and Far is a companion volume to Far Off Things. Issued subsequently, it covers loosely the author's career from the early eighties to the present day. Between 1881 and 1922 Arthur Machen's output has consisted of eighteen titles, including long transla-

## Dreamer and Mystic

tions of the Heptameron, Béroalde de Verville's Moyen de parvenir (Fantastic Tales), and Casanova's Memoirs, in twelve volumes. For this forty-one years of toil Mr. Machen states that he has received £635! For the translation of Casanova he was paid thirty shillings a week and, irony of ironies, he was permitted to finance the publication of the first issue out of a small legacy. The birth pains suffered in writing The Great God Pan, The Chronicle of Clemendy, The Three Impostors, and The Hill of Dreams are duly reported. Herein is also related how the author played the clerk in the court of the Duke of Venice and other minor rôles during a Benson Shakespearean season.

Of all the works of autobiography with which I am acquainted this is the saddest, because it relates, from the calm dignity of advanced middle-age, in beautiful prose, without malice, with superb courage, one of the most tragic and heart-breaking stories in the history of English letters, the story of Arthur Machen's own career as a writer, his intolerable experiences with publishers, his neglect by the public, and, above all, his loneliness and solitude in the formative years, a loneliness that early found expression in his masterpiece, The Hill of Dreams. Did ever, one wonders, another literary artist have so few contacts with his fellow-men?

There are, it must be admitted, alleviating passages, passages of poetic description, like that evocative of a great mystic adventure circa 1900, passages even of humour, as when the author states that his grandfather could not bear radishes or the Adeste Fideles, or when he gives an account of his war with the fleas, but I think it may be safely asserted that few will be able to arise from a reading of this little book without a profound feel-

[167]

ing of pity, a feeling accentuated as the days go by and the recollection of its burning words sinks more deeply into the consciousness. As a matter of fact, this narrative of the conception and birth of Mr. Machen's works contains as much real spiritual drama as his novels and tales, and when we read in Things Near and Far that the author in his early days often dined sumptuously on half a loaf of dry bread, green tea, without milk or sugar, with plenty of tobacco for dessert, and compare this with Lucian Taylor's identical banquet in The Hill of Dreams we begin to see how literature and life become interdependent in the work of this writer, and how Lucian's dreams were the dreams of the lonely boy who came to London from Caerleon-on-Usk.

In this connection it is interesting to recall Machen's account of the inception of that romance: "I started fair. This was to be something different from the former books: I knew that. But I hadn't the remotest notion of what this new book was to be about. I used to go out in the morning and pace the more deserted Bloomsbury squares and wonder very much what it would be like. I got the hint I wanted at last from a most interesting essay by Mr. Charles Whibley, written by way of introduction to Tristram Shandy. Mr. Whibley was discussing the picaresque in literature. He pointed out that while Gil Blas and its early Spanish originals represented the picaresque of the body, and Don Quixote was picaresque both of mind and body, Tristram Shandy was picaresque of the mind alone. The wandering in that extraordinary book, is, in other words, noumenal, not phenomenal. I caught hold of that notion: the thought that a literary idea may be presented from the mental as well as the physical side of things, and said to myself:

## Dreamer and Mystic

'I will write a Robinson Crusoe of the mind.' That was the beginning of The Hill of Dreams. It was to represent loneliness not of body on a desert island, but loneliness of soul and mind and spirit in the midst of myriads and myriads of men."

This then, was the inception of the strange and beautiful book about Lucian Taylor who, in the face of the cruelty of life, the futility of life, the ugliness of life, the uncharitableness of life, the hypocrisy of life, the dishonesty of life, creates beauty for himself, vivid, imaginative beauty, from the casual kiss of a servant-girl, from the bronze hair of a lodging-house woman, from the chimney-pots and streets of London: all are transmuted, as the old alchemists transmuted base metal into gold, into poetic and mystic images.

These three books, Far Off Things, Things Near and Far, and The Hill of Dreams, have, it will be perceived, a significant affiliation, and should be read in the order named, although the autobiographical works are recent, and the novel was written in the late nineties, published in 1907, and now, at last, reissued.

Literature, Mr. Machen asserts with cynical modesty, is an escape from life, like Alpine climbing, chess, methylated spirits, and Prussic acid. In this particular instance, it might be added, it is something more.

*January 5, 1923.*

## Ronald Firbank

Valmouth . . . a young man at an evening party caught my attention. Valmouth, he repeated and, after a significant pause, added, I will send it down to you.

Ignorant as to whether Valmouth was a liqueur or a new variety of dog, with some curiosity I awaited Stuart Rose's gift which, when it arrived, exhibited qualities inherent in both these surmises . . . and yet it was neither. Valmouth was a book. The wrapper, probably with justification, was fashioned of a paper that resembled oilcloth and displayed a quaint design in colour by Augustus John, together with the author's name, Ronald Firbank. I sat down to peruse a page or two. I rose an hour later, having read the book through, a reading interrupted here and there by spasms of merriment or nods of astonishment. Valmouth, indeed, with its lusty, impatient peacocks and parties, its portrait of the always surprising Mrs. Hurstpierpoint, Lady Parvoula de Panzoust and her pursuit of the josephian shepherd, and, above all, that ripping old coon, Mrs. Yajñavalkya, procuress and masseuse, who, in the midst of the most utter nigger jargon, casually inserts such phrases as "plein air!" The opus concludes with an amazing wedding, as smartly attended as that of the Princess Mary, in which the two chief rôles are enacted by a juvenile English naval officer and the young Negro woman, Niri-Esther. Just before this coda, the composer of this jazz concerto has indicated an opportunity for a superb cadenza.

# Ronald Firbank

Arthur Annesley Ronald Firbank, the second and only surviving son of the late Major Sir (Joseph) Thomas Firbank, M. P., and Jane Harriette, daughter of the late Reverend James Perkins Garret of Kilgarron County, Carlow, was born in London in 1886. He was educated "abroad" and at Trinity College, Cambridge. He has travelled extensively.

Elkin Mathews issued Firbank's first book, Odette d'Antrevernes, in 1905. This slender volume of forty-five pages, bound in grey wrappers, stamped in gold, also contains A Study in Temperament, suggestive in manner of his later work. Of Odette, there was also a tall paper edition, limited to *ten copies,* bound in vellum, from which A Study in Temperament was omitted. This story was also excluded from Grant Richards's reprint of Odette (wrappers) in 1916. Firbank's other books, published by Richards, are: Vainglory (1915), Inclinations (1916), Caprice (1917), Valmouth (1919), The Princess Zoubaroff (a comedy in three acts; 1920), Santal (wrappers; 1921), and The Flower Beneath the Foot (1923). Prancing Nigger was published by Brentano's in New York in 1924.[1] These volumes are embellished with designs by Félicien Rops, Albert Rutherston, Augustus John, Michel Sevier, Albert Buhrer, C. R. Nevinson, Wyndham Lewis, and Robert E. Locher.

Sophisticated virgins and demi-puceaux will adore these romances. Married or unmarried persons over thirty will find them either shocking or tiresome, according to the individual temperament of the reader. I have a suspicion that a few delightful old ladies will enjoy a quiet

---

[1] With a preface by Carl Van Vechten, who also suggested the title. For the later English edition, Firbank reverted to his original title, Sorrow in Sunlight.

closet-laugh on the sly. These novels are not suitable for public libraries and Brander Matthews and William Lyon Phelps will never review them.

To be 1890 in 1890 might be considered almost normal. To be 1890 in 1922 might be considered almost queer. There is a difference, however. The colour is magenta. Oscar's hue was green. The fun is warmer; the vice is more léger. Soon or late, one hears a good deal about the light touch in literature. It might be believed, forsooth, that this was no rare quality, so frequently do reviewers apply this ready epithet to writing which has no touch at all. Speaking for myself, I may say that Ronald Firbank is the only authentic master of the light touch I have discovered. His touch is so light, indeed, that after reading one of his books I find even Max Beerbohm a trifle studied, a little composed. Confronted by Prancing Nigger, Aldous Huxley might almost be regarded as an earnest fellow.

Firbank is, perhaps, the only purely Greek writer that we possess today. There is no sentimentality or irony in his work; hardly even cynicism. There is, indeed, a baffling quality about Firbank's very lucidity, his gay, firm grasp of his trivial peccancies. His ellipses serve the same purpose as the descending curtain at the close of the first act of Die Walküre. His form arranges itself for the most part in a diagram of dialogue . . . and such dialogue! No matter how many ancient clouds of glory he trails behind him, and there is Greek, Firbank is more than up-to-date. He is the Pierrot of the minute. Félicien Rops on a merry-go-round. Aubrey Beardsley in a Rolls-Royce. Ronald in Lesbosland. Puck celebrating the Black Mass. Sacher-Masoch in Mayfair.

## Ronald Firbank

A Rebours à la mode. Aretino in Piccadilly. Jean
Cocteau at the Savoy. The Oxford tradition with steam
from the Paris bains de vapeur. The cubists are remembered. Firbank plays Picasso's violin. The decorations
serve more than their purpose. Flippant, impertinent
symbols are the tools of his impudicity. Fruits, flowers,
bees, and even mice play eccentric rôles in these con-
centric comedies. Roses and nightingales impose their
furtive intentions. Cathedral towers and organ recitals
are to be noted among the minor gems in a by no means
despicable collection. At last, apparently, Tinker Bell's
life is no longer in danger. Can it be possible that this
impudent young man is satirizing D. H. Lawrence, or is
this the true picture of English life?

Quotations would serve no purpose—can one quote
from a tapestry?—and they would be unseemly, but
I may permit myself to bring forward a short passage
from Vainglory, in which this jaunty, intrepid, if somewhat pale, original, referring ostensibly to Harvester's
Vaindreams, sums up, perhaps, himself:

" 'He has such a strange, peculiar style. His work
calls to mind a frieze with figures of varying heights
trotting all the same way. If one should by chance
turn about it's usually merely to stare or to sneer or to
make a grimace. Only occasionally his figures care to
beckon. And they seldom really touch.'

" 'He's too cold. Too classic, I suppose.'

" 'Classic! In the Encyclopedia Britannica his style is
described as *odd spelling, brilliant and vicious.*' "

To such affairs of the world as those for which he has
no taste he is utterly indifferent. He does not satirize
the things he hates. He flits airily about, arranging with
skilful fingers the things he loves. Make no mistake:

[173]

# Ronald Firbank

what he wants to do he does, and is a master of the doing of. The delicate tranquillity of his prose, shot through with icy stabs of wit and shimmering gleams of sophistication, is very rare and very original. When you compare him with other authors, logically you can go no further than the binding. His utterly own manner alienates him completely from the possibility of any other form of estimate. He is unique, a glittering dragon-fly skimming over the sunlit literary garden, where almost all the other creatures crawl.

I own a special fondness for The Flower Beneath the Foot, although Caprice is a great favourite of mine, and Valmouth is hors de concours, like the Cathedral at Chartres or a gown designed by Madame Vionnet. The scenario is extraordinarily telling, the characters vividly droll, the flash of wit coruscating, the insinuations incredible. I have read The Flower three times and each time I have dug new worms from under the stones.

The chapter of my choice, possibly, is that which recounts the death of the Archduchess who, as she lies dying, gazes rapturously at the new model for one of her cloacal charities, placed conveniently on the coverlet before her, the while she mutters strange sagas. The Queen, at a desk in the death chamber, occupied in dispatching telegrams announcing the sad eventuality, annoyed by the interruptions, bids the Archduchess to hold her tongue. The form chosen for these wires, after a good deal of careful consideration, is "Lizzie has ceased articulating."

The Archduchess and the Queen, however, are but two in this rich gallery of ripe, rude figures. There is the Flower herself, who learned to read swiftly on the

# Ronald Firbank

"screens at cinemas" and who conquered her Ego in her eighteenth year, whom we leave in the tragic conclusion beating her fragile palms against the broken glass atop the convent wall, as she watches Prince Yousef enter the Cathedral to wed another. This is, indeed, her book, for the title page tells us that The Flower is "a record of the early life of St. Laura de Nazianzi and the times in which she lived." Some times!

Further, there are the Tunisian Bachir and his group of flower-boys, and the Hon. "Eddy" Monteith, who dies of fright at the sight of a jackal while composing a sonnet before the excavations of Chedorlahomor. There is Mrs. Wetme who desires to "climb" from the Café Cleopatra to a royal drawing-room through the purchased aid of the impecunious Duchess of Varna. There is Count Cabinet who makes a curious discovery on the lake, through the telescope of his observatory, just before the sudden tropic night shuts out the view; there are the Nuns of the Flaming Hood and Their Majesties of Date-land, King Jotifa and Queen Thleeanouhee. On the whole, however, I laugh most permanently at the implication of the passage followed by a footnote on page 133.[2]

Ronald Firbank visited Havana in August, 1922. The following month found him in the British West Indies where he wrote the first sketches of Prancing Nigger. He completed the book in Bordighera during the ensuing winter. The novel is typical of his talent. The tropical nights and dawns . . . how many brilliant passages they have evoked! . . . the trumpet-flowers and jasmines, the sapphire and emerald sea, the exotic birds,

[2] The reference is to the English edition.

[175]

seem to have inspired him to write his best. There is possibly more beauty in this book than in any other by this author, and certainly no less humour.

Firbank's treatment of the Negro [3] is his own; he owes nothing, it may be said, to such forerunners as Mrs. Harriet Beecher Stowe, Octavus Roy Cohen, E. K. Means, Waldo Frank, or T. S. Stribling. The Mouth family, whose social advances and amorous adventures form the woof of this tapestry, are as decorative and fantastic as Firbank's more familiar English duchesses. Perhaps, indeed, he moves even more freely in this, to him, esoteric milieu. Prancing Nigger hovers delightfully between a Freudian dream and a drawing by Alastair, set to music by George Gershwin.

*March 6, 1922.*
*June 15, 1923.*
*January 23, 1924.*

[3] It is worthy of note that Prancing Nigger has been greatly admired by Negro intellectuals.

## Sophie Arnould

Although, by way of compensation for his apparently transitory celebrity, it is indubitably true that the actor, the singer, is proportionately awarded more applause during his lifetime than the creative artist, who often moulders in his grave before his books are read, certain interpreters retain a longer lease on fame than equally worthy creators. The irony lies in the axiom that the creative artist who is most applauded by his contemporaries is frequently the first to be forgotten by succeeding decades, while the actor who is the most applauded while he lives is the longest remembered by those who come after. Indeed, if you make up a comparative list of players and playwrights of past periods who still haunt the memory and the imagination, I am willing to wager that the catalogue of actors will be the longer. Nell Gwyn, David Garrick, Mrs. Bracegirdle, Malibran, Pauline Viardot, Giuditta Pasta, Clairon, Peg Woffington, Edwin Booth, Lotta, Salvini, and Rachel have so impressed themselves on the popular consciousness through their lives, romantically recorded by coeval and later memoir writers, that they have taken as definite a place in the minds and hearts of the public as the outstanding characters of fiction, Sancho Panza, Mr. Pickwick, Tartarin, Bazarov, and Daisy Miller. We need harbour no doubts, to introduce a modern note, that the name of Sarah Bernhardt, the French Jewess who defied the laws of the Théâtre Français, who defied the laws of society so flagrantly that on one still-celebrated occasion she permitted her actual lover, Jean Richepin, to enact the rôle of her stage lover in his own piece, Nana-Sahib, who defied the laws of nature, compelling her audience to forget that Marguerite Gautier was seventy-five years old and possessed but one leg—we need harbour no doubt, I say, that this name is not a thousand times more perdurable and amaranthine than that of Victorien Sardou, in whose dramas she won the suffrage of the crowd. Her epitaph, indeed, might be that which Voltaire, or another, wrote for Adrienne Lecouvreur:

> "L'opinion étoit si forte
> Qu'elle devoit toujours durer;
> Qu'apres même qu'elle fut morte,
> On refusa de l'enterrer."

Not the least of the names that have come down to us from the mauve and pale-green past of the exquisite eighteenth century is that of Sophie Arnould, whose fragrant cognomen might have been perpetuated alone through Gluck's statement that without her aid he never could have presented his Iphigénie en Aulide to Paris. But aside from her eminence as the greatest lyric artist of her period, she was beautiful and witty, and the incidents of her life were dramatic and intriguing enough to furnish material for a score of comedies and romances. What verses Alexander Pope might have composed in honour of Sophie, had Clio permitted him to live a little later! Mademoiselle Arnould was the friend of the great men of her day: Beaumarchais, Marmontel, Duclos, Helvetius, Diderot, even Benjamin Franklin, all came to her salon. Jean Jacques Rousseau visited her on at least one occasion, and Voltaire's appearance on her hearthstone assumes, historically, almost the semblance of a pilgrimage. Her wit won the attention of these personages, her humanity, their hearts. Her tongue, at its best, was capable of fashioning epigrammatic masterpieces; her less acceptable sallies were delivered in the form of paronomasia. These aphorisms wormed their way into many eighteenth-century volumes of recollections, memoirs, and letters, and after her death they were collected and issued under the title, Arnoldiana. Many of them are still in daily use in France.

The artists of the epoch were zealous in their desire to reproduce Sophie's beauty. Greuze's portrait is perhaps the most adorable. This canvas also represents Greuze to better advantage than the more celebrated Cruche cassée in the Louvre. The early engravings of this Broken Pitcher, by the way, were dedicated by the painter to Mademoiselle Arnould. Greuze, of course, does not suggest the Iphigénie; it is in La Tour's portrait that we recognize the tragic actress. There is further the bust by Houdon which served Sophie in good stead when the revolutionists broke into her house. She dubbed the head Marat and saved her own.

Sophie Arnould was born at Paris, February 14, 1740. Her parents appear to have been respectable members of the upper middle-class; her mother, as a matter of fact, was a frequenter of literary circles and enjoyed the acquaintance of men who inspired her with the ambition of giving her daughter a thorough education. So Sophie studied reading and writing, foreign languages, the spinet, and singing. At the age of ten, or thereabouts, her charm, her wit, her beauty, and her talent attracted the attention of the Princess of Modena, who thereafter made herself responsible for the child's future instruction.

## Sophie Arnould

It was the custom of the period, more fashionable than pious, for ladies of the great world to seclude themselves in convents during the latter part of Lent. At the beginning of Holy Week, 1757, the Princess arrived at the Abbey of Panthémont to discover the sisters in a state of consternation. They included in their numbers a nun with an exceptionally beautiful voice who had been counted on to supply the music during the retreat, but she had fallen ill. On Wednesday, fashionable Paris would come to hear the Tenebrae and there was no one to sing it. The Princess offered Sophie as a substitute, and the following day, when she sang the Miserere of Lalande, the church was crowded, so quickly the news of the girl's remarkable talent had spread. The Queen learned of this success and sent for Sophie; Madame de Pompadour learned of it and sent for Sophie. The Queen desired to install Sophie in her private choir; the King, through the royal mistress, destined her for the Académie Royale de Musique. Now it was common knowledge that those who entered the stage-door of the Opéra were forced to leave behind them an indispensable element of the quality of maidenhood. Sophie's mother, on this account, strove to conceal her daughter in a convent, but she found it impossible to discover an abbess willing to brave the anger of royalty and its mistress. Sophie, accordingly, was engaged at the Académie. At first, it was intended that she should become a member of the sacred choir affiliated with that institution, but the dearth of talent on the operatic stage afforded this intention a short life. Searching for a novelty to stir the apathetic public pulse, the directors injected Sophie into an opera-ballet called Les amours des dieux on December

# Sophie Arnould

15, 1757. The singer made her début at the age of seventeen and was immediately launched on a brilliantly successful career.

In the meantime her father had become an inn-keeper, and a charming Norman painter, hight Dorval, demanded accommodation at his hotel. Dorval's linen was of the finest; his taste in dress exquisite. Indeed, he must have been quite as rococo as the farmers and shepherdesses of the Trianon. Nevertheless, in spite of the huge baskets of game and fruit which arrived from day to day, the Arnoulds appear to have been lacking in suspicion until the morning dawned when both Sophie and Dorval were missing. A little later, Arnould père received a letter in which Dorval unmasked and appeared in his true character as Louis Léon Félicité de Brancas, Comte de Lauraguais. He adored Sophie, he asseverated, and promised to marry her after his wife died. By way of warning to families who credit such promises, I might state that the Comtesse de Lauraguais expired on the guillotine a full half-century later. Nevertheless, the love of the Comte and Sophie continued unabated for a few years; then there came a break. During one of his absences Sophie packed her two sons and all the Comte's presents into a carriage and dispatched them to the Comtesse, who established a precedent for wronged wives by retaining the children to rear with her own and returning the presents. Later, Sophie presented the Comte with two more children. In fact, they renewed their romance periodically; it was the one grand passion in both their lives, although both were as inconstant as rabbits and guinea pigs and for every new lover of Sophie's Lauraguais retaliated with a new mistress.

## Sophie Arnould

They remained friends, however, until death parted them, a fact to which Sophie's ultimate letter to the Comte bears touching and convincing evidence.

Voltaire once remarked of Lauraguais: "He has all possible talents and all possible eccentricities." He wrote plays, mad five-act tragedies and insane comedies. Delving in the subject of inoculation, at that period regarded as a form of black magic, he issued a pamphlet which caused his detention at Metz. The Comte further dabbled in chemistry and anatomy, endeavoured to bring about reforms in the theatre, and even became a gentleman jockey. One of the early aristocratic radicals, he constantly collided with royalty and the courts. He was a deliciously whimsical paraphrase of the eighteenth-century encyclopedist. It is to his unfading credit that, in one fantastic flight of his winged imagination, in order to rid Sophie of an unwelcome suitor, he actually brought, and substantiated by scientific authority, the charge that the fellow was boring her to death and caused him to be arrested for attempted murder! It is probable that the Comte was the only real love in Sophie's life, although her subsequent turpitudes were many, including relations with the Prince d'Hénin, whom she detested, and Bélanger, the architect, who, with Lauraguais, remained her friend until she died.

Sophie's voice was not powerful. "Nature," she has written in her Mémoires, "had seconded my taste for music with a tolerably agreeable voice, weak but sonorous, though not extremely so. But it was sound and well-balanced, so that with a clear pronunciation and without any defect save a slight lisp, which could hardly be considered a fault, not a word of what I sang was lost, even in the most spacious buildings." It is to be observed

[182]

that clear enunciation is an inevitable part of the baggage of all great dramatic singers. Contemporary critics allot more credit to her than she awarded herself; according to their evidence her voice was sweet in quality and she possessed the gift of imparting to it colour and expression. The Goncourts have summarized the case: "She brought to harmony, emotion; to the song, compassion; to the play of the voice, sentiment. She charmed the ear and touched the heart. All the domain of the tender drama, all the graces of terror, were hers. She possessed the cry, and the tears, and the sigh, and the caresses of the pathetic. . . . What art, what genius, must there have been to wrest so many harmonies from a contemptible voice, a feeble throat." These words are fairly plain. They place Sophie as perhaps the first of the great dramatic singers, among those who act not only with their bodies but with their singing voices as well. David Garrick pronounced her a greater actress than Clairon. What Mary Garden is to the contemporary lyric stage, Sophie Arnould was to the stage of the late eighteenth century.

Prior to Gluck's arrival in Paris, French lyric art was gradually ebbing out its life. Pastiches formed most of the bills, opera-ballets with five acts and five plots, or rearrangements of minor operas. Even from these Sophie wrested an enviable reputation, just as Sarah Bernhardt carved out a magnificent career with the clap-trap of Sardou and Mary Garden has won recognition as the greatest lyric artist of our day largely through her performance in Massenet's meretricious Thaïs. The titles of the trifles in which Sophie appeared, however, are pretty and evoke the powder-puffery, the wigs, the flowered gowns, the regnant artificiality of what must

[183]

ever remain in the memory as a graceful and gracious period. Alphée et Aréthuse, Pyrrhus et Polixène, Dardanus, Pirame et Thisbé, Les dieux d'Egypte, Les fêtes de Paphos, Castor et Pollux, Psyché, Sylvie, Palmire, Aline, reine de Golconde, are a few of the decorative names. Sophie's repertory included works by Lully, Rameau, Monsigny, and Rousseau, in whose Devin de village she appeared in a boy's rôle, but of all the operas she sang, only two works by Gluck retain the stage today.

The causes for Sophie's decline and fall are not difficult to gauge. Her voice, none too reliable in the beginning, began to fail her; further there is reason to believe that on many occasions she made no effort to please the public before which she was appearing. Then her wickedly witty tongue made her an object of fear, dread, and hate to many of her comrades in the theatre, and her caprices were so flagrant that an opera director of today would probably commit suicide in face of them. During whole weeks she would refuse to sing at all, thereby seriously embarrassing a management, already sufficiently embarrassed by the lack of real talent; even the fact that she was announced to sing did not sanction any belief that she would do so. At the last moment she frequently sent word that she was ill; on one occasion she sent no word at all, but came and sat in a conspicuous box and, when pressed for an explanation, declared that she had attended the performance to take a lesson from her understudy. In the circumstances one can understand the hisses that rendered her last appearances tragic. Inspired to some degree by a natural feeling of grievance on the part of the public, these hisses were encouraged, doubtless, by a management which wished to rid itself permanently of such a menace to order and

# Sophie Arnould

discipline. Even the beneficent presence of Marie Antoinette on more than one occasion did not serve to stem the tide of disapproval, for the simple reason that the cold Queen was sufficiently unpopular in her own right.

Poor Sophie definitively retired from the stage in 1778, when she was but thirty-eight years old. Thereafter her life was a constant struggle. Granted a pension by the government, she found it difficult to collect. When a benefit at the Académie was proposed in her behalf, she rejected the offer upon learning that it was conditional upon her personal appearance. The Revolution wrested from her the pitiful remnants of her property, and the last few years of her life were as pathetic as those of any of the heroines she had represented on the stage. She did not, however, lose her friends, Lauraguais and Bélanger, who remained faithful to the end, although both had lost the power to assist her in any material manner. Sophie died on October 22, 1802, and where she is buried no one knows. She was born on St. Valentine's Day, the first words she sang on the stage were "Charmant Amour," and as she was dying the Curé of St. Germain-l'Auxerrois bent over her bed to hear her murmur: "Her sins, which are many, are forgiven, for she loved much."

*September 9, 1919.*

[185]

## Oscar Hammerstein: An Epitaph

### I

Some years ago, passing by the northwest corner of Forty-second Street and Seventh Avenue, I observed a short, stubby figure of a man with a thin, greyish Mephistophelean and slightly rakish, hircine beard, lounging under the lintel of one of the doorways of the old Victoria Theatre. He wore a morning coat with grey trousers. His toes, encased in large, soft-leather boots, were turned out at a wide angle. His linen was immaculate. On his head reposed a top hat of an obsolete French pattern, and from his mouth, which frequently assumed a quizzical expression, a fat black cigar projected. The eccentricity of the figure was apparent at first glance, but magnetism and a certain Napoleonic magnificence raced in as second impressions. It was my first week in New York and I was curious; I asked my companion for a label.

"That," he replied in his most fatidical manner, "that is Oscar Hammerstein."

### II

This happened in the autumn of 1906 when I was a reporter on the New York Times; he was just about to open his new Manhattan Opera House on West Thirty-fourth Street. Later, in the round of my duties, I ap-

[186]

proached him and, as was his wont, almost immediately he familiarly addressed me as Mike. People he liked were sometimes Mike. People he didn't like, he didn't talk to and they were often pilloried on his foulest wit in a manner not reportable. He motioned me to follow him and I did so. I had heard of Mr. Belasco's splendid apartment, laden with spoils from the Ming dynasty, tables upon which Marie Antoinette had written letters to the Chevalier Gluck, fans which had brushed the ether across the face of Lola Montes, mantelpieces which had formerly decorated the drawing-rooms of the Duchesse d'Orléans, and footstools upon which the Abate Metastasio had sat at the feet of La Romanina. Perhaps I expected this other great man of the theatre to be similarly installed.

We walked through the old Victoria, gilded, but shabby, dusty, and dingy: always crowded, afternoon and evening. The smoke from innumerable cigars and cigarettes obscured the atmosphere. On the stage it is possible that acrobats were tumbling, perhaps the Brothers Bard, whose rhythmic feats always awakened wonder and admiration in me, or it is possible that Bert Williams was telling his cat story. You will remember how the Negro bishop, forced to put up for the night alone in a haunted house, sitting before the fire, was visited by pussies: first, a tiny tabby, then a large maltese, then a gigantic, bristling tom, then a cat the size of a leopard, then a cat the size of a lion. And invariably each new visitor seated himself next to the last with the identical remark, "We cain't do nothin' till Martin gits here." The point of the story was that the bishop decided not to wait for Martin. However, on this occasion I did not look at the stage, but followed the short figure, walking, as I recall him, always with his toes very far out, flat-footed, and with rather short steps—he must have been nearly sixty at the time—up the sordid marble staircase of this temple of varieties. He paused for breath at the balcony landing, and then made a wide detour round past the boxes, plodding on through a doorway into a little room. Here he seated himself and, after motioning me to another chair, began to talk at once with communicated enthusiasm about his new operatic venture.

The room was somewhat larger than the average hallbedroom in a New York boarding-house. A window looked into a dismal courtyard. The paper on the walls was soiled and torn. There were no pictures on these walls, but there may have been calendars or maps. There was a desk, littered with papers and books and boxes of cigars and ends of cigars. There was a year's dust spread over all this congeries, save for a square space where Oscar evidently did his work. There was a grand piano, piled with music, music-paper, scores, more boxes of cigars, more books, more letters, more cigar ends, and more dust. The piano was open and the rack held a sheet of music-paper upon which a few hieroglyphics had been scribbled. There were two or three ordinary office-chairs and one arm-chair with broken arms, the upholstery yielding its stuffing. The unswept floor was heaped with boxes, letters, manuscripts, books, and music. Through an archway I perceived another chamber, a brass bed, the sheets tumbled, a bureau. Nowhere order, nowhere cleanliness, except in Mr. Hammerstein's own immaculate person. It was apparent that the man did not permit menials to disturb in any way the disorder of his domain, fearing, no doubt, the accidental destruction of some choice bit of information which he had carefully stowed away in the waste-basket or flung with memory into some corner. Here Oscar Hammerstein did all his work and, at this time, lived. Here he received all his visitors, social or on business. When the Manhattan Opera House was built, his sons prepared for him there a showy apartment furnished with gilt chairs and tables, ormolu clocks, bronze andirons, Tudor trousseau chests, and Carrara marble busts. Certain hours in the morning Oscar consented to occupy these chambers. He held conferences with Campanini on these red carpets and he sometimes signed contracts with singers there, but the nook in the Victoria remained his home. He explained that at night, when he couldn't sleep—and he seldom slept more than four hours out of the twenty-four—he could go out on the fire-escape and watch the busiest corner in New York. On thirty-fourth Street he felt lonesome; besides, the place was too clean and fussy. When, some years later, the old Victoria was practically demolished to make the new Rialto, Oscar clung to his nest as long as he could, although at this time he was living further uptown with his third wife and only employed the place as an office. He was eventually ejected, I believe, by a sheriff's order, when nothing but the sky covered his head and his walls hung over a precipice. Recalling all the conversations, amusing and otherwise, I have held in that little room with him who was always known as the "old man," I can only say that there is a certain pain in my heart when I realize that those days are no more and can never return again.

[189]

# Oscar Hammerstein:

## III

Oscar Hammerstein built the Harlem Opera House, the Harlem Music Hall, the Columbus Theatre, the first Manhattan Opera House, which stood where Macy's department store now stands, the Olympia (the block of theatres now comprising the New York and the Criterion), the Victoria, the Republic, the Harris, the second and more familiar Manhattan Opera House, the Philadelphia Opera House, the London Opera House, the Lexington Avenue Opera House, and probably three or four more theatres, the names of which I have forgotten. He discovered Harlem; he discovered Forty-second Street. The newspaper wits of the day dubbed the Olympia "Hammerstein's Folly." Longacre Square,[1] now the centre of the theatre district, was then quietly restful, uptown. He operated this theatre as a continental music hall and even dared to introduce the promenade in imitation of a similar feature in the London and Paris halls. He had arrived in America in the seventies a penniless immigrant, and it was through his ingenuity in inventing machinery which eventually revolutionized the cigar-making industry that he made his money. Before he died he had patented over one hundred inventions bearing on the manufacture of cigars. It has been said, indeed, that he is in a measure responsible for the present great scope of this industry. He always cherished an ambition to produce opera. Late in life he once remarked, "The tobacco business is prose. Opera is poetry. It's more fun to make Melba sing than to make cigars." The Harlem Opera House was the scene of one of his earliest experiments with opera. Lilli Lehmann sang

[1] Now known as Times Square.

[190]

there for him.  It was there, I think, that he gave one of
the first American performances of Cavalleria Rusticana.
Although he soon dubbed the work, with his characteristically coarse wit, Cavalleria Busticana, from that time
until the day of his death, opera was his only real interest
and he tried persistently and courageously to make it a
successful and popular form of entertainment.  Never,
however, did he give up making cigars; he was making
cigars, I would be willing to wager, the day before he was
taken to the hospital for the last time.  He frequently
wrote comic skits for the German papers (he was a
German Jew, born in Berlin), and he also composed a
good deal of music, some of which has been published.
Once he wagered $500 with Gustave Kerker that he could
write an opera, words and music, in twenty-four hours.
Locked up in a room in the Gilsey House, to the sound of
a hurdy-gurdy which Kerker had engaged to play un-
interruptedly beneath his window, he won the wager.
The opera, subsequently produced, is the worst on record,
probably even worse than Le vieux aigle, another impresario's opera.

But to me, with all this as a vivid and alluring background which occasionally, very occasionally, for it was
not this man's habit to speak of the past, supplied the
material for lively conversation, Oscar Hammerstein
stood for the Manhattan Opera House, in which, during
three seasons (I was in Paris one of its four years)
I enjoyed performances of opera as I have never enjoyed
them before or since.  The scenery and costumes were
often cheap and tawdry, not because insufficient money
had been spent, but because taste in this direction was
not one of the man's qualities; it was the spirit of the
performances that was unforgettable.

[191]

## Oscar Hammerstein:

It was Oscar's invariable habit to sit on a kitchen chair in the right entrance near the proscenium arch. He invariably wore his peculiar top hat; he invariably, in defiance of the fire laws, smoked a long, black cigar. I think we all believed—I know we all said often enough that we believed—that it was his presence that gave the performances their tremendous vitality. Opera was exciting at the Manhattan Opera House; there is no better word to describe it. It seemed, indeed, as though the singers, inspired by the attendance of their manager, were trying to do their best. The facts were, of course, that he knew good performances and enjoyed them and that he knew bad performances and criticized them. His criticism was sharper than that of any of the professional critics. It sometimes took the form of getting rid of some singer who had outlived his usefulness, a severance usually accomplished in some diabolically playful manner.

The list of operas he produced in itself is remarkable; New York may never hear or see French opera given so perfectly again. Carmen, the first season, was a foretaste of joys to come. Thaïs, Pelléas, Louise, Sapho, Grisélidis, Le jongleur, La damnation de Faust, Les contes d'Hoffmann, all received their due, some of them more than their due. Nor was Italian opera neglected; if you heard Don Giovanni at the Manhattan Opera House, you heard the best New York performance of Mozart's masterpiece in recent years. Then there were Salome and Elektra. . . . Nor is it well to forget how many singers he introduced to New York: Mary Garden, Luisa Tetrazzini, Alessandro Bonci, Maurice Renaud, Mariette Mazarin, Jean Perier, Hector Dufranne, John McCormack, Charles Dalmorès, Amadeo Bassi, Emma Trentini, Mario Sammarco, Jeanne Gerville-Réache. . . .

# An Epitaph

It is a matter of record that he stimulated the rival theatre to make great efforts; the Metropolitan Opera Company, too, offered brilliant seasons during the four years of the Manhattan. But surprises, which Oscar loved, were lacking on Broadway. His constantly active brain was continually devising new plans, new sensations. After Chlotilde Bressler-Gianoli had sung Carmen for nearly a full season, he suddenly engaged Emma Calvé for a few performances. Once Mary Garden was successfully launched, he brought Luisa Tetrazzini to America at the height of her meteoric career in London. He allotted the tenor rôle in Le jongleur de Notre Dame to Mary Garden, and later substituted a tenor for a performance or two. He introduced a snake charmer into Samson et Dalila and a juggler into Les Huguenots. . . .

## IV

There never has been any one like him; there never has been a theatrical manager or an operatic impresario (unless it were Richard Brinsley Sheridan) comparable to him in the matter of eccentric greatness or great eccentricity. There was, if you will, P. T. Barnum, at whose name I cannot well scoff. Barnum was famous the world over. Even today his name is probably as well known in Europe as that of any living American. But Barnum was a Yankee and a Yankee business man. All his ventures, beginning with dime museums and ending with Jenny Lind, were money-making schemes. Like Hammerstein, he was a colossal self-advertiser, but there comparison must end. For Hammerstein was a Jewish mystic, or at any rate a mystic Jew. He had his ideals, such as they were. He was an artist; not a

[193]

# Oscar Hammerstein:

a writer, assuredly not a musician, although he loved music and was a competent judge of singing, but an artist in life. He had no desire to make money except to spend it, and he spent it, mind you, not to make more money, but to further his gigantic projects, for, from the very beginning, they were always gigantic. His personal wants, however, were meagre. He was accustomed to lunch or dine on a glass of milk and a box of biscuits. He smoked incessantly, but he never touched intoxicating liquors. There was a time when he frequented a certain corner in the white room at the Hotel Knickerbocker, but he did not go there for the food; he ate at most a plate of tomato soup. He went there to be seen. He was, indeed, on such occasions, the centre of an admiring group. He understood the value of such adulation, he knew exactly how much it was worth, but he was not above courting it. Once, after the Manhattan Opera House was closed, he remarked to me sadly that in the future he would be left pretty much alone. "No one has any use for a man who has quit work," he assured me. "You can't make money out of him any more."

Late in life he owned an automobile and when his leg began to trouble him he found it expedient to use it, but at the height of his career it was his custom to travel in a street-car. He invariably employed a Seventh Avenue car to go to the Manhattan from the Victoria. A street-car, indeed, was the scene of his celebrated encounter with a former chorus girl, who had worked for him at the Olympia. The contractor who was building the Victoria had warned him that day that, unless he raised a certain sum of money before noon, work on the structure would be discontinued. He has told me that he never felt more disconsolate, more discouraged than when he boarded the car . . . to go nowhere, merely to be alone to think. He knew that he could not borrow from any bank or from any business man. "Is Hammerstein crazy," every one was asking, "after the failure of the Olympia to build another theatre in the same square? Nobody will go so far uptown to be amused." The chorus girl recognized him, but he did not recognize her. He did not even look at her. Observing his despondent air, she crossed the aisle to speak to him, to sit down beside him. In a moment he had poured out all his troubles; they were all he had to talk about. But how easy! She had had a stroke of luck, was affluent, had money in the bank. Could she help him? . . . The Victoria eventually made more money than any other of his many theatres.

I have described his personal surroundings. So far as I am aware he never bought anything. I never met him in any kind of shop. Most of the music and books in his room had been presented to him. I do not think reading was one of his habits, but for a man who read so little he was astonishingly well informed. One thing only he desired and it was this that he was always seeking; he wanted fame; he wanted to be considered a public benefactor; he wanted to be talked about as the man who had done more for opera in New York than any one else. In a way he had his wish; in a way he had his successes, many of them, although I believe he was never satisfied. He occupied more space in the newspapers than any other American of his time, unless it were Theodore Roosevelt. He made millions of dollars and lost them. It was impossible for him to retrench. At a time when the Manhattan Opera House was losing money he built the still larger Philadelphia Opera House.

## Oscar Hammerstein:

He probably considered himself a composer. He wrote a good deal of music, dreadful stuff that never would have been heard, had he not been in a position to command a hearing; in this respect he was like a king. His favourite opera was La Traviata. He has often told me that he felt there was more sentiment and beauty in the last act of Verdi's opera than in all of Wagner. This was not bad taste. The last act of La Traviata is shopworn, perhaps, but we recognize its faded loveliness. One would not, however, expect the admirer of the last act of La Traviata to appreciate and engage Mary Garden, to produce Pelléas et Mélisande. That is what I mean when I say that Oscar Hammerstein was in his way an artist, an idealist. He had a certain kind of gnosis. Before his time impresarios had avoided novelties so far as they were able to do so; he opened new doors and awakened public curiosity. In Maurice Grau's day the announcement of a novelty was the assurance of an empty house; now it is the assurance of a full one. To Oscar Hammerstein is due this new condition.

By some curious manner of percipience all his own, he understood voices and singing. He used to say that all he wanted was to hear a singer once to know whether he (or she) was good or bad. Not all the singers he engaged were good, but their average quality was high. He certainly had a flair for knowing what the public wanted.

'He could be arrogant and hard—in this mood he had a habit of wagging his head emphatically from side to side; he was always egotistical and selfish, and yet to a certain degree he drew men to him and he was extraordinarily humane at unexpected moments. I happen to know of an instance in which a trusted employee (all his em-

[196]

# An Epitaph

ployees were trusted to the most absurd degree; he never took the time or trouble to watch anybody working for him; his suspicion was all directed towards those working *against* him) defaulted. He did not prosecute the man. He never spoke of the matter at all, but I afterwards learned that the fellow was ill in a hospital and that Hammerstein was footing the bills. He could be charming, although he seldom could be persuaded to talk about anything but himself and his own plans. He probably lacked a sense of humour, but he possessed an amazing sense of wit; there are hundreds of recorded examples of that. Some one, indeed, should collect them and entitle the collection Hammersteiniana. Frequently this wit was coarse, but almost invariably it hit its mark. Of all the clever things I remember he has said I think I prefer his reply to the invitation to dine with the directors of the Metropolitan Opera Company after they had bought him out for a period of ten years, the tragic ten years. This reply was one line long, a line written in long hand, for in his busiest years he never employed a secretary, although a stenographer sometimes copied the statements he prepared for the newspapers. "Gentlemen," so read his letter, "I am not hungry." Letter writing was one of his major talents.

His arrogance, his pride, his egoism, assisted him to success; he permitted no obstacle to stand in his way. They also caused his downfall. He sometimes scolded the public for not being better customers. He refused backing unless it were made unconditionally; occasionally, doubtless (although I do not know this to be true), he asked rich men for money, but he asked for it as Beethoven might have asked for it, to consecrate his own ideals. He scorned advice and he would never submit to working co-operatively with others; a board of directors was an obnoxious idea to him.

He shared one fault with all other impresarios I have met. Singers were great only when they were singing for him. If they drew large salaries without drawing large audiences he lost his enthusiasm. There is a legend to the effect that he paid a certain tenor only half his salary for singing in Cavalleria Rusticana. "You have worked only half the evening," was his explanation! His treatment of a famous soprano, who made a few appearances at the Manhattan Opera House, was perhaps not chivalrous, but to him it was natural. Most of his singers were loyal to him. Mme. Melba and he were great friends. He quarrelled with Mary Garden, but she called to see him only a few weeks before he died. Almost his last words to me were about her. "She does not know," he said, "how great she is. She knows she is greater than any of the others, but she does not know how much greater."

His philosophy was all-embracing; he even had a philosophy in regard to free tickets for his theatres. "I like to give a man passes when my theatre is crowded," he said. "Then I am doing something for *him,* but if I give a man seats when the house is empty, he makes me feel that he is doing something for *me.*"

He was interested in women; he married three times. He liked to talk with women; he enjoyed bantering with them. A clever woman, I think, interested him more than a clever man, and only women fooled him; men he saw through.

It was part of his greatness that he was never too busy to receive callers. He never kept newspaper men waiting. For three years I looked in on him nearly every day and he not only admitted me readily but usually found time for a long talk.

## V

The last ten years of his life he was slowly dying; there were times during this period when he seemed to have some realization of his fate, when discouragement sat heavily upon him. He was ill when the contract was signed in which he pledged himself not to give opera in New York for ten years and he never really recovered. He tried in various ways to avoid the issue. He produced opera in London, in a new house, and quite characteristically he instructed the architect to cause his portrait to be carved in one of the stone lintels. He imported a light opera for the Manhattan Opera House. These ventures were failures. Indeed, all his life his ventures were failures. It was typical of his ideas that they were too big to succeed. Only the Victoria, his vaudeville theatre, made money, and that never interested him. He planned a circle of theatres for cities the size of Cleveland and St. Louis, each of which was to be constructed identically so that he might carry an opera company and its scenery from one to the other in rotation. He submitted this scheme, which he had prepared in detail, even to the extent of employing an architect to draw up the plans, to the Boards of Trade in the various cities, but although in some instances a good deal of interest was expressed, the project fell through. Then, relying on a somewhat vague implication of certain directors of the Metropolitan Opera House that he might give opera in English before his ten years expired, he built the Lexington Avenue Opera House. It is probably the ugliest theatre he erected—his taste in such matters was execrable—but its brilliant acoustics are a matter of record. These, he assured me, were no accident, but the result of his experience in building theatres. In the concrete foundation of the balcony and the orchestra pit he had caused powdered glass to be sprinkled. All of his later theatres enjoyed fine acoustics, a fact which leads me to believe that he had solved a problem which has always puzzled architects, the solution of which, indeed, is usually left to chance.

He never was destined to give opera at the Lexington Avenue Opera House. He never, indeed, entered its doors. His bitterness regarding his loss of this house tinged his talk for many months.

When he was forced to leave the Victoria, Oscar moved to a dingy office on the second floor of a building across Forty-second Street. On the third floor he had rigged up his cigar-making machines, and he continued to experiment with his inventions. I think it was his habit also to fabricate his own cigars. Any man occupied with any kind of creative work knows the advantage of having some such employment which leaves the mind blank but satisfies the nervous fingers. Less than a year ago, I think, he moved again, this time to a room on the first floor of a building on West Thirty-eighth Street. Again he installed his machines on the floor above. Not many, I fancy, went to see him there, but I made it a habit to drift in every month or so. About six months before his death he had in a measure recovered his health. He was the old Oscar Hammerstein, bouyant and enthusiastic. He planned to present opera again; he was surrounded by scores, libretti, prospectuses, and blank contracts. His conversation fairly bubbled. It seemed to me that in 1920 the Metropolitan would again find him a very dangerous rival.

One hot day about three weeks before his death I called again. His office was open but empty; a man from above shouted down to demand my business. "Ask Mr. Hammerstein," I replied, "if he will see Mr. Van Vechten." I heard a limping step on the floor above. Then the familiar figure appeared at the top of the stairs and descended slowly, very slowly. His foot was worse; he was suffering pain, severe pain, I could see that. He led me into the office and sat down, heavily, hopelessly. He was tired, sick, worried. The long ten years would expire in April, but he could not be certain that the lessee would be willing to give him the Manhattan Opera House in April. Suppose he had a success installed there. On the other hand Oscar could not afford to refuse to rent the theatre until then. Difficulties, difficulties, difficulties! Matters of no moment to the man of forty, fifty, and sixty, but hard to bear for the man of seventy, ill, discouraged, alone, as the man of genius is always alone. We spoke of Mary Garden. We spoke of many things, but he was vague, hopeless, fatigued, dying. . . . Yes, I knew that he was dying. I knew the end had come. I knew that he would never give opera again. He shook my hand with his customary flabby handshake, and asked me to return soon, but as I walked away I knew I never would. When I heard that he had been taken to the hospital and lay at the point of death, I was not surprised. His death did not shock me. . . .

It was not in Oscar Hammerstein, I think, to inspire affection. His manner was often too arrogant, his egoism too colossal, his genius too apparent. These qualities made men stand a little away from him. A few, indeed, disliked him; a few, alas, derided him. To some, even, who did not know him, he seemed a trifle ridiculous. He was never ridiculous, however, to those who knew him; his dignity was too perfect; he was even, in a sense, magnificent! He could and did command admiration, admiration for his achievements, more than that, admiration for the way he failed. He was not, as a matter of fact, what is called a good loser. He groaned and moaned over loss, but in a few days the board was erased and with a clean piece of chalk he was drawing a new diagram, making a new plan. I admired him; more than that I liked him. He was a figure, he lived his own life; sometimes he fashioned it with difficulty, but he always carved it out. He was an artist; he was a genius. I have met few men who have seemed to me as great. Some day, I hope, his statue will stand in Times Square. He would like that.

*August 3, 1919.*

*Léo Delibes*

# I

I am tired of the "Six." I am weary of Erik Satie. I am fed up with Malipiero. The music of Zoltan Kodaly has begun to pall on me. I have consigned my Arnold Schönberg scores to the flames and tossed Alfredo Casella into the dustbin. I have presented such examples of the genius of Poulenc as I possessed to my grocer's daughter and my erstwhile copy of Lord Berners's Three Little Funeral Marches is now the property of the policeman on the corner. I am gorged with Ornstein and Prokofieff. De Falla and Stravinsky are anathema to me. Béla Bartók is a neo-zany. I am sick of Greek tunics and bare legs, satiated with oriental dancing, Persian, Javanese, Chinese, and Polovtsian, surfeited with turkey trots and bunny hugs and fox trots, bored with tangos and maxixes, boleros and seguidillas, Argentine and Spanish dances of whatever nature. I have had my fill of "ball-room dancing," cakewalks, pigeon-wings, clogs, jazz, and hoe-downs. Terpsichore has been such a favourite of late, literary, pictorial, musical, and even social, that the muse has become inflatedly self-conscious, afflicted with a bad case of megalomania. Personally, I wave her away. There is, of course, a reason for this reaction, a stimulant for this new litany: in cleaning out an old music cabinet today I stumbled upon the score of Coppélia: the distinguished, spirited, singing, luminous,

[203]

melodies of Delibes rang again in my ears, the eyes of memory focused on the fluffed tarlatan skirt, the suggestive fleshings terminating in the pointed toe, and, quite suddenly, all "modern" music and dancing assumed the quality of fustian.

"Every dance recalls love. Every ballet leaves us sighing with regret," writes André Suarès. "This mad Mænad becomes intoxicated in her own fashion; she burns only with the wine she drinks; she does not aspire to an internal intoxication, that which the vine of the heart opens to the spirit. She has no subjectivity; she is not meditative; she is wholly carnal and voluptuous; she is not even melancholy, her nature is light. Thus, having humbly grasped the hand of music, held music in her arms, the dance betrays music. She asks music for his great heart, passionate and tender, of which she makes nothing. She does not even offer music her own heart in return, because she has no heart to offer. Like youth, she can only bestow élan and caprice. What is she then, for art and the supreme desire of man, but the most charming body, even if she be bereft of soul?"

The classic costume, the tutu, serves to accentuate this fantastic, carnal quality of the ballet. What fascinations of the imagination it immediately evokes, metamorphosing the dancer into a dragon-fly, a great moth, or a flower swaying in the wind, suggestive of nymphs and banshees and faraway, faded, immortal things! The fluffy tarlatan and the tight bodice emphasize the wasp-waist, the frailty of the arms and legs. Sex is both concealed and awakened. The pointed toe gives the illusion to this mythological creature of an airy defiance of the laws of gravity. She becomes, indeed, a brilliant insect, hovering between heaven and earth. "The ballet," wrote

# Léo Delibes

Théophile Gautier in a happy phrase, "is music that one can see." See in a dream, he might have added, for surely there is a sense of unreality about this art, created artificially and consciously by its devotees, which makes it, thanks to its very conventions and limitations, something rich and strange.

Turning the leaves of this crepuscular score, I recall the names of dancers, some of them born and dead before Delibes's day: Maria Taglioni, the glamorous, Fanny Elssler, the saucy, Fanny Cerito, Carlotta Grisi, beloved of Gautier, Rita Sangalli, and Rosita Mauri, who foreswore caviar because the Tsar, at one of her representations, turned his gaze from the stage to converse with his companions. What pictures of pleasant periods are brought before the eye of the mind by the very names of these ladies! And the names of these ladies and other lulling reveries have been awakened in me by a glimpse of a tattered score by Léo Delibes.

The significance of Delibes, albeit he himself assuredly owed something to Auber and Offenbach, in the history of French music is not, perhaps, generally recognized. More frequently, probably, it is entirely ignored. It was an agreeable experience, therefore, to discover a review by Emile Vuillermoz, apropos of a recent Parisian revival of Le roi l'a dit, in which the statement is made: "Such works as Le roi l'a dit and Lakmé have a considerable importance in our musical history. Delibes is the great forerunner of the 'artist-writer' from which our modern school has evolved. It is he who has given to our musicians the taste to dispose the notes of a chord, the timbre of an orchestration, the voices of an ensemble, with an attentive ingenuity which multiplies discoveries with each measure. His influence, and that of Edouard

[205]

# Léo Delibes

Lalo, have been decisive on the musicians of our time."

Another debt which music owes to Delibes is not owed exclusively by France; it is an international obligation. Before he began to compose his ballets, music for dancing, for the most part, consisted of tinkle-tinkle melodies with marked rhythm. Dancing in France, and often elsewhere (I am speaking, naturally, only of the ballet), was not deeply expressive in its nature. Its spectators were satisfied with technical feats of virtuosity. Dancers were compared on their respective abilities to execute the entrechat and the pirouette. Taglioni and Elssler, to be sure, transcended the technical limitations of their art, evolving an imaginative and spirituelle contribution to the dance fully appreciated in early nineteenth century literature. They accomplished this through their own personalities, aided by the traditional, mystic costume, the garb of their priesthood, which endowed their movements with an element of fantasy. They received meagre assistance from the music to which they danced. For these sublime rites, the simplest and most banal tunes, the baldest rhythm, the most threadbare harmony, sufficed. Nay more, music with any true verve or character was repudiated .as actually likely to exercise a detrimental effect. It was Delibes who revolutionized this peurile ideal of ballet music, introducing in his scores a symphonic element, a wealth of graceful melody, and a richness of harmonic fibre, based, it is safe to hazard, on a healthy distaste for routine. Coppélia and Sylvia, then, are the forerunners of such elaborate contemporary scores as Tcherepnin's Narcisse, Debussy's Jeux, Ravel's Daphnis et Chloë, Strauss's The Legend of Joseph, and Stravinsky's Petrouchka. Beyond any manner of doubt, Delibes is the father of the modern ballet.

# *Léo Delibes*

## II

Clément-Philibert-Léo Delibes was born on February 21, 1836 at Saint-Germain-du-Val, a village situated in the Sarthe, near La Flèche. The death of his father having left the family without resources, his mother took him to Paris in 1848. He was admitted to the Conservatory, and at his first contest he won the second prize for solfège; the following year (1850), he won the first prize. During this period he was a choir boy at the Madeleine. He studied pianoforte with Le Coupey, organ with Benoist, harmony with Bazin, and advanced composition with Adolphe Adam. In 1853, the latter exerted his influence to secure for his pupil a position as repetiteur at the Théâtre-Lyrique. He also became organist at St. Pierre de Chaillot and elsewhere before his appointment at St.-Jean-St.-François, where he was organist from 1862 to 1871. This appears to have been a traditional occupation with French composers. César Franck, Charles-Marie Widor, and Camille Saint-Saëns were all organists in Paris churches.

Very early in his career, Delibes began to write for the theatre, modestly at first, operettas and opéras-bouffes, which have been forgotten. His first effort appears to have been a piece in one act, Deux sous de charbon, produced at the Folies-Nouvelles in 1855. He wrote other operettas for the Kursaal d'Ems, the Bouffes-Parisiens, the Variétés, and the Athénée: Les deux vieilles gardes (1856); l'Omelette a la Follembûche (1859); Le serpent à plumes (1864); l'Ecossais de Chatou (1869); etc. Two of his one-act light operas, Monsieur Griffard (1857) and Le jardinier et son seigneur (1863), were written for and produced at the Théâtre-

# Léo Delibes

Lyrique. He also composed several choruses and a mass. In 1863, he was engaged as repetiteur at the Opéra, and, in 1865, second chorus-master, under Victor Massé. In 1865, his cantata, Alger, was performed.

Having been commissioned to compose a ballet, La Source (performed for the first time, November 12, 1866), in collaboration with Minkus, the Polish musician, his share of the score [1] proved so melodious and so much more distinguished and original than that of his confrère, that Minkus found himself completely eclipsed. Delibes was next asked to write an interpolation, Le pas des fleurs, for a revival of Adolphe Adam's ballet, Le corsaire, on October 21, 1867. His masterpiece, Coppélia, was produced May 25, 1870. His principal songs were published in 1872, the year of his marriage to a daughter of Mme. Denain, an actress of the Comédie Française. These include the celebrated Les filles de Cadix and Bonjour Suzon (on poems by Alfred de Musset), Avril (Rémy Belleau), and Myrto (Armand Silvestre). Le roi l'a dit was produced at the Opéra-Comique, May 24, 1873, and Sylvia, at the Opéra, June 14, 1876. La mort d'Orphée, a "grand scena," was performed at the Trocadéro concerts in 1878; Jean de Nivelle, at the Opéra-Comique, March 8, 1880, and Lakmé, at the Opéra-Comique, April 14, 1883. He wrote incidental music for a revival of Le roi s'amuse at the Comédie Française, November 22, 1882, and a five-act opera, Kassya, on which Massenet put the finishing touches, including the composition of the recitatives, after the composer's death, was performed at the Opéra-

[1] The second and third scenes, in this ballet in four scenes, are the work of Delibes.

# Léo Delibes

Comique, March 21, 1893. For a time, under the name of Eloi Delbès, he contributed musical criticism to the Gaulois.

In 1877, Delibes was made a Chevalier of the Legion of Honour. In January 1881, he succeeded Henri Reber, recently deceased, as professor of advanced composition at the Conservatory. In December 1884, he was elected a member of the Institut, succeeding Victor Massé, and in 1889, he was promoted to the grade of officer of the Legion of Honour. He died at Paris, January 16, 1891, and a memoir by E. Guiraud was published in 1892.

## III

His operas, constructed according to a formula that was once fashionable, are a little tarnished. Lakmé, awakening bizarrely confused memories of Marie Van Zandt, Bessie Abott, Luisa Tetrazzini, and Maria Barrientos, retains some of its vitality and still remains in the repertory of the Paris Opéra-Comique. Occasionally, this lyric perversion of Le mariage de Loti is given elsewhere so that some florid soprano may warble The Bell-Song. Pauline L'Allemand was the first New York Lakmé; Adelina Patti, the second. The score has the monotony and the clotting languor of the East. After the first act, all souls who are sensitive to suggestion are likely to fall asleep. Le roi l'a dit is interesting in its historical aspects; I have already quoted M. Vuillermoz in this regard. I heard Jean de Nivelle at the Gaieté-Lyrique at Paris fourteen or fifteen years ago when Arlette was sung by Nicot-Bilbaut-Vauchelet, the daughter of the soprano who created this florid rôle in 1880.

[209]

# Léo Delibes

This Louis XI lyric drama is Delibes's contribution to Tannhäuserism. Russia, Germany, France, all suffered from this quaint disease.

Saint-Saëns once remarked with contemptuous bitterness: "French criticism has not reproached Delibes for not being a melodist; he has made some operettas." The gift of melody, however, is rare and it is a gift the gods bestowed on Delibes to the partial exclusion of Saint-Saëns. It is not in his operas that this gift may be studied most advantageously, although neither The Bell-Song nor the Barcarolle in Lakmé is to be scoffed at. The best pages in the score, however, are those devoted to the ballet, the exotic Terâna, the Rektah, and the Persian dance, and it is in his music for the ballet generally that Delibes excelled and in which, as has been intimated already, he made certain innovations. Ballet music, heretofore, had been subservient to the dancers, and it was believed, it would seem (we may take Giselle for a typical example), that banality was essential to its success. Delibes's ballet music is piquant and picturesque, nervous and brilliant, shot with colour and curious instrumental effects, subtle in rhythm; above all, his melody has a highly distinguished line and the texture is symphonic.

Sylvia, ou la nymphe de Diane, created by Rita Sangalli (who ten years later became the Baronne de St.-Pierre) at the Paris Opéra, June 14, 1876, is an evocation today (it has recently been revived) of a period; it is Second Empire classicism, if you like, but the music remains as pimpant, as exhiliratingly fresh as ever. A happy fragrance, a delightfully artificial, if somewhat heartless, charm hovers over this score. Delibes, aware of his limitations, or governed purely by his taste, deliberately excluded the barbaric and the savage from his work.

## Léo Delibes

Les chasseresses, the Valse lente, the Cortège de Bacchus, all retain their peculiar seductions, and the pizzicati divertissement of the slave has achieved a world-fame.

Coppélia, ou la fille aux yeux d'émail, is assuredly his masterpiece. From the Prélude and the Valse lente, to which the adorable Swanilda floats across the scene almost as soon as the curtains part, through the Csárdás, the Mazurka, on to the end of the work, it is a model of concise and witty music, spirited and delicate melody. There are, to be sure, sentimental passages, but on the whole Delibes is less sentimental than Gounod. His tunes usually move at a brisk pace. They have all the lustre of a polka bý Offenbach, and something more in the way of glamour. Perusing this old score, I dream again of the languorous delights of the ballet, the *real* ballet and, for the moment, I am no modern. It has even occurred to me to wonder if any composer gifted with the power to create melody has ever found it necessary to try to create anything else.

*May 9, 1922.*

## Sir Arthur Sullivan

In her preface to the new edition of the most enchanting of her books, Eighteenth Century Studies, Vernon Lee points out the fact that comparatively little "available immortality" (thrice wondrous phrase!) is reserved for the musician. Museums preserve and cherish the work of painter and sculptor; libraries house poet and prose artist, not alone the work of the masters, but also that of the inferior men, the forerunners and imitators of the geniuses, as well. The case of the musician, whose work remains incomplete until it is interpreted, is exceptional. However limited the space, room can always be made for more objects, but time is inexorably circumscribed and music occupies time rather than space. So, in our concert halls, the great names gradually crowd out the feebler ones. Moments can no longer be spared for Piccinni, Sacchini, and Hasse. Of the glories of eighteenth century music, Bach, Gluck, Handel, Haydn, and Mozart alone have survived. In the mid-nineteenth century Bellini, Donizetti, Rossini, and Meyerbeer held the stage almost exclusively at the old Academy of Music. In the early twentieth century three men, Wagner, Verdi, and Puccini, had acquired a virtual monopoly of the repertory of our singing theatres, until, temporarily, the war drove Wagner out and the names of his heroes became the names of German railroads and trenches in France. Much that is lovely in music must therefore inevitably be removed from the knowledge of

# Sir Arthur Sullivan

auditors, unless the revival of such a work as Monteverdi's Orfeo or Pergolesi's La Serva Padrona may help to teach a careless public that many such carved chalices of pure gold lie buried in seventeenth and eighteenth century treasure houses.

An extremely meagre portion of this available immortality has been allotted to English composers. Even in England, the Italian or the German has consistently held the centre of the stage or the concert platform. Handel lived in London for many years, and Beethoven, Haydn, Weber, and Mendelssohn all wrote works for the English public. The greater genius of these and other foreign musicians has driven British music off the boards. Even a superior figure like Purcell only exists in the musical histories or in the minds of antiquarian enthusiasts, while Balfe and Wallace, once the favourites of the London playhouses, have been sent on tour in the provinces or entrusted to the mercies of amateurs or church choirs. As for the moderns, Delius, Holbrooke, Bantock, Scott, and Ireland have found the competition of Richard Strauss, Igor Stravinsky, Rimsky-Korsakoff, Ravel, Puccini, and Debussy too strong to combat effectively. Even Elgar, who seemed for a time to be conquering new worlds with his symphonies and oratorios, is fast falling into deserved disrepute. Ten years from now, probably not one of these men will be able to command more than sporadic particles of time in the concert room. England,[1] however, boasts one composer who, I think, will still be heard when all of us, young and old alike, are dead. That composer is Sir Arthur Sullivan.

No adequate life of this musical genius has yet ap-

[1] Sullivan was born in Ireland and has been called a Jew.

peared. There have been many biographers, but not one of them discusses Sullivan's music with any discernment or authority, not one of them writes with a trace of literary charm. The longest and most recent,[2] Gilbert, Sullivan, and D'Oyly Carte, by François Cellier and Cunningham Bridgeman (Sir Isaac Pitman and Sons; London; 1914), scarcely refers to the music at all. Cellier died while the work was in progress and Bridgeman, who completed it, frankly admits that he knows nothing whatever about the tonal art. It is also obvious that he knows nothing about the art of writing. Of the others, B. W. Findon's Sir Arthur Sullivan and His Operas (Sisley's Ltd.; London; 1908) is the best, slight as it is. C. Willeby's volume in the Masters of Music Series (London; 1893) is practically worthless, and the same may be said for H. Saxe Wyndham's Arthur Sullivan (George Bell and Sons; London; 1903). Arthur Lawrence's Sir Arthur Sullivan (Bowdon; London; 1899) is padded to a decent length, but it does not contain two illuminating or suggestive phrases. The bibliography is useful, however. H. Augustine Simcoe's Sullivan versus Critic (Simpkin, Marshall, Hamilton, Kent and Co., Ltd.; London; 1906) is a compilation of criticism, adverse and favourable, of the man's work, but as the emphasis is laid on Ivanhoe and The Light of the World, the book falls under the classification of literary curiosities. Louis Engel's paper in From Handel to Halle is entirely negligible and the article in Grove's Dictionary, written by Sir George himself, while sufficiently appreciative, is little more than a catalogue.

Percy Fitzgerald's The Savoy Opera (Chatto and

[2] In 1923, W. S. Gilbert: His Life and Letters, by Sidney Dark and Rowland Grey, was published by Methuen.

## Sir Arthur Sullivan

Windus; 1894) is better. Unfortunately, Mr. Fitzgerald was not a musician and he therefore stresses Gilbert's contribution to the collaboration. However, he gives a better account of the method by which the men worked together than is to be found elsewhere and his infrequent musical judgments are sufficiently acute. He is not taken in, for instance, by Sullivan's oratorios. "Unfortunately for the development of his talent," writes Mr. Fitzgerald, "he was attracted by the forms of oratorio, usually written for some great festival, whose rather stilted academical style often checks all airiness and spontaneousness." Of The Martyr of Antioch, Ivanhoe, and The Golden Legend he writes with rare perspicacity: "These are excellent, scholarly works, but they seem to lack inspiration, and are academical in style and treatment. It may be laid down that every trained musician can write his cantata or oratorio, just as every littérateur can write his novel or biography. . . . Without inspiration these things are mere exercises. Ivanhoe was certainly a ponderous work, more like a vast symphony protracted through several acts than an opera."

The other biographers of Sullivan tend for the most part to exaggerate the importance of his minor work. It would perhaps be too much to say that the composer of Onward, Christian Soldiers would be forgotten, had that been his only contribution to musical literature, but to say, as some have said, that the Sullivan of the hymns, the Sullivan of the string quartet, the Sullivan of The Golden Legend and The Light of the World, the Sullivan of the In Memoriam overture, the Sullivan of the score for The Tempest, the Sullivan of the Irish Symphony, the Sullivan of the ballet, The Enchanted Isle, the Sullivan

[215]

of the concerto for cello, the Sullivan of the Te Deum, or the Sullivan of Ivanhoe is a greater Sullivan than the Sullivan of the Savoy operas, is equivalent to saying that the Wagner of the C major symphony is a greater Wagner than the Wagner of Tristan und Isolde. Some of this music is excellent, but none of it is important enough to carry its composer over the treacherous sandbars of a decade in the memory of man. A good deal of it is simply well-made academic music in the standard forms.

The great Sir Arthur Sullivan then, the lasting composer, was the creator of the series commonly known as the Savoy operas, although several of them were not in the first instance produced at the Savoy,[3] more particularly the collaborator of Gilbert. For, curiously enough, Sullivan failed, comparatively speaking (occasionally outright), even here, in his own field, when some one other than Gilbert supplied him the book on which to work. Box and Cox, The Beauty Stone, The Chieftain, The Emerald Isle, and Haddon Hall are all but forgotten. They will soon pass into the limbo of things, become outcasts in the universe of art. No immortality is available for them. It is but just to state that W. S. Gilbert was quite as much lost without his friend. The plays which he wrote alone, the books he offered to other composers, are no longer the source of much more than a little innocent merriment. To be frank, Gilbert's satire, his sense of parody, burlesque, and caricature, palls unless diluted, stimulated, pointed, and refined by

---

[3] The Pirates of Penzance, for instance, was produced at the Fifth Avenue Theatre in New York, December 31, 1879. A single performance, for purposes of copyright, was given at Paignton, England, on the previous afternoon, and the London production was made at the Opera Comique, April 3, 1880. At Paignton, Richard Mansfield was the Major General.

the melody of Sullivan. Nowhere else, except perhaps in the case of the Goncourts, can we find an example of artists so well fitted to work together. Trial by Jury, Pinafore, The Pirates of Penzance, Patience, Iolanthe, The Mikado, The Yeomen of the Guard, and The Gondoliers, probably even The Sorcerer, The Princess Ida, and Ruddigore,[4] operas with which this generation is strangely unfamiliar, will brave the indifference of time as steadfastly as any contemporary French or Italian works. Indeed, aside from The Barber of Seville, Die Meistersinger, and Der Rosenkavalier, can one point to other comic operas composed during the nineteenth century as good as these?

Sullivan has been called the English Auber and again, the English Offenbach. Neither epithet is just, neither is apposite. Auber wrote light music and insofar as that matters in a question of comparison Sullivan may be called Auberian; Offenbach wrote burlesques and insofar as that matters in a question of comparison Sullivan may be called Offenbachian. Sullivan once remarked to Findon: "This epithet, 'the English Offenbach,' was first given me in a burst of ill-natured spleen by G. A. Macfarren, and he used it in his article on Music in the Encyclopedia Britannica. It was never used as a compliment." Dr. Hanslick must have heard the epithet

---

[4] Ruddigore is the only one of the series never revived at the Savoy. It has commonly been regarded as a failure, but the work was performed 288 times during the original run. It contains some of Sullivan's most enchanting music, but the enormous cost of mounting and dressing this opera was out of ratio to the drawing power in a small theatre. Originally, £6,000 was spent on the dresses and properties, £2,000 on the scenery. Ruddigore was performed in New York in 1920 during the Gilbert and Sullivan seasons inaugurated by the Society of American Singers at the Park Theatre, and it has recently been revived in London, not, however, at the Savoy.

somewhere because he refers to it in his review of The
Mikado: "Sullivan has been reproached with imitating
Offenbach. It shows at any rate more sense to learn
from Offenbach than to abuse him. Offenbach's exuberant richness of melody and sparkling wit certainly
cannot be acquired; but what might and should be
learned from him are the terse forms, the well-chosen
rhythms, the adaptability to the voice, the judiciously
arranged orchestra. In all these things Sullivan has
taken the composer of Fortunio as his pattern, without
giving up his own independence. That the Englishman
has not attained the sparkling liveliness and piquant
charm of the Frenchman (sic) is easily to be understood;
but on the other hand Sullivan shows himself in concerted numbers to be the more thoroughly cultivated
musician." It seems fairly obvious now that Sullivan
never attains the champagne-like bubbling, the boulevard
dash, of Orphée aux enfers; nor is there to be found in
his music any parallel to the poignant and touching
emotion of the last act of Les contes d'Hoffmann. On
the other hand, Sullivan is seldom, if ever, vulgar, while
page after page of Offenbach is sheer flummery. The
composer of Patience writes with delicacy, grace, and
refinement, qualities which, except occasionally, are not
to be met with in the music of the composer of La Grande
Duchesse. Sullivan's style, indeed, may be regarded as
classic rather than romantic. It might be stated, justifiably, that the musical idioms of the two are as distinct
as those of Wagner and Verdi. Offenbach, albeit a German Jew, gave a new impetus to the lighter form of
French music, while Sullivan's music breathed as truly
insular an air as that of William Shakespeare. One

thing is certain, that Sullivan's operas are much more
alive today than those of Auber and Offenbach.

Comparing Sullivan with his Viennese contemporaries,
Hanslick is on surer ground and he makes an excellent
point: "Sir Arthur Sullivan's music . . . adapts itself to the words in an unconstrained and natural manner; it is always melodious, lively, and uniform in style,
and upon this point we lay great stress. From year to
year we have had occasion to lament over the false exaggeration and deterioration of operetta which, mistaking
its very being and limits, makes a show of tragic pathos,
with instrumentation à la Wagner, and with grand tenor
and prima donna parts. . . . Any one who can call to
mind the Vienna operettas of the last ten or fifteen years
will confess that charming details are almost always
spoiled by a complete absence of style. Ballads with the
popular harp accompaniment take turns with grandiose
noisy finales; love duets between Hans and Grethe end
in loud unison à la Verdi on the high B flat or C; merry
scenes at a fair rival the conspiracy in The Huguenots.
Most of the composers who write for our smaller
theatres appear to wish above anything to show that they
know how to write grand opera, while in reality they only
show that they do not know how to write operetta. Al-
luding to a remark of Berlioz, I may compare them to
troubadours, who wander through the land with trom-
bones on their backs instead of guitars.[5] . . . The songs

[5] As true today as it was in the time of Dr. Hanslick. The orchestration and scoring for the voices in Dr. Leo Fall's Die geschiedene
Frau, produced in English as The Girl in the Train, the plot of which
is as boisterous and gay as that of any book that Offenbach set, are
frequently as heavy as those of a Wagnerian music drama. Lehár,
perhaps misled by semi-serious subjects, made the same mistake in

in The Mikado are so intelligible, and kept within such modest limits, that .powerful lungs and technical perfection are almost as little needed for them as for the music of Adam, Hiller, Monsigny, and Grétry. The orchestra is subservient to the singing, without failing to lend a brighter colouring or sharper characterization in the right places."

It may safely be stated that the ballad is the form most natural to the English composer. Without going into a discussion of the work of such a man as Molloy, it is sufficient to recall that The Beggar's Opera (a pastiche, to be sure) and the works of Balfe and Wallace, whose operas pleased poet and peasant in the Victorian era, are based on the ballad. The ballad, assuredly, is an outstanding feature of Sullivan's operettas. Such numbers as The nightingale's song and A maiden fair to see in Pinafore, or Frederic's air, Oh, is there not one maiden breast, in The Pirates, are capital examples. Sometimes Sullivan transcends the form, as in Jack Point's I have a song to sing, O! in The Yeomen of the Guard, Sullivan's favourite among his own works. Here Gilbert's exceedingly ingenious metrical scheme is handled with extraordinary effect. The tragic recapitulation of this ballad in the final scene of the opera, in which the mood is varied by a change in the situation of the characters, is as fine an example of a device of this kind as is to be found anywhere in lyric drama. Yet it must be admitted that the song is purely English in style. Recall Take a pair of sparkling eyes, in The Gondoliers.

Ziguenerliebe and Eva. Even Oskar Straus fell in Ein Walzertraum. It is perfectly clear to all of us today (as it was to Dr. Hanslick at the time the work was originally produced) that the music of Die Fledermaus goes beyond all the reasonable bounds of operetta.

# Sir Arthur Sullivan

This air, redolent of lanes and lassies, hawthorns, briars, and holly branches, is as English as pounds, shillings, and pence, and yet (perhaps I should say therefore) it is equal to any tenor air in Italian opera. I myself prefer it to Spirto gentil, La donna è mobile, Una furtiva lagrima, yes, reader, even to Dalla sua pace. There are many examples of the old English glee form also to be noted. Of these, probably the best is A British tar is a soaring soul in Pinafore. One of the truest indications of the English spirit in the music of Sullivan is the almost complete neglect (a neglect only emphasized by the few examples such as Mabel's air, Stay, wand'ring one, in The Pirates and Buttercup's song in Pinafore) of ¾ time in his work, for ¾ time is almost as foreign to the real feeling of England as anything else is to the real feeling of Vienna. Pinafore, therefore, is mostly written in common time, just as Der Rosenkavalier is mostly written in waltz rhythms.

It does not seem necessary to insist further on this point of Sullivan's insularity. Proofs of it are to be encountered on every page of his scores. It is as silly, therefore, to compare his music in point of style with that of Offenbach or Auber as it would be to institute a similar comparison between the plays of Shakespeare and Molière. His early German training, which might have left its mark upon his manner, served only, as best it might, to make of him a thorough musician. In no way is this musicianship more evident than in .his treatment of recitative. As these parlando passages almost invariably accompany burlesque dialogue in the operettas, he goes to the Italians for his model. If you compare the style of Buttercup's entrance, Hail, men-o'-wars-men, with the declamation of Donizetti or the early

Verdi, you will discover very little essential difference. Once, at least, Sullivan used his vast talent for this sort of joke to effect in a situation which another composer would doubtless have set in a quite different manner: I refer to Bunthorne's soliloquy.

For the most enduring proofs of Sullivan's inspiration and musicianship, his unflagging vitality, and his unfailing mastery of his material, it is perhaps wisest to inspect his concerted numbers, of which, I fancy, the quartet in The Gondoliers, In a contemplative fashion, is the most justly celebrated example. This quartet, indeed, is a masterpiece of technical achievement. Beginning with a measured movement, the music works up to a polyphonic climax unparalleled in light opera.[6] Indeed, you will look far to find its rival in serious opera, and yet never for a moment does it suggest anything pretentious. Therein lies its charm. The brilliant duet of Frederic and Mabel in the first act of The Pirates, in which the lovers sing in ¾ time while the chorus chatters in ⅔ time is another case in point. Remember also the delightful treatment of the principals with the chorus in the finale, This very night, of the first act of Pinafore. These musical feats are not accomplished, as so many dull musicians would accomplish them, at the expense of clearness and amusement. Sullivan possessed an unerring sense of the fitness of things and when he wrote music of a complicated character it was always suitable to its situation in the score. He never made mistakes. These

---

[6] This quartet really suggests work of the great madrigal period in England, although, of course, madrigals were sung unaccompanied. William Byrd, John Dowland, or Thomas Greaves might have signed this music with profit to their reputations. There are other charming examples derived from the madrigal form in Sullivan's work, notably Brightly dawns our wedding day, in the Mikado.

numbers are not the least popular in the operas in which they occur. On the contrary, they are always rede-manded vociferously.

His capacity for setting verses of divers sorts appears to be have been endless. When Gilbert offered him a sentimental ditty, he bathed it in lovely melody, a quar-tet, the words of which were relatively unimportant, he treated in a retiary, polyphonic fashion, while he set a comic song in the extreme of simplicity, emphasizing the words and pointing the wit, but never allowing the music to usurp first place. This patter song music, heard with-out the text, means next to nothing, but the text without the music is about one-third as effective as the two in combination. Any of the Savoy operas contains one or two examples of this kind of song. The best, perhaps, are I am the monarch of the seas, in Pinafore, the Major General's song, in The Pirates, in which a scale is re-quired to do duty for a tune, and the celebrated dream of the Lord Chancellor, in Iolanthe, with its nervous, Freudian accompaniment. Edward's song, A policeman's lot is not a happy one, and the rollicking duet between Grosvenor and Bunthorne, also deserve special mention. In songs of this character, written in most instances for voices of less than an octave, in which it is impossible for the auditor to miss a word if the interpreter be cap-able of decent enunciation, so crystal is the composer's music, it was Sullivan's habit to utilize the orchestra for descriptive purposes. Note, for example, the eupeptic self-assurance, the rocking-horse jauntiness of the ac-companiment to The Duke of Plaza-Toro in The Gon-doliers. The Grand Inquisitor's air in the same work, No probable, possible shadow of doubt, no possible doubt whatever, is irresistible. Of course, the words are excruciatingly droll and the skill of the performer counts for a good deal, but the fresh and simple music is so artless in its emphatic rhythm that it seems to bear in its flow the meaning of the catch phrase with which the song concludes. The second air of the Inquisitor, There lived a King, is only less good. The legendary nature of the lyric sets Sullivan's muse to work in the old ballad form. Consequently, the melody is well-defined; there is, indeed, a bit of florid music for the interpreter to deliver. Sullivan has embedded three musical jokes in the instrumentation of this tune. On the word "toddy" the orchestra imitates a bagpipe; on the word "admiral" we hear a reminiscence of the hornpipe; while a scoriac scale illustrates the word "shoddy." This sort of thing has been done by every composer from Haydn, who imitated worms, to Strauss, who imitated peacocks. Musorgsky's music teems with such effects. By themselves, they perhaps mean nothing and are scarcely worth the doing, but in Sullivan's case, at least, where they serve to embellish his inevitably appropriate music, they more than justify their presence. Perhaps, indeed, they are useful in keeping the operettas alive, for just such details, which may pass unnoticed at first hearing, are immensely valuable in reviving an auditor's interest at the second. Examples of suggestive imitation are not rare in Sullivan's music, but the notation of three more will suffice. After the words, "and the tar who plows the water," in the trio in Pinafore, the orchestra imitates the creaking of nautical buckets; in the song, The magnet and the churn, in Patience, both churning and scissors grinding are simulated; while the introduction of the flageolet above the words, " the criminal cried," to convey the suggestion of Nanki-Poo's death in The Mikado, is a forerunner of a similar effect in Strauss's Till Eulenspiegel. As W. S. Rockstro once sapiently wrote, in reference to a Sullivan opera: "It overflows with witty passages—passages which would make the words sound witty were they ever so tame. The fun of very clever people is always the richest fun of all. Its refinement is a thousand times more telling than the coarser utterances of ordinary humour. Arthur Sullivan has made every one in London laugh; yet the predominant quality in his comic opera music is reverence for Art—conscientious observance of its laws in little things. It may sound absurd to say so, but no one who takes the trouble to examine his scores can deny the fact. . . . His treatment of the orchestra shows an intimate acquaintance with the nature of its instruments and a genius for their combination such as few contemporary masters have surpassed."

Sullivan's father was a bandmaster, and when Arthur was a lad of eight, so runs the legend, he inveigled the members of his father's band into permitting him to experiment with their instruments, with assistance and instruction in each case. At fourteen, therefore, he was capable of performing on most of them, an accomplishment which proved an immense advantage to him later in colouring his scores. His skilful use of the oboe and the bassoon is especially to be noted. Nevertheless, although his instrumentation is delightful, and frequently fantastic, it never obscures the voice of the singer or diverts the mind of the listener from the words. Sullivan never forgot that he was writing operetta. His method of work was interesting. He orchestrated a number only after he had attended several rehearsals; only, in fact, after the business of a scene had been finally set by the stage director. By that time he had penetrated to the depths

[225]

of its humour or sentiment and with unerring touch he
was able to give exactly the desired colouring to his
instrumentation.

The burden of this ballad, the plea of this paper, is not,
after all, in behalf of a hearing for Sullivan's music.
There never has been a time as far back as I can remember (I was born after the original production of
Pinafore) when these operettas were not being performed
somewhere.[7]  It is rather more grace and honour in their
presentation that I bespeak.  It would be delightful
if a theatre could be devoted to them, a theatre in
which, turn and turn about, each Savoy opera might
be presented, but as no one seems likely to dedicate
a playhouse to such a pleasant project I see no reason
why the Metropolitan Opera House should not offer
us at least two of them.  It will be urged at once that
the theatre is too large.  To which I reply that it is
certainly too large for L'Elisir d'Amore and The Secret
of Suzanne; still these operas, or others which require a
similarly small frame, are constantly included in the
repertory.  It may be alleged that spoken dialogue is
lost in this vast temple, but we have heard Der Freischütz,
Manon, The Bartered Bride, and Fidelio performed there
without great objection being raised on this score.
There are those who will shamelessly assert that the
music is too light for so serious a theatre; to which I may
respond that the music is no lighter than that of The

---

[7] It is an unfortunate fact that the overtures to the operettas do
not bear transplanting. They consist, for the most part, of potpourris
of the airs from the works which they preface, without musical
development or working out of the themes. Musically, therefore, they
are uninteresting and scarcely one of them would stand the test of
association with standard works on a symphonic program.

## Sir Arthur Sullivan

Daughter of the Regiment or La Bohème. It also happens to be better music. If comic songs are to be ostracized, what shall we say in defence of Beckmesser's serenade, Leporello's catalogue air, or Figaro's Largo al factotum? The ultimate form of disapproval would be based on the fear that it would be difficult, or impossible, to provide suitable casts for these operettas without engaging extra singers, but I should venture to cast any one of them from the Metropolitan roster.

With Pinafore or The Pirates, the obstacles are minimized. These works are travesties of a type of Italian opera with which both audiences and interpreters at the Metropolitan are entirely familiar. Such music as the duet in Pinafore, Refrain, audacious tar, or the duet in The Pirates, Stay, Fred'ric, stay, would arouse even an unpaid claque to applause. Any one who has heard Trovatore could not fail to appreciate The Pirates. It can further be urged in support of this work as a choice that there is very little spoken dialogue in the first act, and still less in the second. Indeed, I think there is less spoken dialogue in The Pirates than there is in Fidelio.

The Mikado holds the distinction of being the best lyric drama yet written to a Japanese subject. I make this statement categorically, bearing in mind not only The Geisha, but also certain operas by Puccini, Mascagni, and Messager. I make no boast of a talent for haruspicy, but I venture to predict that The Mikado will be sung two centuries after Iris, Madama Butterfly, and Madame Chrysanthème are forgotten. Furthermore, The Mikado is probably the best opera ever written to an English book. No possible alternative occurs to me save the other operas of Sullivan himself, and Oberon.

Iolanthe reminds one of Oberon, because it is a fairy

[227]

opera, and after Oberon, the best. It is infinitely more significant than Crispino e la Comare or Cendrillon, both of which have been produced under high auspices. At the beginning of the overture, Sullivan pays a graceful tribute to Weber with a horn motif. Doubtless, the score throughout owes a good deal both to Weber and the Mendelssohn of A Midsummer Night's Dream, and yet this delicious fairy music has a delicate shimmer all its own. The opening chorus is an inspiration of genius. The pastoral interludes in this opera are charming, the parliamentary satire as happy as when the work was first produced. I should say that Sullivan lavished more loving care on the orchestration of Iolanthe than he did on any other of his operettas.

The music of Patience is, in some respects, the loveliest Sullivan ever penned, but its performance preconizes difficulties quite beyond the powers of a "grand opera" company. I should fancy that either The Yeomen of the Guard or The Gondoliers would prove a more suitable choice for the Metropolitan. The Yeomen is more serious in intention than the others in the series; the end, indeed, leaves a frankly melancholy impression, while the delightful orchestration of The Gondoliers, with its ingenious treatment of the drums, the oboe, and the bassoon, its Spanish and Italian tunes, its opulent musical colour, and its airs for soprano and tenor, make it the most brilliant. There is even a number for the ballet. Perhaps a better opportunity is offered by The Gondoliers to study Sullivan's style and method than is to be found elsewhere. From the opening chorus, Roses white and roses red, to the final repetition of the Cachucha, it is a gay masterpiece. Louis Engel speaks with amazement of the thirty musical numbers in the score: "I very well

remember that Donizetti once told me that he never contemplated writing more than thirteen pieces for any of his
grand operas. But then, he lived in less exacting times,
when the public was not as blasé as they are today and
they were satisfied with finding two or three melodies
easily sticking to their memory." . . . Certainly nothing
better than this work can be discovered in the field of
operetta. For comparison, one must turn to the musical
comedies of the eighteenth century Italians or to the
best opéras-comiques of the French. . . . It is not entirely clear why the directors of our Opera always turn to
the continental stage for the lighter pieces in their
repertory, while these products of English genius, the
highest musical genius that England has produced, are
forbidden entrance.

*January 5, 1919.*

## Isaac Albéniz

### I

Since the day in the eleventh century when, so the
legend has it, Guido d'Arezzo improved the monochord,
through the lifetime of the virginal, the clavicytherium,
the harpsichord, the clavichord, and the spinet, the invention of the pianoforte by Cristofori, to that more modern
period of Bechstein, Broadwood, Pleyel, Steinway, Chick-
ering, and Knabe, composers for these stringed instruments of the same family have sought inspiration from
the folk-dance. Pavans and galliards abound in the
music of the old English virginalists. Henry Purcell
often chose such titles as chaconne, courante, jig, menuet,
rigadoon, march, and hornpipe. Couperin's fancifully
named pieces, among which I might mention La prude,
La séduisante, and Le bavolet flottant, are actually
dances; some of them he has frankly labelled gavotte,
gigue, and menuet. Moreover, the sonata form is based
on suites of old dance tunes, a fact to which the titles of
certain movements in the sonatas of Haydn, Mozart, and
Beethoven, scherzo, menuet, and rondo, bear witness.
Schubert wrote polonaises and rondos, and many of
Schumann's melodies move gracefully to dance rhythms.
Chopin's profession of faith was made to the Muse
Terpsichore. He penned the proudest polonaises, the
most majestic of mazurkas, waltzes which Schumann
refused to play for dancers unless half the women were

# Isaac Albéniz

countesses. What are the Liszt Rhapsodies but gipsy dances, arrangements of the Csárdás form in which the dancer, by signalling the violinist-leader of the orchestra, moves faster or more slowly at will?

It is not therefore an innovation for the modern Spanish composers to seek inspiration from the dance, but there is perhaps a more logical reason for this procedure in their case than in that of the composers I have cited, for the dance is assuredly the national musical form of Spain, where singing, most frequently, serves to accompany waving arms and tapping feet. The founder [1] of this modern school of Spanish composers, at least insofar as the pianoforte is concerned, was Isaac Albéniz who, like Liszt and Rubinstein, made a name for himself as a virtuoso, and who left behind him, besides several hundred pieces for the piano, a number of operas and zarzuelas, and a good-sized pile of orchestral and chamber music. During his lifetime Albéniz was certainly not regarded as a composer of the first, or even second, rank, although it cannot be said that he lacked for appreciation of a kind, and even since his death no one has attempted a thorough classification of his work or an accurate appraisal of his special qualities.[2] It is begin-

---

[1] Of course, no one ever actually "founded" anything. What I mean to imply is that, to a certain extent, the Iberia of Albéniz is the modern Spanish composer's Bible, but it is well to remember that Iberia, which ultimately bloomed in France, grew from Spanish seed. To Felipe Pedrell, who died in 1922, Albéniz probably owed the most of his interest in nationalism.

[2] The musical dictionaries are not very fortunate in their references to Albéniz. In the latest edition of Grove a short, inadequate paragraph is allotted to him; the added notes in the appendix are inaccurate. The third edition of Baker's Dictionary, a work on a much smaller scale, gives him a little more space. Riemann, too, is more generous, but neither of these accounts is illuminating or sufficiently

# Isaac Albéniz

ning to be bruited about, however, that here is a fine example of the national composer, like Musorgsky or Chopin, and it is occasionally whispered, although as yet in secluded spots, that he has written a series of pieces which add rich clang-tints to the technique of the piano, and which for emotional content, nervous rhythm, and descriptive power may be set beside only the very great works composed for that instrument.

These pieces, collectively entitled Iberia, written shortly before Albéniz's death, after a course of study with Vincent d'Indy (it may be said of this composer that he was studying all his life; the list of his instructors reads like the faculty pages in the catalogue of a large university), will successfully preserve his name against the erasures of time. They are more and more becoming an essential part of the slowly growing repertory of concert pianists and there is reason to believe that they form a link in that chain which began with Bach, was carried

informing. More is to be found in Espasa's Spanish Encyclopedia, but the volume containing Albéniz's biography was published before his death.

Pedrell has a fine paper on Albéniz in his book, Músicos contemporáneos y otros tiempos. Luis Villalba Muñoz, another, in Últimos músicos españoles del siglo XIX; Madrid; 1914. G. Jean-Aubry's Isaac Albéniz, in the Musical Times (London; December 1, 1917) is interesting from a biographical point of view. F. Forster Buffen in the second series of his Musical Celebrities (Chapman and Hall; London; 1893) describes the virtuoso at the height of his London career. H. J. Storer's Isaac Albéniz, in the Musician (Boston; May 29, 1916) is not important. Hermann Klein writes of Albéniz's opera, Pepita Jiménez, in the Musical Times (London; March 1, 1918) and Ernest Newman published a paper on the opera Merlin, in the New Witness (London; September 20, 1917). The most satisfactory attempt yet made to sum up the work of Albéniz is Joseph de Marliave's essay in his book, Etudes musicales (Paris; 1917). It will readily be apparent that these articles lie out of the reach of the general reader.

# Isaac Albéniz

on through Mozart, Beethoven, Weber, Schumann, Chopin, Liszt, and Brahms, and which at the present day includes beyond question Debussy and Ravel. Iberia is not only the best piano music which has yet come out of Spain (other Spaniards have surpassed Albéniz in the composition of songs, orchestral pieces, operas, and zarzuelas), but also music which, I am inclined to believe, may be placed side by side with the best music written for the piano anywhere.

## II

The history of Albéniz's career has a picaresque flavour which is truly Spanish. Artist-Spaniards, it would appear, never remain at home, or if they do, they embark on wild and extravagant adventures. The life of Cervantes reads like a romance, and Cervantes, perhaps, was the typical Spanish artist. The novelist, Alarcón, was a soldier and man of the world. Blasco-Ibañez is a politician and revolutionist. It is said that he has been in jail thirty times. Some Spanish composers, like Victoria, have gone to Rome; others like de Falla and Usandizaga, have gone to Paris. Albéniz even travelled to America. He was born on May 29, 1860,[3] at Camprodón, province of Gerona, one of five children of Angel, a government official at Barcelona, and Dolores Albéniz. Soon after his birth events occurred which forced his father, on a very stormy night, to carry him, wrapped in a cloak, to a nurse capable of satisfying his enormous appetite, which did not diminish as he grew older.

---

[3] There is some dispute about this date. Grove's Dictionary, Baker's Dictionary, and H. J. Storer give it as 1861. I prefer to follow Espasa, Riemann, and G. Jean-Aubry.

# Isaac Albéniz

Neither of his parents was musical, but his eldest sister played the piano and young Isaac listened to her with such delight that she began to teach him to play while he was yet a baby. He gave his first recital at the Roméa Theatre in Barcelona at the age of four,[4] and performed so well that the audience suspected a trick, a player concealed behind the screen. Later, his mother took him and his sister to Paris, where they studied with Antoine-François Marmontel. The boy soon conceived the ambition of competing for a Conservatory prize and actually did so at the age of a little more than six. After he had finished playing, he rose from the bench, drew a hard rubber ball from his pocket, and hurled it with all his force at one of the large mirrors in the room, which was shattered to bits. This mad, juvenile prank, a foreshadowing of his later fantastic exuberance, his love of practical jokes, qualities which fight with rich emotion and deep sentiment for predominance in his music, locked the doors of the Conservatory to him for two years.

Returning to Spain in 1868, he began to study at the Conservatory of Madrid, whence his family had removed from Barcelona. It is probable that his teacher at this period was Ajero y Mendizábal. A year later he ran away from home, but, with the good fortune that usually attended his movements, he encountered the Alcalde of Escoriál who was so amused and impressed by the boy that he arranged that Isaac might give a concert at the Escoriál Casino. Albéniz's playing on this occasion made something of a sensation. Now the good Alcalde sent

[4] Buffen says that this appearance was made at the age of seven, after his return from Paris. He played Dussek's sonata, Les Adieux, and the last movement of Weber's Concertstück in F minor.

him home, but Isaac, with the proceeds of the concert in his purse, quit the train at Villalba and caught one going in the opposite direction. He gave concerts at Avila, Zamora, and Salamanca. Then a whim urged him to return to Madrid, and he would have followed this fancy had he not been set upon by bandits who robbed him of his savings. So, for two or three years, el niño Albéniz, as he was dubbed at this epoch, wandered over Spain, giving concerts. At length, he returned to his father's house, only, however, to run away again, this time to Cadiz. From this port he embarked as a stow-away on a vessel bound for Porto Rico. This must have been about the year 1872 when Isaac was eleven or twelve. Soon after the ship left the harbour he was discovered, but his playing and his very considerable amount of charm awarded him such popularity that he left the steamer with a sheaf of letters of introduction from influential passengers. In Porto Rico he gave more concerts, and then sailed for the United States, where he was often without funds and, indeed, suffered great privations. He met with some success, however, particularly in San Francisco.

During the winter of 1873 his father made a business trip through South and Central America. Visiting Havana, he was surprised to see the announcement of a concert to be given by his son. He attended this concert, a reconciliation was effected, and it was arranged that the boy should go to Germany for further instruction. So Isaac sailed for England, where, according to G. Jean-Aubry, he performed publicly in Liverpool and London; his English friends seem to believe that he made his first appearance there in 1889. Be that as it may, he went on to Leipsic where he studied piano with

# Isaac Albéniz

Salomon Jadassohn and composition with Carl Reinecke, paying for these lessons with money he had earned in America and Havana. When his funds were exhausted, he applied to his father for aid, which was refused, but returning to Madrid in 1876, he sought an audience with the King (Alfonso XII), who granted him a pension, sufficient for his immediate needs. Young Isaac now departed for Brussels where he studied harmony with Joseph Dupont, counterpoint and fugue with H. F. Kufferath, composition with François Gevaërt, and piano with Louis Brassin. Brassin, painter as well as musician, afterwards remarked that his brushes flew faster when he could get Albéniz to play for him. The financial results of a concert at Brussels enabled the boy to carry out a long cherished ambition, to study with Franz Liszt. He departed for Weimar about the year 1877. Biographers of Liszt seemingly have omitted to be impressed by this incident. There is no record of the two years Albéniz spent with Liszt, but it is known that the student followed the master first to Rome and later to Buda-Pesth.

Already the pupil of many professors, Albéniz was destined to experiment still further with pedagogues, a fact which may be open to misinterpretation. Pedrell asserts that as a composer he was largely an autodidact. "Artistic temperaments like his are not teachable," he continues. "They bear their fate within themselves. One can only guide them to prevent their wasting the flow of their inspiration. Dry, hard, cold rules only upset them." Pedrell admits that the lessons he gave Albéniz were in reality only "half-humorous colloquies between two friends. We talked about music, good and bad taste, etc. There was not a hint of pedagogy."

# Isaac Albéniz

It is highly probable that Albéniz was a fine pianist, with unique gifts and a personal style. "He was," avers Joseph de Marliave, "without show, virtuosoism, or pose, a dazzling pianist, a male, vigorous, magnificently passionate pianist, judicious in his interpretation, profoundly artistic and comprehending." Pedrell testifies: "I heard Rubinstein play for a roomful of friends, but I did not experience the cold shiver which went through me when Albéniz performed his own compositions for us with a fire which, as can be easily understood, drove the London public mad." The following is from one of the London criticisms: "He is one of the best pianists we have heard since Liszt. He reminds us of Rubinstein in his delicacy and Hans von Bülow in his vigour." He made, it appears, his greatest effect when he performed his own music.

In 1880, Albéniz undertook a series of tours as pianist through Cuba, Mexico, the Argentine Republic, and Spain. Then he managed a zarzuela company, an unsuccessful venture. To recoup his losses, he set out on another concert tour. In 1883, he married Rosina Jordana who bore him two daughters and a son. In 1884, he was proclaimed "court pianist." After his marriage he had hoped to settle down in Barcelona, but financial difficulties drove him forth on another concert tour. This persistent, crying need of money seems to have harassed Albéniz like the sting of a whip. During one period he actually carried a piece of music every day to a Madrid publisher who gave him enough silver in return to pay for the day's meals. It may be judged whether or not this enforced haste had any effect on the quality of his early work. Yet the inscription on the reverse side of the medal informs us that this was the

[237]

# *Isaac Albéniz*

very incentive needed to keep his music from becoming precious. Even at the end, he was able to breathe spontaneity and freshness into his Iberia, which offers no external evidence of calculation.

In 1889 he toured Germany, Holland, and Scotland, and at London was heard at Lady Morell Mackenzie's. He played on this occasion Schubert's Impromptu in E flat and several of his own compositions. His success was so considerable that he soon afterward announced a public concert at Albert Hall.[5] Although London now claimed him for several years, it did not adequately employ his genius. Owing to the enthusiasm which greeted the incidental music he had composed for a play by Armand Silvestre, he was commissioned to write the score of an operetta called The Magic Opal, performed at the Lyric Theatre, January 19, 1893 (Madrid, 1894), and later at the Prince of Wales'. It was during this same year that he decided to forsake the career of virtuoso for that of composer and appeared for the last time in a piano recital at Berlin. Following the production of The Magic Opal, he was engaged as composer in ordinary and conductor at the Prince of Wales' Theatre. It was probably at this time that his health became undermined, as he certainly overworked, often finding it necessary to compose at the theatre where copyists seized the sheets as they fell from his hands. He wrote and produced three more operas, Enrico Clifford (produced in Italian at the Liceo at Barcelona, May 8, 1895), Antonio de la Florida (Madrid, October 26, 1894; produced in Brussels as l'Ermitage fleurie, 1904), and Pepita Jiménez (Barcelona, January 5, 1896). Shortly before his death he was

[5] Buffen says it was Princes' Hall and he gives the date as June 12, 1889.

[238]

working on a King Arthur trilogy; the first part, Merlin, he completed and the piano and vocal score has been published. I am uncertain as to the state in which he left Lancelot and Ginevra. This work, so far as I can learn, has not yet been produced.

In the early nineties Albéniz returned to Paris to study and there he found the inspiration he needed to guide him through the mazes of his future masterpieces. Mr. Jean-Aubry describes the fertility of the ground: "It was but three years before, in Paris, that Franck had died, and more recently, Lalo, in 1892, while poor Chabrier, in 1894, stricken with illness and almost unconscious at the first performance of Gwendoline, was shortly afterwards also to die. But in 1893 Fauré had just completed La bonne chanson; the first eight songs of Duparc were shortly to be published; d'Indy was writing Fervaal; Chausson had finished his symphony and was working on the quartet and the Poème for violin and orchestra; Charpentier had recently published his Impressions d'Italie; Debussy had had his quartet performed and had begun Pelléas et Mélisande; and Bordes had founded in 1892 the Chanteurs de Saint-Gervais and, with Vincent d'Indy, laid the foundation for the Schola Cantorum. Is there in the history of French music a period richer in fulfilment and in promise?" From this time on, indeed, Albéniz walked among the great. His most important work for orchestra, Catalonia, was composed in 1898 and performed by the Societé Nationale at Paris, May 27, 1899. In January 1900, it was played by the Colonne Orchestra.

By this time, overwork, worry, the strain of a crowded career, had begun to tell on him. In 1900 his health broke down. Returning to Spain, where his condition improved, he began to work slowly on King Arthur, but found he could not overtax his failing strength. When he became worse, he was taken to Nice and it was there, ill himself, his wife also ill, his daughter at the point of death, that he wrote the book for pianoforte which bears the proud title Iberia, a book of memories of his beloved Spain. He lived to complete this work and, indeed, almost finished two more pieces, but he never regained his health and died at Cambo, on the Franco-Spanish border, May 25, 1909.

G. Jean-Aubry, who knew the man, paints his portrait for us: "He who met Albéniz, were it but once, would remember him to his dying day. At first his effusiveness could surprise, yes even displease, but soon one felt that a living fire inspired all his gestures, and that the great soul of the man dominated his outward frame; and to astonishment would succeed an affection which nothing could alter. I do not think it possible for any other personality to show such singular harmony between head and heart. His eager intelligence never outran his feverish love of life and things. On each one of the few—far too few—occasions I saw him he revealed to me some phase of personality that endeared him to me. He was one of the first to give me an estimate of the young Spanish school, and in what glowing terms he spoke of the love he bore the musicians of France.

"The kindness and the generosity of the man were unsurpassable; I could give a thousand proofs. He was sensitive without wishing it to appear, and the goodness of his heart was a thing of much charm. He was unstinting in his praise of others; his talk was always of friendship, affection, or joy. I never saw him otherwise. He steeped himself in music as the source of all strength, but nothing in life itself escaped him, and behind his joyous exterior vibrated a heart responsive to the least modulation of the soul. We find it in all his work. What man can take the place of this marvellous fount of vitality? As for myself, I have never known in another such joy at being happy. Even at the gates of death he retained this joyous boyishness. In Brussels I heard tales of a thousand pleasant adventures of which he was the soul; jests, planned with much skill, which the grave Gevaërt himself did not escape. He enjoyed himself with juvenile gaiety, and the victims of his jests only loved him the more for them. One would have forgiven him anything, for one was always his debtor.

"It was wonderful to see Albéniz at the pianoforte, playing his own pieces in the last years of his life. The virtuoso of former years had lost his cunning, his fingers were not equal to the difficulties, and we were given the spectacle of Albéniz singing, stamping with his foot, talking, making up with looks and laughter the notes his fingers could not play. Dear Albéniz! what performances of Iberia will ever have for us the charm of these, when all your poet's soul passed into those chords, that singing, that laughter!"

### III

As a composer Albéniz was exceedingly prolific.[6] No complete, or semi-complete, catalogue of his music has yet been compiled. It may be stated, however, with comparative safety, that he wrote altogether between five

[6] He was, by the way, an excellent improviser, and it is said that Liszt derived an especial enjoyment from his impromptu performances at the piano.

and six hundred pieces; perhaps, two hundred of these are temporarily lost. They were published everywhere, Spain, Germany (Breitkopf and Härtel), England, France, even America. Probably the greater number were issued by the Casa Dotésio at Barcelona and Diaz at San Sebastián.

It has become the fashion for musical dictionaries, casual essayists, and even concert pianists, to speak slightingly of his youthful work, but it is possible that this superficial conviction may be reversed. Jean-Aubry protests: "I do not like the opinion of those who set too little store by this early output in order to esteem only the later. In the middle of the music in his first manner will appear suddenly in many places an unexpected intonation in the turning of a facile phrase. One is conscious not so much of hasty workmanship as of too great a facility; but in all that he produced, what joy of life, and still more, what voluptuous beauty!" Marliave, for whom the composer during his last days at Nice played as many of these early pieces as he could recall, found some of them very beautiful. "Everything is interesting," he writes. "These are impressions hastily sketched on paper, short sketches produced instinctively, assuredly more valuable as invention than as finished work, but which denote a marvellous facility, and at the same time a most subtle and most musical sentiment." Ernest Newman's dictum is, "Most of his minor piano pieces, I should think, were the potboilers of a man who, even when he was writing a potboiler, could not forget that he was an artist."

Nature aroused artistic sensations in Albéniz. Spain and its landscapes were an inexhaustible source of inspiration to him. More than half of his pieces bear the name of some village or province, melodies composed from day to day, each dedicated to the town of its birth. Often, it is true, the insufficience, even the absence, of art makes itself felt. The sentiment of these numbers, too, is frankly popular, but the themes are personal to the composer. Nevertheless, occasionally these tunes are so imbued with the spirit of a region that they have vied in favour with the folksongs of the place. Spaniards, as a matter of fact, usually prefer this early music to the Iberia which, they assert, is more French than Spanish. Ernest Newman, who scoffs at the theory of nationalism in music, brings forward Albéniz's operas as proof that he was not a nationalist composer, but these operas have never been successful on the stage. Assuredly, his piano music is nationalistic in the best sense, as the titles will plainly show was his intention, but he is indebted to some degree for his form to the modern Frenchmen and Russians.

The list of these early pieces is of formidable length. Perhaps the two most popular numbers are an Orientale and the Serenata española. Marliave describes the latter as possessing "marvellous local colour." Albéniz himself preferred his Seis pequeños valses de salón. The Tango in D is striking, and crosses some pretty stiles, despite its brevity. The Spanish Suite embraces impressions of Cuba, Granada, Seville, Cadiz, Asturia, Aragon, Castile, and Catalonia. Another suite of "characteristic pieces" includes Gavotte, Minuetto á Silvya, Barcarola, Plegaria, Conchita, Pilar, Zambra, Pavana, Polonesa, Mazurka, Staccato, and Torre Bermeja. There are at least five sonatas.[7] There is a book called Souvenirs de voyage which includes En el mar, Leyenda,

[7] Buffen says there are twelve.

# Isaac Albéniz

Alborada, En la Alhambra, Puerta de Tierra, Rumores de la Caleta, and En la playa. There are more dances, Jota Aragonesa, Bolero (Andalusia), Sevillanas, etc. There are more pictures of places, Córdoba, Burgos, Mallorca, etc. There is a Spanish Rhapsody for two pianos, and two concertos, one a Concerto fantástico. There is a Zambra granadina, in which Marliave asserts one can hear the "tuning of guitars under an oriental breeze." Marliave further announces that Véga (from the Alhambra Suite) belongs to Albéniz's transition period; it is connected with his past and yet it foreshadows his future. In this long, poetic nocturne, the composer evoked the spirit of the plain of Granada, lying tranquil under the high stars, sleeping to the murmur of brooks and to the soft sweep of the breeze over the gardens and groves of blooming orange trees.

The songs are not numerous, nor are they well known. I have neither seen nor heard any of them. Several of them were composed to French, English, and Catalan words. Francis Money-Coutts supplied the verses for a few; there is a book of Rimas by Bécquer, and at least one of the songs is by Pierre Loti.

All his ideas, Marliave informs us, were *thought* for the piano, a fact which explains the relative weakness of his music for orchestra, but the same general statement might be made of Chopin and Schumann. Nevertheless, one continues to hear the Chopin concertos and the Schumann symphonies. Albéniz himself was not ignorant of this fundamental trait. For the Spanish Rhapsody, mentioned above, he wrote only an accompaniment for second piano, although he had originally planned the work for piano and orchestra. The second piano part was orchestrated in 1911 by Enesco. Buffen mentions

# Isaac Albéniz

a symphony in A and Espasa lists under orchestral works, a Suite: Scherzo, Serenata morisca y capricho cubana. Marliave asserts that Catalonia is as good as Chabrier's España. This tone-poem has been performed in Paris and London, but although I have been pleading for a number of years for a New York performance, conductors remain deaf to its and my blandishments.[8] Chamber music assuredly was not Albéniz's forte; his only published effort in this direction is the Trio in F, for violin, cello, and piano. The composer could never bear to have this work even mentioned. His inspiration forsook him when he tampered with classical or academic forms. . . . I cannot find any enthusiasm expressed for his oratorio, El Cristo.

His operas, on the other hand, have their adherents, one no less a personage than the lively Ernest Newman. The Magic Opal and San Antonio de la Florida have as yet found no distinguished friends. Enrico Clifford, a conventional work, a melodramatic episode from the War of the Roses, sung and published in Italian, was, I believe, a complete failure. His last produced opera, Pepita Jiménez, was his first success on the lyric stage. Edmund Gosse says of Valera's novel, which furnishes the theme for this music drama: "This book still remains, after a quarter of a century, and after the large development of fiction in Spain, the principal, the typical Spanish novel of our day. . . . Pepita Jiménez is Spain itself in a microcosm—Spain with its fervour, its superficial passion, its mysticism, its graceful extravagance.

[8] Catalonia was performed for the first time in America by the Boston Symphony Orchestra, Pierre Monteux conducting, on October 10, 1919, in Boston, and by this same organization in New York, on December 6, 1919.

# Isaac Albéniz

The story may be summarized as that of a theological student, full of ancient Catholic fervour, training to be a missionary, delivered, all unarmed, to the wiles of a young, innocent, and beautiful woman." The conflict is not alone between religion and passion, for Don Luis's father is also a suitor for the young widow's hand, and father and son are therefore rivals. Hermann Klein, who heard the first performance, finds this opera delightful, bubbling over with charming music, which he admits, unfortunately is not particularly Spanish. Is not this the principal cause, perhaps, for the neglect of Albéniz's operas, that they lack provincial colour, the colour he lavished so prodigally on his piano music? Nevertheless, Pepita has been produced at Prague, Karlsruhe, Leipsic, Brussels, as well as at many Spanish cities.

Another excuse for the comparative failure of these operas is to be found in the librettos prepared by Francis B. Money-Coutts (later Lord Latymer). These (and I include the King Arthur) are wretched affairs, the equal, it would seem, of some of our American efforts in that line. It is not necessary to discuss this point at length; I simply offer in evidence a sample (I copied the following verses from the first pages that flipped open of Breitkopf and Härtel's piano score of Pepita):

> "All is ready!  All is ready!
> All is weariness!
> Waiting the steady stirring of cheeriness!
> Love with his madness
> Turns all to sadness!"

In September 1917, a performance of Nivian's Dance from Merlin, at a Queen's Hall Promenade Concert in London, moved Ernest Newman to the following out-

[246]

# Isaac Albéniz

burst: "The music is . . . no more 'Spanish,' no more a 'mirror of nationality' than if it had been written by an Englishman, a Frenchman, or a Choctaw; it is simply music, and very good music—the finest on the whole that Albéniz ever wrote. . . . I warmly recommend the score to any one on the look-out for something at once original, strong, and beautiful, and who can chuckle with me over the fact that the best opera on our sacrosanct British legend has been written by a Spaniard."

Marliave does not share Newman's enthusiasm for this work. He considers the King Arthur a mistake in judgment: "a Wagnerian libretto in situation, sentiment, and characters, the last thing to propose to his inspiration. The concentrated psychic force that such a work demanded was not in him; as a consequence he lost his own personality in that of the German colossus."

Albéniz seems to have been at work on this trilogy from 1897 to 1906. His other operas were crowded into a few years in the early nineties. He also wrote several zarzuelas, just how many it is difficult to determine. Espasa gives the names of three: Cuanto más viejo, Catalanes de Gracia, and El canto de salvación.

Whatever critical opinions may be professed regarding the ultimate worth of his operas, the fact remains that none of them has held the stage. The King Arthur trilogy has not even been produced. As a matter of fact, his operas, his early piano music (not, however, to be unappreciated), his songs, and his orchestral music would probably award him no very high place in the history of music. That he achieved that place before he died is due to Iberia.

Albéniz began Iberia in 1905. It is published in four books by the Edition mutuelle at Paris. The contents are: Book I, Evocation, El Puerto, Fête-Dieu à Séville; Book II, Rondeña, Almeria, Triana; Book III, El Albaicin, El Polo, Lavapies; Book IV, Malaga, Jerez, Eritaña. These pieces, without exception, are all masterpieces of pianoforte literature. More, they are the corner-stone, the Koran, of the modern Spanish school. They are the songs and dances, the sights and sounds, of the peninsula, translated with peculiar felicity into the language of the piano, a language which Albéniz has even successfully extended for his purposes. In rhythm, in emotion, in harmony, in themal content, and in their polyphonic complexity (which sounds simple when played, as all good music should), they are almost unique. They far transcend in importance all but a few other modern works for the piano. Indeed, they allot Albéniz a seat in blessed company, near Chopin and Schumann.

In The Soul of Spain, Havelock Ellis observes, "It has been said that a Spaniard resembles the child of a European father by an Abyssinian mother." There is certainly a wild, African strain in Albéniz's European music. Marliave detects therein the two essences of Iberian music, one, vigorous, hardy, passionate, the jota; the other dreamy, sensual, languid, the malagueña. "You cannot walk through a little town in the south of Spain without hearing a strange sound, between crying and chanting, which wanders out to you from behind barred windows and from among the tinkling bells of the mules," writes Arthur Symons in Cities and Sea-Coasts and Islands. "The Malagueña, they call this kind of singing; but it has no more to do with Malaga than the mosque at Cordova has to do with the soil on which it stands. It is as Eastern as the music of tom-toms and gongs, and, like Eastern music, it is music

## Isaac Albéniz

before rhythm, music which comes down to us untouched by the invention of the modern scale, from an antiquity out of which plain-chant is a first step towards modern harmony. And this Moorish music is, like Moorish architecture, an arabesque. It avoids definite form just as the lines in stone avoid definite form, it has the same endlessness, motion without beginning or end, turning upon itself in a kind of infinitely varied monotony. The fioriture of the voice are like those coils which often spring from a central point of ornament, to twist outward, as in a particular piece of very delicate work in the first mihrab of the mosque at Cordova. . . . The passion of this music is like no other passion; fierce, immoderate, sustained, it is like the crying of a wild beast in suffering, and it thrills one precisely because it seems to be so far from humanity, so inexplicable, so deeply rooted in the animal of which we are but one species.

The Evocation, as the name implies, weaves the mood of Iberia; "bright burning daylight beating down upon the rows of white houses, a blaze of heat over it all; then in the evening the fragrance of orange blooms arises from the gardens and the thrum of merriment is heard in the streets through long and sleepless nights"; [9] citron trees, myrtle hedges, rows of acacias, tamarisks and pomegranates; véga and sierra; we peep through the iron bars of a gate into a patio; we inhale the aroma of jasmine blown across to us through the heavy night air; a serenade is heard in the distance, the faint tinkle of guitars; this is the Spanish Invitation to the Dance! . . . Triana: the gipsy quarter of Seville; we are in a

[9] John Garrett Underhill.

maison de danses; a gipsy girl is performing the romalis, coiling, stamping, now slowly sensual, now fast and fiery; crotals, castanets, tambourines . . . the sparkle of spangles . . . stamping heels . . . accroche-cœurs . . . and a certain savage dignity reminds us that Trajan was born at Triana. . . . El Albaicin: the gipsy quarter of Granada; guitars, strumming, thumping . . . an old gipsy woman sings a plaintive melody . . . interrupted by the guitars . . . nostalgia . . . wanderlust . . . wildness and woe . . . the dirty huts, poverty, the life of the bohemians. . . . Rondeña, in which ¾ and ⅜ time alternate in the graceful and peculiar dance of Ronda, the town built high on a cleft rock, in turn invaded by Phœnicians, Carthaginians, Goths, Moors, and Christians . . . the market rich in fruit, grapes, peaches, medlars . . . a famous bull-ring. . . . El Puerto: the mountain portal from which the robber bands were formerly accustomed to descend and infest the high road from Seville to Cadiz. . . . The rhythm runs in the quick, decisive trot of mules . . . El Polo: the sobbing strain of an old Andalusian song, "speaking directly to the spine, sending an unaccountable shiver through one" . . . Eritaña: an inn outside Seville. Can this be Lillas Pastia's? Marliave says that this music "waddles, good-humoured and joking, like Sancho Panza's donkey approaching the rack of a Sevillan inn." To Marliave, the gem of the series is Jerez, a picture of the city of sherry, "an absolute masterpiece of pure musical beauty." I would find it difficult to choose my own favourite. Indeed, as is the case with the Gilbert and Sullivan operettas, it is usually the latest one I have heard.

Only very brilliant pianists need attempt to play these pieces. To master their depths requires an astounding technique, a technique that must be forgotten by the auditor during the performance. Ernest Newman has made some remarks on this point: "Albéniz, I think, sometimes makes matters needlessly difficult for the player by his way of notating his music. He has always had a preference for the flat keys, particularly those with five, six, or seven flats in the key signature (the bulk of the pieces in Iberia, for instance, are in flats); and not content with this he is for ever doubling the flats, or doubling some and chromatically raising others in the same chord, till the most skilled reader may be pardoned for getting confused at times, while the ordinary amateur becomes hopelessly befogged. Albéniz could have saved us a lot of trouble by writing many passages in the equivalent sharp keys. But setting this aside, the difficulties of his music all come from the nature of his thinking. His music is not self-consciously sophisticated, as that of so many of the modern Frenchmen tends to be; his mind was one of extraordinary subtlety, and his ideas so far removed from the customary ruts, he had to find a correspondingly personal mode of expression. In some respects he has carried the idiom of the piano further than any other composer of his time; I do not know, for example, where else we shall find such tremendous resonance, as of organ and orchestra combined, as in the Fête-Dieu à Seville. His originality is invariably of the same kind; that is to say, no matter how unusual a passage may sound at first, it is always found to talk simple sense when we have become accustomed to it. . . . Albéniz had the real logical faculty in music. He thinks continually and coherently right through his seemingly complicated harmonies, and he has a technique that enables him to say lucidly anything, however remote from the ordinary track, that he may want to say. In the Lavapies, for instance, he suggests to perfection the animation of the popular quarter of Madrid, with all its clashes of sound and of colour. Musorgsky tried to do a somewhat similar thing in the picture of the Limoges market-place in his Tableaux d'une Exposition, but he had nothing like Albéniz's technical command. The Lavapies is not only good fun and good description but good music. Great as are his descriptive powers, however, he is at root an emotionalist, an eloquent evoker of moods."

After Iberia, although he was dying, Albéniz contrived to write two more pieces for the piano, or at least to sketch them out. These pieces, Azulejos and Navarra, he regarded as his masterpieces, and there are those who agree with him. After his death, the first was completed by Granados and the second by Déodat de Sévérac.

## IV

I am frequently informed that there are rules by which art can be measured, justly appraised, and pigeon-holed. I have frequently expressed doubt, publicly and privately, that this be true. I am the more inclined to doubt by the solemn discussions of the subject which have been published. Arthur Machen's Hieroglyphics makes pleasant and stimulating reading. It is written with grace. Yet the avowed purpose of the volume appears to be to present the reader with a formula by which he can test works of art. By the aid of this magic formula, Mr. Machen blithely proceeds to prove that Jane Austen and Thackeray are not artists and that Dickens is akin to Homer. By this same formula I could prove that Murillo

# Isaac Albéniz

was a greater painter than Velázquez. Mr. W. H. Hadow
prefaces his valuable Studies in Modern Music with a
critical essay in which he attempts to lay down the rules
for musical criticism and to offer us a formula by means
of which we can judge and appraise music. Employing
this formula, Mr. Hadow proves beyond any possible
shadow of doubt that Sir Charles Hubert Hastings Parry
is England's musical Messiah. [10]

With these dire examples in mind as a warning, I refrain from making any attempt towards assigning Albéniz
too definite a position. It seems to me that the "impressionistic critic" who expresses his personal preferences is much more likely to light up his subject. He, at
least, is not tied down by a theory. Now artists seldom
fit theories and so it becomes the business of the form-
ulist to make them appear to do so. "To try and approach truth on one side after another, not to strive or
cry, nor to persist in pressing forward, on any one side,
with violence and self-will,—it is only thus, it seems to
me, that mortals may hope to gain any vision of the mysterious Goddess, whom we shall never see except in outline, but only thus even in outline. He who will do nothing but fight impetuously towards her on his own, one,
favourite, particular line, is inevitably destined to run his
head into the folds of the black robe in which she is
wrapped." To which wise words of Matthew Arnold I
reverently add, Amen!

It is agreeable, therefore, to conclude this informal
paper on a note of mere rhapsody. I have made some

[10] "There has arisen among us a Composer who is capable of re-
storing our national Music to its true place in the art of Europe . . .
There is little presumption in the forecast when we already have such
first fruits as St. Cecilia, and the De Profundis, and the English
Symphony."

[253]

small attempt to give an idea of Albéniz's music, to describe the gradual flowering of his genius. Unless I am very much mistaken he will soon be borne from the rather obscure corner into which he has been shoved by more thriving modernists, and presently be installed on a pedestal somewhere nearer the centre of our musical Pantheon, and on this pedestal we could do no better than inscribe these lines of Marliave: "En lui, sensuelle et mélancolique, joyeuse et passionnée, agreste et chevaleresque, l'âme de l'Espagne se trouve et se résume, et si l'école ibérique existe aujourd'hui, consciente d'elle-même, vraiment nationale, débordante de sève jeune et vivace, c'est au délicieux génie d'Isaac Albéniz qu'elle le doit."

*April 4, 1919.*

## Erik Satie

Paul Verlaine's Sagesse appeared in 1881 (although it was not until 1893 that Edmund Gosse tracked the dissipated poet to the basement of the Café Soleil d'Or on the Boul' Mich'); the Sâr Péladan published Le vice suprême in 1884; in the same year Joris K. Huysmans issued A rebours; Les complaintes of Jules Laforgue dates from 1885; Les illuminations of Arthur Rimbaud was offered to the public in 1886, together with George Moore's Confessions of a Young Man; 1887 was the year of the Poésies complètes by Stéphane Mallarmé. Degas, Monet, Renoir, Manet were all painting in the eighties, while Augusta Holmès presided over her celebrated salon where Catulle Mendès, "with his pale hair, and his fragile face illuminated with the idealism of a depraved woman," was an outstanding figure. Were not Méphistophéla and Le roi vierge romances of this epoch? Symbolism, mysticism, vers libre, impressionism, decadence, disillusion were in the Parisian air. Painters and writers alike were indulging in acrobatic intoxication: sipping their absinthe on the high wire. Only the musicians clung to the earth, refusing to be lured to the giddy trapeze-cafés. Massenet and Saint-Saëns were the popular French composers . . . Gounod, Bizet . . . To be sure, César Franck, believer and mystic, belonged to the epoch (during the eighties he wrote his best piano music and the Symphony in D minor). There was also another voice, a wee small voice, it seemed then, even

[255]

# Erik Satie

to its possessor, especially to its possessor. Erik Satie
did not regard himself as an innovator, and for the time
being his music was swept into the maelstrom of unheard
tones. Nevertheless, his Ogives were composed in 1886,
his Sarabandes, in 1887, his Gymnopédies, in 1888 and
his Gnossiennes, in 1890 (the year that Villiers de l'Isle-
Adam published his Axël). Save by his own circle,
however, Satie passed unnoticed until twenty-five years
later when it was recalled, with some astonishment, that
Claude-Achille Debussy had stepped very modestly
futureward in 1893 with his La damoiselle élue.[1]

A strange figure, Erik Satie, a shy and genial fantasist,
who has been writing curious music with curious titles
in Paris for thirty years, music which has only recently
been published in any quantity or any buyable form
(Roland-Manuel asserts that a clerk in the largest Paris
music shop told him in 1909 that Satie had written
"some waltzes and two cake-walks," while an old lady
assured him that Satie was the proprietor of a bathing
establishment on the Avenue Trudaine), music yet to
be heard in most of the great concert halls of the
world. . . . Beginning with the classic form of the sarabande, Satie, whose talent is wantonly blended from the
decadent literary and artistic impulses of his epoch, at
first to have so little influence with other composers, has
written a mass for the poor, trumpet calls for the Salon
de la Rose-Croix, ditties for a music hall divinity, preludes to plays by Jules Bois and the Sâr Péladan, and
dances for the Russian Ballet and Valentine de Saint-
Point. He has celebrated the family lives of unfamiliar
sea-creatures, the Holothurie, the Edriophthalma, and the

[1] In l'Harmonie moderne, René Lenormand gives Satie the credit
of having initiated the French renaissance in music.

[256]

# Erik Satie

Podophthalma, and he has composed a fugue "in the form of a pear." Over music as simple in its melodic line, and as French, as the music of Massenet, he has inscribed the most extraordinary directions to the performer. "Sur du velours jauni" "lourd comme une truie," "sec comme un coucou," "léger comme un œuf," and "comme un rossignol qui aurait mal aux dents," are a few of these original signals. Satie has been heard to remark, "Il faut être rigolo!" Incorrigible Satie: Scotch and French, product of Honfleur, a village organist's instruction, Montmartre cabarets, the Conservatoire, and the Schola Cantorum; played on by impressionism, Catholicism, Rosicrucianism, Pre-Raphaelitism, the science of black magic, theosophy, the theory of androgyny, the camaraderie of the Place Clichy; part-child, part-devil, part-faun, all intelligence (you may sense the paradox in the portrait by Antoine de la Rouchefoucauld),[2] there is no other such figure in modern music; there is no other such figure in all the annals of music. The publisher of Lombroso would do well to include Satie in a new edition of The Man of Genius; Gérard de Nerval would die of envy were he alive to regard him; Jules Laforgue, in hell, must feel that he did not write his Moralités Légendaires in vain; and Max Nordau must be chortling, "I told you so!" Yet the bearded and bespectacled countenance, the tête de blagueur, of Erik Satie is rarely seen on the Paris boulevards, and his name is seldom celebrated with that of his contemporaries. Only in obscure corners of papers on modern French composers will you discover it, usually mentioned without pregnant comment. At least three literary portraits exist in French, however. Jean

[2] Or in the more recent portraits by Picasso and Jean Cocteau.

# Erik Satie

Ecorcheville, Roland-Manuel, and G. Jean-Aubry have all written about him [3] with sympathy, and his name is often on the lips of Debussy and Ravel. Each of these composers has orchestrated works of Satie [4] and every Saturday, I have been informed, he pays a visit to the creator of l'Après-midi d'un faune [5] in perpetuation of a friendship which dates back to the late eighties when Satie played the piano at the Auberge du Clou, Avenue Trudaine.

Eric-Alfred Leslie Satie (he doubtless owes this remarkable collection of names to a mother of Scotch descent) was born at Honfleur (where the aunt in the play comes from) May 17, 1866 (G. Jean-Aubry gives this date incorrectly as 1855). On his published music he has changed the c in his first Christian name to a k, and dropped the Alfred Leslie. One of his childhood friends was Alphonse Allais, perhaps an early instigator of that subtle buffoonery which later became a notable characteristic of Satie's music. His first teacher was the organist (Vinot, a pupil of Niedermeyer) of the church of Sainte-Catherine in the village of his birth, and it was from Vinot, possibly, that he derived the Gregorian spirit which permeates a good deal of his music. His musical education is said to have begun at the age of eight, but neither then nor later did he manifest signs of precocity or even of aptitude. At the age of twelve, Satie left Honfleur for Paris where his first teacher was Guilmant.

[3] Since this paper was published Rudhyar D. Chennevière '(Musical Quarterly; Vol. V, page 469), Ernest Newman (A Musical Motley; 1919), Jean Cocteau (Le coq et l'arlequin; 1918), André Cœuroy (La musique française moderne; 1922), Paul Rosenfeld (Musical Chronicle; 1923), and others have written about Satie.

[4] Debussy orchestrated the first and third of the Gymnopédies.

[5] No longer, of course. Debussy died March 26, 1918; Satie, July 1925.

# Erik Satie

At the Paris Conservatoire, which he entered in 1879, Satie proved himself an indolent pupil and there is a legend to the effect that he was dropped from one piano class on the ground of sheer incompetence. His instructors in harmony assured him that his métier was the piano; his piano professors advised him to stick to composition; Mathias,[6] the Hungarian, a pupil of Chopin, in despair one day counselled Satie to study the violin! Decidedly this young man was not regarded as talented at the Conservatoire. In the classes of Mathias he was a co-pupil with Chevillard, Paul Dukas, and Philipp, but there is no evidence to show that he ever acquired any great proficiency in the art of piano playing; rather the contrary. Next we find him in the cabarets of Montmartre (one chronicler mentions the Chat Noir where he may have been contemporary with Yvette Guilbert, unless she were singing at the Divan Japonais at this epoch) and at the Auberge du Clou, to this day a popular eating place for artists. It was at the latter, according to Jean-Aubry, that he encountered Claude-Achille Debussy, who may have heard Satie play his Ogives (1886) and the now celebrated Sarabandes (1887), of which there are three, "les deux manches et la belle." The mystic harmonies and refined melodies in these curious pieces for the piano spell (and antedate) much of the mysterious wonder in Debussy's later work. Was this the result of the Gregorian influence? Satie did not know that he was revolutionary; he did not want to be an anarchist. He wrote his round clear notes on clean, white sheets of paper. He did not ask any one else to play his music, he made no effort to get it published, and so he remained obscure.

[6] James Huneker was a pupil of Mathias in 1878.

[259]

# Erik Satie

It was during this same period, or a little later, that Satie encountered the Sâr Péladan and the second cycle of his career began. One of the phenomena of the early nineties in Paris was the foundation of a mystic sect, half-artistic, half-theosophic, called the Salon de la Rose-Croix. A youth with an ascetic, Assyrian face, a mop of black hair, a wealth of black beard, and piercing, penetrating eyes, the eyes of Maurice Renaud as Athanaël in Thaïs, Joséphin Aimé Péladan, was the founder. The son of a writer and mystic, Adrien Péladan, he was born at Lyons in 1859. He began, as a fervent disciple of Barbey d'Aurevilly, by writing romances; later, he travelled in Italy and to Bayreuth and wrote about Leonardo da Vinci and Richard Wagner; then he proclaimed himself Sâr, became a magician, donned flowing robes, established the Salon de la Rose-Croix (1892–98), invited guests to æsthetic soirées, at which esoteric dramas of his own devising were performed, and generally held the attention by his eccentricities. His books, written in a blatant, metaphoric style, were compounded of the not very clearly seen visions of a magician, the faith of an obstinate Catholic, a hallucinatory idealism, glorification of the flesh, and erotic sensualism. His knowledge of music, of painting, of the life of the Greeks, of all the subjects he touched upon (and they were many) was seemingly a little confused; his philosophy was neither scientific nor literary. The novelists regarded him as a mystic and a man of ideas; to the mystics he remained a novelist; to the public at large he loomed as another of those fantastic figures which always amuse the Paris crowd. His principal work is the series of novels which appeared under the general title of La décadence latine. It includes: Le vice suprême (1884),

# Erik Satie

Curieuse (1886), l'Initiation sentimentale (1887), A cœur perdu (1888), Istar (1888), La victoire du mari (1889) [7] Cœur en peine (1890), l'Androgyne (1891), La gynandre (1892), Le panthée (1893), Typhonia (1893), Le dernier Bourbon (1895), La lamentation d'Ilou (1896), La vertu suprême (1896), and Finis Latinorum (1899). Other of his books bear the titles: Comment on devient mage (1892; let us hope he did not advocate the method of Bouvard and Pécuchet), Comment on devient fée (1893), l'Art idéaliste et mystique (1894). In 1916, he published l'Allemagne devant l'humanité.[8] His plays include Le fils des étoiles (1895), Prométhée, Sémiramis (1897), Œdipe et le sphinx (1898), and Le mystère du grail. It is interesting to read the letters in which the directors of the Odéon (Porel) and the Comédie française (Jules Claretie) rejected his play, Le prince de Byzance. They are printed in the volume with the play. Le fils des étoiles was also rejected by both these theatres. St. Francis of Assisi was translated into English "and adapted" by Harold John Massingham. Péladan gave a performance at Paris (March 17, 1892) of Palestrina's Pope Marcellus Mass. Gustave Moreau was interested in his Salon and I believe that Odilon Redon exposed pictures there. Among the painters identified with the Rose-Croix movement, Jean Delville, Alphonse Osbert, Carlos Séon, Egusquiza, Aman Jean, Fernan Khopff, and Armand Point may be mentioned. A feature of the Salon of 1893 was the portrait of Péladan by Marcellin Desboutins. Was Albert Samain one of the poets of the movement? Erik Satie composed music for two of the Sâr's plays

---

[7] Reviewed by Anatole France in La vie littéraire: Vol. III, page 233.
[8] Péladan died June 27, 1918.

[261]

# Erik Satie

(this fact is not mentioned in the books of the plays; of so little importance was the name of Satie at the time), Le fils des étoiles and Le prince de Byzance, and he created trumpet calls, emulating the fashion of Bayreuth, for the Salon de la Rose-Croix. Roland-Manuel professes to discover a revolt against Wagnerism in this music; personally I do not believe that Satie consciously harboured such an intention. Ravel orchestrated the prelude to Le fils des étoiles, the "Wagnerie kaldéenne" of the Sâr Péladan (performed at Durand-Ruel's during February, 1892).

About this period Satie composed the music for a ballet, Uspud, which was the cause of a quarrel with the direction of the Opéra. He is said to have proposed a duel, but his whim was not humoured. Another incredibly uncharacteristic act was his attempt to become a member of the Institut, to fill the place left vacant by the death, in 1892, of Ernest Guiraud, the same Guiraud who completed Les contes d'Hoffmann, left unfinished at Offenbach's death. Gustave Moreau is reported to have been the only member of the august body in favour of admitting him.

A long silence ensued. Satie was seemingly forgotten. A few years later, feeling the need of technical invigoration, he immured himself for a time in the Schola Cantorum, from which institution he emerged with a series of pastorals, chorals, and fugues, in typical d'Indy forms, if not quite in the d'Indy manner. Then, on January 16, 1911, Ravel played three of Satie's compositions, including one of the Sarabandes, at a concert of the Societé Musicale Independente. This baffling figure was now dragged into the view of the public eye, and to the musical publishers, and a series of remarkable works for

# Erik Satie

the piano has been the result. At present, Erik Satie lives at Arcueil, near the fortifications of Paris.

The list of Satie's compositions is a long one. A few of the pieces listed below, however, have not as yet been published. Of a few others even the manuscript has disappeared. Here is the catalogue:   Valse-Ballet (1885), published in Musique des familles; Les anges, Sylvie, and Les fleurs (1885; songs, all of which are lost); Ogives (1886); Trois sarabandes (1887); Trois gymnopédies (1888); Trois Gnossiennes (1890); three preludes for Le fils des étoiles (1891); l'Hymne au drapeau for Le prince de Byzance (1891); prelude to Le Nazaréen of Henri Mazel (1892); Uspud, "Christian ballet for one dancer" (1892); prelude to a play by Jules Bois, La porte héroïque du ciel (1893; orchestrated by Roland-Manuel); Danses gothiques, neuvaines pour le plus grand calme et la forte tranquillité de mon âme, mise sous l'invocation de Saint-Benoit (1893; the excerpts from these dances published in S. I. M. are incorrectly printed); La messe des pauvres (1895); in 1896 Satie, in collaboration with Jules Dépaquit, made some sketches for an English pantomime, Jack in the Box (mss. lost); Pièces froides (Airs à faire fuir and Danses de travers, dedicated to Mme. J. Ecorcheville, 1897); Le Piccadilly, for piano, and arranged for small orchestra (out of print); Je te veux, waltz for piano; also arranged as a song and for small orchestra (1897); Poudre d'or, waltz (1897); Tendrement, valse chantée (1897); La diva de l'Empire, song (1900); Ecorcheville mentions sketches for a piece entitled Poisson reveur (1900); Trois morceaux en forme de poire, avec une manière de commencement, une continuation du même et un en plus, suivi d'une redite, piano, four-hands (1903; orchestrated

# Erik Satie

by Roland-Manuel); Pousse l'amour, music for a play by M. de Féraudy (1905); En habit de cheval, pièces en forme de fugue (choral-fugue litanique—autre choral-fugue de papier), piano, four-hands (1911); and Aperçus désagréables (pastorale, choral, and fugue), piano, four-hands (1911).

Since 1912 Satie has written: Véritables préludes flasques (pour un chien) (1912); Les pantins dansents, for Valentine de Saint-Point (1912); Descriptions automatiques (April 1913); Embryons desséchés (June 1913); Croquis et agaceries d'un gros bonhomme en bois (July 1913); Vieux sequins, vieilles cuirasses (1913); Pièces enfantines (1913); Le piège de Méduse, dances for a comedy by the composer (1913); Choses vues à droite et à gauche, for piano and violin (1913); Les heures séculaires et instantanées (1914); Trois valses distinguées du precieux dégoûté (1914); Trois poèmes d'amour, words by the composer (1914); Jeux et divertissements (1914); Avant-dernières pensées (1915); and Daphénéo, Le chapelier, and La statue de bronze (1916).[9]

[9] Before the war began Jean Cocteau, Paulet Thévenaz, and Stravinsky were planning a pantomime, called Parade, for the Russian Ballet. It did not progress beyond the idea. Later, Cocteau transferred his attention to Satie and Picasso. Parade was produced by the Russians at Paris, May 18, 1917. Miassine was responsible for the choregraphy.

This is Cocteau's scenario, as it was printed in the program: "The scene represents the houses of Paris on a Sunday. Street Theatre. Three music hall numbers serve as the free show. Chinese magician. American girl. Acrobats. Three managers organize the publicity. In their illiterate manner they explain to the crowd that it is confusing the free show with the spectacle inside. Nobody is convinced. After the final number, supreme effort of the managers. The Chinaman, the acrobats, and the girl come out of the empty theatre. Aware of the failure of the managers, they exert their own charms, but it is too late."

# Erik Satie

You will find the name of Satie furtively poking its head out of odd manuscripts yet too radical for magazine publication, touched on casually in the books of James Huneker and the program notes of Philip Hale, and mentioned in obscure paragraphs of newspaper feuilletons devoted to a discussion of modern French music, but his delicate melodies are seldom performed in public: their structure is too ethereal, too gauze-like, too butterfly-winged, too gauche, too angular, at once too refined and too barbaric, and in some instances too in-

Picasso's costumes did not please the critics. That does not mean that they were not good. Satie's music caused a disturbance similar to that provoked by the original production in Paris of Le sacre du printemps. The typewriter was employed as an instrument in the orchestra. It is possible that one of Marinetti's disciples had thought of this device before Satie. Jean Cocteau (Le coq et l'arlequin, page 37), asserts that the work was not performed as written. "The score originally included automobile sirens, aeroplane engines, dynamos, etc. In the haste of rehearsals, material difficulties arose, and these suggestive sounds were nearly all suppressed." Cocteau has written further of this score in Vanity Fair, September 1917. Henri Quittard, in le Figaro, declared: "La musique de M. Erik Satie ne mérite pas moins de louanges (this after a paragraph devoted to the demolition of Picasso). Ce compositeur a reçu du ciel la grace singulière de conserver toute sa vie l'heureuse facilité des personnes très jeunes à prendre le plus vif plaisir aux blagues d'atelier et aux grosses charges des plus innocentes. (As Ernest Newman with some justification has said, "Satie is sometimes charmingly childlike, but often merely childish.") Il s'est donc diverti, avec une fantasie tant soit peu laborieuse, à reproduire les effets burlesque qu'une douzaine de musiciens de foire produisent sans effort et même sans y penser le moins du monde. Il lui a fallu, pour un résultat si plaisant, beaucoup de travail et un nombreux orchestre d'excellents artistes. Mais il a fort bien réussi. Et je ne doute pas qu'il n'ait pris un grand divertissement à si belle besogne." It is interesting to note that Stravinsky and Satie both regard clowns as excellent impersonal mediums for the expression of the comic spirit.

In 1920, Socrate, "drame symphonique pour quatre soprani et orchestre," was performed at Paris. Satie has published other compositions since this bibliography was compiled.

[265]

completely realized, to please the tympanum of the public ear. It *is* vague music, but has not vagueness become the whispered slogan of a school since Satie began to write? Musicians know, and some of them appreciate, this music, and recognize its relation to that of Debussy. There is more than a casual use of the wholetone scale to recommend this comparison to the critical ear, there is a fragile melodic line, and there are sonorous harmonies, concocted untraditionally, to be played diminuendo. Satie's limitations have actually added to his artistic stature. Like Musorgsky, had he been more of an expert with the cliché and technique of his art, he might not have developed his own personality so successfully. From the very beginning he imagined strange procedures. He hit, for instance, almost at once, on the plan of abolishing the bar line.[10] Here, of course, he betrays his acquaintance with mediæval church music. The tyranny of the bar line in music dates back no farther than the seventeenth century. There are then no separations in Satie's music. Nothing is dichotomized. The notes flow along. It is Satie's agreeable habit to employ few accidentals; in many of his compositions practically all the notes are of the same or of a closely related value. Appogiatura, syncopation, bravura, he is not friendly with. The pieces are written in facile keys for pianists. They are sometimes difficult for the ear and brain, never for the fingers. "Their particular colour," writes Jean Ecorcheville, "is made up of harmonic blemishes, subtly combined, sonorities juxtaposed without regard for the permitted cadences or the required

[10] It is interesting, in this connection, to recall that Stéphane Mallarmé ignored punctuation in many of his poems; a modern English poet, Mina Loy, has followed his example.

resolutions." He has written tunes for Paulette Darty, divette de music hall . . . even a banal waltz called Tendrement . . . and one breathes the atmosphere of the music hall, the cabaret, even in the Gymnopédies (did these dances for nude Spartan babies, inspired by the Salammbô of Flaubert, in turn inspire Isadora Duncan?). This is a part of his joke, for he is very gamin, this composer, and he loves the rigolo. Certainly the first Sarabande bears a strong resemblance to the prelude to Tristan. The family of the Edriophthalma, "crustaceans with sessile eyes, extremely sad by nature, who live in holes pierced in the cliffs," weep softly to a paraphrase of the middle section of the funeral march from Chopin's B flat minor sonata, over which Satie has written "Citation de la célèbre mazurka de Schubert." In Sur un vaisseau, the opening bars of the sextet from Lucia are incongruously introduced. The Tyrolienne turque is a ridiculous parody of a familiar Chopin waltz. The Greek Danse cuirassée is simply a bugle-call eccentrically harmonized. There are further jocular references to Puccini and Chabrier. The mystic side of Satie's nature, revealed in his Gothic Dances and his Pointed Arches, with their angular lines, is worthy of consideration. His pale, frail Gnossiennes (Gnosse was a town in ancient Crete), the second of which is a veritable masterpiece of definite indecision (like a miniature picture in tone of Flaubert's l'Education sentimentale), were partly inspired by the spectacle of the Javanese dancers at the Paris Exposition in 1889, partly by the Greek chorus of Saint-Julien-le-Pauvre (Satie, I am informed, spends long hours in the churches, listening to the chanting of the priests). Timorous, meticulous, mincing, neat, petulant, petty, are a few of the adjectives one might

[267]

# Erik Satie

apply to this music, and yet none of them exactly describes its effect, half-spiritual, half-mocking! Is there any other music like it? I am reminded that Baudelaire once wrote: "Have you observed that a bit of sky seen through an air-hole, or between two chimneys, two rocks, or through an arcade, gives a more profound idea of the infinite than the grand panorama seen from the top of a mountain?"

Three periods are to be noted in the style of Satie. First, the period of the Sarabandes and the Gymnopédies (by no means the usual immature output of a composer's nonage); second, the period during which he applied himself to the task of finding fantastic expression for the vagaries of the Salon de la Rose-Croix; third, the period in which he appeared before his little world bearing before him his printed music, embellished with the most extravagant titles and programs. These titles and programs have little enough to do with the music. Obstacles venimeux, from Heures séculaires et instantanées, offers a typical example: "Cette vaste partie du monde n'est habitée que par un seul homme: un Nègre. Il s'ennuie à mourir de rire. L'ombre des arbres millénaires marque 9 h. 17. Les crapauds s'appellent par leur nom propre. Pour mieux penser, le Nègre tient son cervelet de la main droite, les doigts de celle-ci écartés. De loin, il semble figurer un physiologiste distingué. Quatre serpents anonymes le captivent, suspendus aux basques de son uniforme que déforment le chagrin et la solitude réunis. Sur le bord du fleuve, un vieux palétuvier lave lentement ses racines, répugnantes de saleté. C'est n'est pas l'heure du berger." True ironist that he is, Satie conceals his diffidence beneath these fantastic programs. He ridicules his own emotion at just the

[268]

# Erik Satie

point at which the auditor is about to discover it. He also protects himself against the pedants and the philistines by raising these barriers. Is not this a form of snobbery? "Il est de toute évidence," Satie is quoted as saying to Roland-Manuel, "que les Aplatis, les Insignifiants, et les Boursouflés n'y prendront aucun plaisir. Qu'ils avalent leurs barbes. Qu'ils se dansent sur le ventre." It is more than probable, moreover, that these titles and programs are aimed as ridicule at certain of the more outrageous extravagances of program music.

The joke, however, is a secret between composer and performer; even the printing of one of his programs or of a catalogue of his fantastic directions will not help the auditor to appreciate this intellectualized fun because he will be unable to synchronize the directions with the performance. In his theatre at Petrograd, Evereïnoff has given performances of Bernard Shaw's Candida during which a little Negro page-boy read all the stage directions. This Russian producer believed that the author's comments were the best part of the play, and he was determined that his audience should share them. A performer of Satie's later music might resort to a similar expedient if he wished his audience to participate in the titillation. Vladimir de Pachmann, Huneker's "naughty fairy of the keyboard," should be perfectly willing to play and recite the program simultaneously. You may easily fancy Pachmann performing Sur une lanterne, muttering occasionally, with a cunning leer: "N'allumez pas encore: vous avez le temps . . . Vous pouvez allumer, si vous voulez . . . Eclairez un peu devant vous . . . Votre main devant la lumière . . . Retirez votre main et mettez-la dans votre poche ; . . . Chut! Attendez . . . Eteignez."

[269]

# Erik Satie

The significance of Satie, if he has significance, lies in the fact that he, apparently, quite unconsciously was the founder of the French impressionistic school. He liberated French music from the monarchy of the major-minor. This is admitted by the impressionists [11] themselves today, thirty years too late, perhaps, but they are endeavouring to make amends. The new art was born of irresolution, a circumstance, as Ecorcheville notes, which is analogous to the transmutations which occurred at the close of the sixteenth century.[12] The artist finds pleasure in fugitive dissonances which the academicians describe as licentious, but a new movement results. Ecorcheville, with a bit of a smile, compares Satie to Monteverdi. His influence upon his successors, possibly, has been equally noteworthy, and while the pedants may refuse to take him seriously and the great public on the whole is quite unaware of his name, future historians must reserve a few paragraphs for this esoteric figure.

*November 16, 1916.*

[11] The "Six" also claim Satie, and allege that his music is a revolt against impressionism, forgetting that much of it was written before the impressionist school came into being. His later manner, it is true, has probably influenced Auric, Milhaud, and the others.

[12] For a learned discussion of this theory in its more general aspects, read Ernest Newman's A Musical Critic's Holiday.

## A Note on Dedications

Antoine Furetière, writing early in the eighteenth century, declared that the inventor of dedications must have been a beggar, a point of view echoed by Dr. Young in his Universal Passion:

"All other trades demand—verse-makers beg;
A dedication is a wooden leg."

That this aspersion is reasonably truthful, at least in regard to the coevals of these gentlemen, there can be no denial. Records exist which serve to prove that dedications were bought and sold even in the old Roman days. Sixteenth, seventeenth, and eighteen century inscriptions in books were almost invariably aimed at a patron's vanity, sometimes that of a noble lord, sometimes that of the king himself, and before the ink was dry on the page embellished with fulsome flattery, frequently equivalent to canonization or coronation, the thrifty author, or his agent, had called at the patron's door to collect a sum commensurate with the dignity conferred. Few poets of these other days, it would seem, were proud enough to hold themselves above taking advantage of this custom. John Dryden accepted his dedication fee with the graceful nonchalance of a barber of today accepting a vail.

Naturally, there were certain ungrateful fellows who refused to pay this involuntarily accrued debt. Among

# Dedications

these was the eminent Emperor Augustus who was willing enough to send a purse to an author whose book had pleased him, but who, upon receipt of a worthless book, of which he had been appointed the official patron, substituted a set of verses of his own for the gold. For one patron, however, who set up his back against the flattery, there were a hundred who were delighted by it. This result, quite normally, inspired authors to write books for the deliberate purpose of catching these guileless fools. The practice of these blithe cheats is described in Dekker's O per se O (1612). In the Lettres héroïques, aux grands de l'estat, by Rangouze (Paris; 1644), the pages were left unnumbered so that their order might be variously arranged in different copies and each person addressed might regard himself honoured by being awarded first place. Thomas Jordan invented an even more lucrative scheme. He prefixed flowery prefaces to his works, above which, with a hand-press, he printed a new name in each copy. Of a scurvy history he published an edition of two thousand copies. He chose two thousand retired tradesmen, whose names he had culled from a directory, as patrons, and each received his own particular exemplar. The majority of these chuckleheads hastened to requite him with substantial cheques for the trumpery glory with which he had endowed them.

Others than Dekker derived pleasure from exposing the system, for muck-raking was not an entirely unfamiliar pastime even in the days of Shakespeare. Witness, for a classic example, Thomas Gordon's anonymous Dedication to a Great Man Concerning Dedications:

I have known an author praise an earl, for twenty pages together, though he knew nothing of him, but that he had

[272]

# Dedications

money to spare. He made him wise, just, and religious for no reason in the world, but in hopes to find him charitable; and gave him a most bountiful heart, because he himself had a most empty stomach.

He goes on to make out a fantastic itemized bill in return for the good qualities bestowed on the anonymous patron. It seems unnecessary to add that a few authors existed, even at an epoch when it was considered no disgrace to call a man a hero for a few pieces of silver, who utilized their dedicatory pages quite unselfishly. I doubt, indeed, were a complete catalogue of dedications to be compiled, if a single object, animal, group of human beings, or profession could be discovered which had escaped the honour, so that an author of today who would dedicate his book in some new fashion is forced to create a new play of words to express an idea that probably has already been expressed in some form or other. In two respects, however, taking into account the exceptions already noted, current dedications differ in a marked manner from those of a century or two ago: they are offered for value received, to pay a debt of friendship rather than to create one, and usually they are shorter. Again there are exceptions to be noted. Several books by Vernon Lee are headed by lengthy dedicatory epistles and one of her volumes is really a dedication from beginning to end. Arthur Symons and George Moore, too, have sometimes seized the opportunity to be attractively garrulous in this form.

The most familiar dedication in all literature is undoubtedly that which Thomas Thorpe prefixed to Shakespeare's Sonnets (1609):

[273]

# Dedications

TO . THE . ONLIE . BEGETTER . OF .
THESE . INSUING . SONNETS .
MR. W.H. . ALL . HAPPINESSE .
AND . THAT . ETERNITIE .
PROMISED .
BY .
OUR . EVER-LIVING . POET .
WISHETH .
THE . WELL-WISHING .
ADVENTURER . IN .
SETTING .
FORTH .

The controversy that has raged around this innocent inscription might be bound, I fancy, in several thick tomes, for, with the passing of the centuries it has become a matter of considerable importance to discover the identity of Mr. W. H. All the Shakespearean commentators and a few others, notably Oscar Wilde, have tried their wits at solving this baffling problem. Certain modern authors, Edgar Saltus for one, whether through a sense of discretion or to hatch another mystery, have followed this celebrated example of blazoning in initials only.

Spanish and Italian poets frequently dedicated their books to the Virgin Mary, Jesus Christ, and even God himself. James I conformed to this custom when he consecrated to Jesus his reply to the work of Conrad Vorstius on the nature and attributes of God, addressing the Saviour of mankind in an exceedingly familiar manner. Yvette Guilbert inscribed her autobiographical Struggles and Victories to God, whom she addressed in a long epistle. That curious Dada romance, Joseph Delteil's Choléra, is also dedicated à Dieu.

# Dedications

There have been dedications to abstractions. Dr. Pinckard inscribed his Notes on the West Indies (1806) to Friendship:

Looking round, as it is said authors are wont, for a great personage, to whose name I might dedicate my work, I have not found it possible to fix upon any one to whom I could with so much propriety consign it, as . . . to its Parent! Accept then, Benign Power! thine offspring; cherish it even as thou hast begotten it; and cause thy warmest influence ever to animate the heart of thy faithful and devoted servant,

THE AUTHOR.

The cynical Herman Melville dedicated Israel Potter to the Bunker-Hill monument and Pierre to a mountain.

Kinsfolk have always been among the most frequent recipients of complimentary inscriptions. Dedications to fathers, to mothers, to brothers and sisters, to aunts to uncles, even to grandparents and cousins, abound in literature. One of the best of these, perhaps, is that which Alphonse Daudet devised to give a tone of morality to his Sapho:

Pour mes fils quand ils auront vingt ans,

which a Paris wag, not unjustifiably, altered to:

Pour mes fils quand ils auront vingt francs.

Joseph Delteil's Sur le fleuve amour is dedicated:

A maman
A la Vièrge Marie
Au Général Bonaparte

An entire volume might be compiled on the variations of dedications to wives, for it has long been traditional for an author, in an encomiastic address, to ascribe his success, or his potential success, to his wife's influence. A typical example is to be found in Coventry Patmore's The Angel in the House:

This Poem
is inscribed
to
the memory of Her
By whom and for whom I became a poet.

Certain writers have delighted to inscribe all their books, or almost all of them, to their spouses. Of these, the name of Thomas A. Janvier comes readily to mind. I have seen only one of his books in which the initials, To C. A. J., did not appear on the proper leaf.

It is a pleasure to observe that a few of our moderns are breaking away from this tendency to hail the wife as the seat of all inspirational power. George Creel, for instance, has caused to be printed on one of the early leaves of Ireland's Fight for Freedom:

To my wife
BLANCHE BATES CREEL
who has long begged me to give
up controversy in favour of
"nice, unargumentative things like books,"
this volume is lovingly dedicated.

Quite as lovingly, perhaps, and quite as ironically too, Francis Hackett has dedicated The Invisible Censor:

To
my wife
SIGNE TOKSVIG
whose lack of interest
in this book has been
my constant desperation.

# Dedications

Philip Guedalla's conjugal dedication to Supers and Supermen is cryptic:

> To
> N. or M.
> in either case
> to
> my wife.

There have been other dedications flavoured with the spice of mystery. The inscription in Lord Beaconfield's Vivian Grey (1828) is a masterpiece in this category:

> To
> The Best and Greatest of Men
> I dedicate these volumes.
> He, for whom it was intended, will accept and
> appreciate the compliment;
> Those, for whom it was not intended, will——
> do the same.

Kipling inscribed his Plain Tales from the Hills,

> To
> The Wittiest Woman in India,

which reminds me of an earlier dedication in Alfred Allendale's The Man of Sorrow,

> To
> The Prettiest Girl in England.

James Huneker inscribed his Bedouins,

> "A la très-belle, à la très-bonne, a la très-chère."

[277]

# Dedications

Did he mean Mary Garden? H. Dennis Bradley's Not for Fools is dedicated:

To
The Inarticulate, Splendid
Nameless,

but possibly the most mysterious inscription of all is that in Grant Overton's The Island of the Innocent:

[Privately Dedicated].

Many modern dedications are to friends to whom the author owes an obligation, literary, social, or even financial, or to some celebrated personage who may be expected to feel an interest in the book. Thus certain of Huneker's dedications are to Philip Hale, Richard Strauss, Remy de Gourmont, H. E. Krehbiel, Georg Brandes, Rafael Joseffy, Henry T. Finck, Vance Thompson, and John Quinn. Certainly James Branch Cabell's dedication of Taboo to John S. Sumner, who was responsible for the temporary suppression of Jurgen, falls under this head, and so does Philip Moeller's graceful dedication to Sophie:

To
Carl Van Vechten
who first gave me the key to
Sophie's dressing room
and to
Emily Stevens
who was waiting when the
knob was turned.

This playwright's dedication to Madame Sand is in a similarly charming vein:

[278]

# Dedications

To
Mrs. Fiske
for whom the play was written
and to
Arthur Hopkins
for whom I wrote the play.

Christopher Morley, in Pipefuls, gives this theme a new variation:

This book is dedicated
to
three men
HULBERT FOOTNER
EUGENE SAXTON ,
WILLIAM ROSE BENÉT
Because if I mentioned only one
of them, I would have to
write books
to inscribe to the other two.

This frankness is delightful and rare, for others have indulged in multiple dedication without the explanation, possibly, indeed, for a different reason. It was the lavish custom of Donald Evans to inscribe each of his poems to a separate person; in Two Deaths in the Bronx he lumped his honours together on the dedication page, where not less than twenty-four names appear. The inscription in James Branch Cabell's Figures of Earth is also inclusive:

To six most gallant champions is dedicated this history of a champion: less to repay than to acknowledge debts to each of them, collectively at outset, as thereafter seriatim.

On the half-titles preceding each part are emblazoned the names: Sinclair Lewis, Wilson Follett, Louis Untermeyer,

[279]

# Dedications

H. L. Mencken, Hugh Walpole, and Joseph Hergesheimer.
Many authors have dedicated their books to nations.
Victor Hugo blazoned his William Shakespeare to England, while Ouida, in a spirit of gratitude towards that land where she entertained so many readers, inscribed her Tricotrin to the American People. Morrie Ryskind's dedication to Unaccustomed as I am is in a slightly different spirit:

Dedicated to the Great American Democracy—may it bring me royalty.

Dedications to the class at which the book, in some sense at least, is aimed, are among the most interesting. Such a one is the curious inscription in Richard Brathwayte's Strappado for the Divell (1615):

To all usurers, broakers, and promoters, sergeants, catchpoles, and regrators, ushers, panders, suburbes traders, cockneies that have manie fathers; ladies, monkies, parachitoes, marmosites, and catomitoes, falls, high-tires, and rebatoes, false-haires, periwigges, monchatoes, grave gregorians, and shee-painters—send I greeting at adventures, and to all such as be evill, my Strappado for the Divell.

William Hornby's Scourge of Drunkenness is dedicated:

To all the impious and relentless-harted ruffians and roysters under Bacchus' regiment Cornu-apes wisheth remorse of conscience and more increase of grace.

The most ironic and terrible dedication that I know is that to Octave Mirbeau's scorching masterpiece, Le jardin des supplices:

[280]

# Dedications

Aux Prêtres, aux Soldats, aux Juges,
aux Hommes
qui éduquent, dirigent, gouvernent les hommes,
je dédie
ces pages de Meurtre et de Sang.

This dedication, of course, is an arraignment. Mirbeau's La 628-E 8 is inscribed to the manufacturer of the automobile whose licence number gives the book its title.
The inscription in Elliot H. Paul's Indelible is worthy of citation here:

> Blithely I dedicate this first of my novels to that group of acquaintances who have, during the lean season which marks the start of a literary career, been most solicitous for my health and hopeful for my success—My Creditors.

I think I could do no better than to conclude this group with James Huneker's dedication to Painted Veils:

> This Parable, with its notations and evocations of naked nerves and soul-states, is inscribed in all gratitude to the charming morganatic ladies, les belles impures, who make pleasanter this vale of tears for virile men. What shall it profit a woman if she saves her soul, but loseth love?

We must turn back to Restoration Drama for a parallel to this: Wycherley inscribed The Plain Dealer (1677) to a notorious procuress of Covent Garden, Mother Bennett, whom he addressed as "my Lady B——" in a coarse epistle six pages long.

The author is not always successful in pleasing the person whom he thinks to honour. Mrs. Elizabeth Carter, for example, was greatly annoyed by Hayley's dedication to his Philosophical, Historical and Moral Essay on Old Maids (1785):

# Dedications

Dear Madam,—Permit me to pay my devotions to you, as the ancients did to their threefold Diana; and to reverence you in three distinct characters; as a Poet, as a Philosopher, and as an Old Maid. Although the latter may, in vulgar estimation, be held inferior to the two preceding, allow me to say, it is the dignity with which you support the last of these titles, that has chiefly made me wish you to appear as the Protectress of the little volumes which I now have the honour to lay before you. Your virtues and your talents induce me to consider you as the President of the chaste community, whose interest I have endeavoured to promote in the following performance.

The inscription in Whistler's The Gentle Art of Making Enemies reads:

To
The rare Few, who, early in Life,
have rid Themselves of the Friendship
of the Many, these pathetic Papers
are inscribed.

Thackeray dedicated Pendennis to Dr. John Elliotson, the physician who had saved his life, and there is at least one case on record of a theatrical press agent who was the recipient of a dedication. It is a good one, too:

To
Scheherazade, Baron Munchausen,
Jacques Casanova,
and
Glenmore Davis
These feeble attempts of fancy to
Rival fact are humbly
Dedicated.

This was Gelett Burgess's pleasant way of sending Find the Woman into the world.

# Dedications

Otway dedicated a book to his publisher, a custom followed by James Branch Cabell in Beyond Life, by Joseph Hergesheimer in Balisand, and by myself, in The Blind Bow-Boy. I suppose that hundreds of volumes have been inscribed to beloved animals. I recall at once the dedication to Ouida's Puck which, it will be remembered, purports to be the autobiography of a dog:

To
A faithful friend
and
A gallant gentleman;
Sulla Felix.

Sulla was the Newfoundland presented to Mlle. de la Ramée by Mr. Hamilton Hume shortly after the death of her Beausire, to whom she was greatly attached. Oliver Herford dedicated A Kitten's Garden of Verses to his celebrated Persian cat, Hafiz, and Agnes Repplier, The Fireside Sphinx to her Agrippina. W. L. George's Kallikrates shares with Mrs. George the dedication to Blind Alley, and my own Feathers shares with Edna Kenton the dedication to The Tiger in the House.

Ouida's dedications were more frequently addressed to ladies of quality, like the following to Ariadnê, an excellent example of her florid dedicatory style:

A mon amie
DONNA ADA COLONNA
LA DUCHESSE DE CASTIGLIONE
connue dans le marbre comme
"Marcello"
qui, à tout le charme de la femme, a su réunir
le force de l'art.

# Dedications

And while dwelling on the agreeable subject of Ouida, it may be well to set down the most charming dedication I know, that to Max Beerbohm's More:

To
MLLE. DE LA RAMÉE
with the author's compliments
and to
OUIDA
with his love.

Hogarth proposed to publish a History of the Acts as a supplement to the Analysis of Beauty and he composed the following amusing dedication for it:

The No-Dedication; not dedicated to any prince in Christendom, for fear it might be thought an idle piece of arrogance; not dedicated to any man of quality, for fear it might be thought too assuming; not dedicated to any learned body of men, as either of the Universities or the Royal Society, for fear it might be thought an uncommon piece of vanity; nor dedicated to any particular friend, for fear of offending another; therefore dedicated to nobody; but for once we may suppose nobody to be everybody, as everybody is often said to be nobody, then this work is dedicated to everybody.

Henry James followed this principle quite literally. Not one of his novels or books of criticism contains a dedication.

Perhaps the most amusing way of dedicating a book is to inscribe it to yourself, for do not all good writers write to please themselves? Colley Cibber's daughter, Charlotte Clarke, dedicated her autobiography (1755) to herself. Earlier examples are those of Marston, the playwright, who dedicated his Scourge of Villainy:

# Dedications

To his most esteemed and beloved Selfe,
Dat Dedicatque,

George Wither who caused to be printed in the front of his abuses Stript and Whipt (1628) the following sentiment:

To himselfe G. W. wisheth all happinesse,

while the biographer of Samuel Johnson inscribed his anonymously published Ode to Tragedy:

To James Boswell, Esq.

The wittiest of the autodedications, however, is indubitably that created by Oliver Herford for The Bashful Earthquake:

TO THE ILLUSTRATOR
In grateful acknowledgment of his
amiable condescension in lending
his exquisitely delicate art to
the embellishment of these poor
verses from his sincerest admirer
THE AUTHOR.

*March 4, 1921.*